Neighbourhoods of Poverty

Neighbourhoods of Poverty

Urban Social Exclusion and Integration in Europe

Edited by

Sako Musterd

Alan Murie

Christian Kesteloot

First published 2006 by
PALGRAVE MACMILLAN
Houndmills, Basingstoke, Hampshire RG21 6XS and
175 Fifth Avenue, New York, N.Y. 10010
Companies and representatives throughout the world

PALGRAVE MACMILLAN is the global academic imprint of the Palgrave
Macmillan division of St. Martin's Press, LLC and of Palgrave Macmillan Ltd.
Macmillan® is a registered trademark in the United States, United Kingdom
and other countries. Palgrave is a registered trademark in the European
Union and other countries.

ISBN 13: 978–1–4039–9316–8
ISBN 10: 1–4039–9316–5

This book is printed on paper suitable for recycling and made from fully
managed and sustained forest sources.

A catalogue record for this book is available from the British Library.

Library of Congress Cataloging-in-Publication Data
  Neighbourhoods of poverty : urban social exclusion and integration in
  Europe / edited by Sako Musterd, Alan Murie, Christian Kesteloot.
      p. cm.
  Includes bibliographical references and index.
  ISBN 1–4039–9316–5 (cloth)
    1. Urban poor–Europe. 2. Poverty–Europe. 3. Marginality, Social–
  Europe. 4. Neighborhood–Economic aspects–Europe–Case studies.
  5. Neighborhood –Social aspects–Europe–Case studies. 6. Urban
  geography–Europe. 7. Space in economics. I. Title: Neighborhoods of
  poverty. II. Musterd, Sako. III. Murie, Alan. IV. Kesteloot, Christian.
  HV4084.A5N45 2006
  362.5'2094091732–dc22   2005044653

10   9   8   7   6   5   4   3   2   1
15   14   13   12   11   10   09   08   07   06

Printed and bound in Great Britain by
Antony Rowe Ltd, Chippenham and Eastbourne

Contents

List of Tables

List of Figures

Acknowledgements

This book has been developed on the basis of a four-year international comparative research project called: The Spatial Dimensions of Urban Social Exclusion and Integration: A European Comparison (URBEX). Eleven cities and 22 neighbourhoods were our targets of research. We are grateful to the European Commision who financed this project in the final phase of the Fourth RTD Framework Programme, in the domain of Targeted Socio-Economic Research (SOE2-CT98-3072).

Many people have played an important role in this project, not least several hundreds of neighbourhood inhabitants and other key persons we interviewed who allowed us to collect the information we required. People back-stage were also highly important to the success of this project. We would like to mention Dick van der Vaart, who has managed the non-scientific part of the programme and allowed us to focus on the academic side; and we also would like to thank Brooke Sykes, who corrected most of the English in the final phase of this project.

The book also owes to the Flemish Fund of Scientific Research, FWO-Vlaanderen. They financed for a 5 year period a scientific network on 'Social integration and exclusion processes and urban policy in Europe' in which all URBEX teams worked together with additional Flemish and Brussels research teams. Most of the book chapters were thoroughly discussed at several meetings of the network in Brussels, Leuven and Naples. We especially thank Yuri Kazepov, Pieter Saey, Henk Meert, Katleen Peleman, Maarten Loopmans, Filip De Maesschalck, Sarah Luyten, Matti Korteinen, Fulong Wu, Ugo Rossi and Jonathan Pratschke for their helpful comments.

Sako Musterd
Alan Murie
Chris Kesteloot

List of Contributors

Alberta Andreotti: Researcher, Sociologist, Department of Sociology, University of Milan-Bicocca, Milan, Italy.

Justin Beaumont: Researcher Urban Planning, Department of Planning, Faculty of Spatial Sciences, University of Groningen, The Netherlands.

Joos Droogleever Fortuijn: Associate Professor in Human Geography, Department of Geography, Planning and International Development Studies, University of Amsterdam, The Netherlands.

Hartmut Häussermann: Professor of Sociology, Department of Urban and Regional Sociology, Humboldt University Berlin, Germany.

Andreas Kapphan: Urban Sociologist, Bureau SMS (Urban research, migration and social analysis), Berlin, Germany.

Christian Kesteloot: Professor of Urban Geography at the Institute of Social and Economic Geography, Catholic University of Leuven, Belgium.

Martin Kronauer: Professor of Sociology at the Fachhochschule für Wirtschaft Berlin, Germany.

Peter Lee: Researcher, Centre for Urban and Regional Studies, University of Birmingham, United Kingdom.

Pascale Mistiaen: Researcher at the Institute of Social and Economic Geography, Catholic University of Leuven, Belgium.

Enrica Morlicchio: Professor of Sociology, Department of Sociology, University of Naples FedericoII, Naples, Italy.

Alan Murie: Professor of Urban and Regional Studies, Centre for Urban and Regional Studies, University of Birmingham, United Kingdom.

Sako Musterd: Professor of Urban Geography, Department of Geography, Planning and International Development Studies, University of Amsterdam, The Netherlands.

Inge van Nieuwenhuyze: Researcher, Department of Sociology and Social Policy, University of Antwerp, Belgium.

Peter Noller: Urban Sociologist, Institute for Sociology, Technical University Darmstadt, Germany.

Riette Oosthuizen: Researcher, Office for Public Management, London, United Kingdom.

Wim Ostendorf: Associate Professor of Urban Geography, Department of Geography, Planning and International Development Studies, University of Amsterdam, The Netherlands.

Elise Palomares: Researcher, National Demographic Institute (INED), Paris, France.

Enrico Pugliese: Professor of Sociology, Department of Sociology, University of Naples FedericoII, Naples, Italy.

Patrick Simon: Researcher in Social Science, National Demographic Institute (INED), Paris, France.

Ronald van Kempen: Professor of Urban Geography, Urban and Regional research centre Utrecht, Faculty of Geosciences, Utrecht University, The Netherlands.

Berthold Vogel: Sociologist, Institute for Social Research, Hamburg, Germany.

Jan Vranken: Professor of Sociology, Department of Sociology and Social Policy, University of Antwerp, Belgium.

1
The Spatial Dimensions of Urban Social Exclusion and Integration

Sako Musterd and Alan Murie

Neighbourhoods of poverty

Urban social questions are often related to issues of participation, inclusion and integration of the population in the urban society. When formulated the other way around, it regards a 'fight' against social exclusion, often also against segregation, separation and disintegration. Urban-oriented policy makers and politicians, who are operating at the level of the city, urban region or metropolis, frequently consider the understanding and reduction of social exclusion and the stimulation of integration or inclusion of sub-sections of the population as their most important tasks. An interesting element is that most of them appear to think, some explicitly, others impli-citly, that 'space matters' in these urban questions. The state and city they are in; the place where people are; the space they are in; the composition of the space they use; the location relative to other important locations; these are all considered of crucial importance to understand the life chances of cit-izens. In the European realm, proof of this assertion can easily be found at various geographical levels. We simply have to refer to the welfare state comparisons (Esping-Andersen, 1990); or to studies, which address the eco-nomic prospects of cities (Parkinson *et al.*, 1992). We may also refer to the enormous volume of area-based policies, which have been developed over the past decade and which often are legitimized by the idea that the spatial setting has extra and independent effects upon people's opportunities (Burgers and Vranken, 2003). Examples are the Social City Programme in Germany and the French Politique de la Ville with its 'Contrats de Ville', the Flemish Social Impuls Fund (SIF) and the Brussels' 'Contrats des Quartiers', the UK New Deal for Communities programme as well as the New Commitment for Neighbourhood Renewal, the Kvarterløft programme in Denmark, and the Big City Policies programmes in The Netherlands.

Many scientists have expressed their interest in these matters as well, although they underline the 'understanding' element when they search for elaboration of the theoretical knowledge in this sphere. Among the best known scholars in this scientific arena is William Julius Wilson. He referred to the changing social and ethnic population composition in central city areas as a crucial factor in the socialization process of citizens. He concluded that central cities, which were left behind by white middle class inhabitants who moved to the suburbs, especially the central cities that were losing jobs at great speed, were transformed into territories with a very weak opportunity structure. For those who lack the skills to apply for a good job elsewhere, and for those who cannot afford the trip to jobs elsewhere, these inner city areas seem to provide virtually no stimulus at all (Wilson, 1987).

However, this is not to say that concentrations of poverty are always related to areas without opportunities. In Europe, cities have their own historically grown physical, economic, cultural and social characteristics. There too, numerous areas can be found with – relative – concentrations of poor or excluded people. European researchers also talk about segregation, spatial inequality and excluded spaces (Madanipour *et al.*, 1998, Marcuse and Van Kempen, 2000; Musterd and Ostendorf, 1998). However, not all of the urban areas that are being discussed, perhaps not even most of them, are isolated; few are heavily abandoned; few are completely without activities; and many still have their commercial and public infrastructures. We can refer to neighbourhoods such as the famous Quartieri Spagnoli in Naples, which is a lively area where a lot of activity is taking place, an area that is well connected to the main infrastructure, and also is perceived as a territory with new prospects; that area is also well-known for its strong social networks. We might also think of similar types of areas in other European cities, like Brussels. Some of these areas may be characterized by specific spatial attributes that help them provide a new opportunity structure for those who try to integrate in the urban society. Meert (2002) discussed some Brussels neighbourhoods and referred to social networks and social territories that may develop at the local level and may stimulate integration in society.

There are other examples of relatively poor neighbourhoods that do not have to follow the trajectories that were sketched by Wilson. In concentrations of relative poverty in the city of Amsterdam, for example, we can find areas, which are well linked to the economic centres by private and public transport and that consist of good quality housing, where abandonment is not part of the vocabulary.

In short, space matters indeed, but not all spaces that are characterized by concentrations of people who are defined as socially excluded produce similar effects. Perhaps the spatial dimension aggravates the problems, as is suggested in the American example; the spatial dimension may have a weaker role in other contexts, as the Amsterdam example suggests; but perhaps the spatial dimension may even help to solve the problems in other contexts, as is suggested in the examples of Naples and Brussels.

The interest in these issues about the relationship between social exclusion, cities and space was the driving force behind the development of a large-scale European research programme that focused on the spatial dimensions of urban social exclusion and integration. This book is about the findings of that research programme (URBEX). These findings are all put into a wider academic and analytic framework. In the programme the focus was on four issues or questions in particular:

1. What are the relevant spheres of social exclusion and integration?
2. What are the levels of social exclusion and what are the integration opportunity structures or resources available to those who are (potentially or already) socially excluded, in various European urban contexts?
3. What is the role of the neighbourhood in stimulating integration?
4. What are the (new) policy responses to reduce social exclusion in European cities?

In this book we will present some of the answers to these questions. This will not be done in a repetitive way for each of the cities respectively. While carrying out the research, which is underlying the content of this book, it became clear that there are similarities between cities in terms of problems and processes, but also that there is a lot of specificity, which often is rather structural. We decided to highlight the specific spatial and other contextual dimensions for each of the 11 case studies. As a result, the 11 case study chapters roughly follow the guidelines, which were set for the research programme. The case studies also all pay specific attention to the spatial settings; but at the same time, specific impacts, factors, forces and outcomes will be dealt with elaborately as well. This results in a series of contributions that can be regarded as a narrative of similarities and dissimilarities between European cities as far as the relation between space, social exclusion and integration is concerned.

Some say that cities are actually too complex to compare. We take another position. We will do justice to the individual cases studies by presenting them per chapter. However, in the final chapter we will challenge the complexity and draw some conclusions based on a cross comparison of the most clear differences and similarities between the cities as far as their position relative to social exclusion, integration and space are concerned. In that chapter, we will also connect the academic debate with policy and politics about social exclusion and integration in cities, again highlighting the spatial dimensions that are regarded relevant.

In this introductory chapter we will briefly present the theoretical framework. Following that introduction, the spatial contexts that are regarded to be important for each of the opportunity structures will be clarified. We will also touch upon the three target groups we have distinguished. We will also introduce the individual case study chapters.

Theoretical framework

Debates about neighbourhood differences and urban poverty have a long history. At the beginning of the twenty-first century they have an enhanced importance. Cities are widely regarded as more unequal than in the past. This is partly because of a number of important economic changes: the economic crisis occasioned by the oil shocks of the 1970s, changes in the advanced economies of Europe and North America with the restructuring and decline of manufacturing industry and the growth of service sector employment, flexibility in the new production and consumption processes and globalization with its increased competition between places. Alongside this the welfare state has generally been under attack. Neo-liberal thinking has become much more dominant in informing debates about economic and social policy. We have moved beyond the full employment, welfare state-based social rights of the earlier postwar years into a period referred to in the literature as post-Fordist and postindustrial.

It is not only changes in the economy and the welfare state that have been important. Changes in the nature of marriage and the family and increased life expectancy mean that the demographic structure of cities is significantly different to that 50 or more years ago. There is a much larger population of elderly people and of childless households. People's life histories no longer follow the predictable family life cycle that informed policy thinking in the past. There is greater volatility in family and domestic arrangements and greater volatility in employment and security of employment. At the same time European cities have been changed by a succession of waves of migration that reflect demand for low-skilled labour forces on the urban labour markets under Fordism, colonial histories or changes in the politics of eastern Europe, as well as the attraction of European cities because of their relative affluence and the economic and employment opportunities they provide.

All of these changes have affected European cities as well as those in America and beyond. The concerns about their effects are evident in the titles of some of the important contributions to research and academic debate related to cities: *The Global City* (Sassen, 1991), *Divided Cities* (Fainstein *et al.*, 1992), *Globalizing Cities* (Marcuse and Van Kempen, 2000). Academics as well as policymakers have been concerned by the significance of a series of social and economic changes, but much of the attention, and this applies to the titles referred to above, analyses change at a city level. The debate between Sassen, Fainstein, Hamnett and others about the real nature of the changing social and occupational structure of New York or London involves an exchange relating to data at a city level. It does not address the nature of changes at a neighbourhood level. Nor does it give much attention to the influence of policy or for example the welfare state. In relation to the latter, the American literature in particular tends to neglect the welfare state (and particularly national welfare systems) in discussions of what factors shape cities. Perhaps because of the residual nature of the welfare state in the USA market processes are the focus for explanations of why cities are as they are and for how they are changing. In European cities the state has been more interventionist and exercised more control and influence across the economy during and following wartime emergencies and through political coalitions that have supported stronger welfare states. In these cities changes in welfare state arrangements are more likely to be an important element in explaining differences and changes. These issues are also relevant when it comes to interest in uneven patterns of change within European cities.

The debate between Sassen and Hamnett, for example, involves a discussion of whether economic change has polarized the occupational structure or professionalized it and there are other versions – whether there has been a professionalization of the economically active population but at the same time a growth in the economically inactive population. But this debate says little about whether the polarization or professionalization has an uneven geographical impact across the city. Other contributors, notably Massey and others, have emphasized the uneven geography of economic change. But again this is a debate largely at a regional and sub-regional level rather than a neighbourhood one. An uneven pattern of economic change could have no impact at all upon residential patterns within the city. Those in employment would still live in the same areas but would have different journeys to work.

So we have a debate that identifies growing inequality as a key feature of cities but does not provide us with very much understanding about the importance of neighbourhood. Do different neighbourhoods provide resources that mitigate the effects of other changes and assist coping strategies of households? Is it preferable to live in these kinds of neighbourhoods in cities that are becoming more unequal and are undergoing change than it is to live in the neighbourhoods with different kinds of resources?

Much of the policy debate emanating from this evidence does identify the most deprived neighbourhoods and an increasingly sophisticated industry has developed to measure and map deprivation. What it tends to generate is a league table of neighbourhoods that are most deprived. If you were to read the league table alone you would imagine that these neighbourhoods are essentially the same: that in Rotterdam if you visited Hoogvliet it would be almost the same as Rotterdam Oud-Zuid (both in the 2003 list of most deprived neighbourhoods, presented by the Ministry of the Environment) or in Birmingham if you visited Aston it would be the same as Sparkbrook. The indices constructed from characteristics of the population suggest that this is the case but anyone visiting these neighbourhoods or having lived in them will immediately be aware that they are enormously different. They are located in different parts of the city, they have a different built environment and physical infrastructure, they have populations of different age and ethnicity, and they have different dynamics and a different character. Are these things unimportant or do they call into question the implication that neighbourhoods that are similarly deprived have similar resources and would be affected by similar policies?

These considerations take us on to a further debate. Much of the literature about American cities highlights the importance of race and issues such as housing tenure do not emerge as important. In European cities the conflict has been much more around the welfare state and the housing produced by not for profit and state agencies (Rex and Moore, 1967).

The organizing principles of residence in American and European cities then appear to be quite different. Rather than the market and race, residential patterns in European cities have been organized around the welfare state and social class. But this is a dynamic situation. The share of the market in housing provision has increased and new patterns of immigration have introduced a race element into the operation of housing markets in Europe. European cities have seen neighbourhoods with a changing racial composition and increased segregation, but these levels of segregation have come nowhere near meeting those that are apparent in American cities and there is evidence of considerable dispersion of ethnic minority households as their affluence and employability changes.

So we have four interrelated dominant concerns:

1. increasing inequality and differentiation within European cities;
2. the geographical or neighbourhood element in this differentiation;
3. the importance of the welfare state and differences between welfare systems as factors contributing to neighbourhood differentiation; and
4. issues of class and redistribution as well as the operation of the market and ethnicity.

The theoretical framework adopted for the project is one that gives attention to all of these dimensions of neighbourhood change and social exclusion.

Concepts: Integration and exclusion

Integration is a multidimensional concept encompassing people's position relative to the labour market; their relationship with governmental or related institutions, including institutions in the domains of education, health, housing, finance, culture, and so on, and a person's position in social networks. These dimensions are also referred to as 'spheres of integration'. The concept tends to be used in a wide variety of meanings and is often also referred to in terms of the type and level of participation in society (socially, economically, culturally, politically); people are usually regarded to be integrated if they participate in the labour market, if they have build social net-works and regularly visit friends and relatives; if they participate politically, for example via voting during elections; and if they use the public facilities and institutions that have been created for their own benefits.

Social exclusion implies being cut off from relevant sections of society; this includes, for example, being unemployed; being in a position where social networks are weak and the risk of becoming socially isolated is serious; or it may be related to a situation in which individuals have lost their connection with important institutions in society (including the health system, public housing and the school system).

In this book we address socially excluded people, and – in some chapters more than in others – also the trajectories that brought them to the position they found themselves during our interviews. We restrict the definition of socially excluded people to the unemployed. Within the category of unemployed, we focus the attention on three groups; these will be introduced below.

The main body of this book is about the way unemployed people seek to integrate economically in the urban society, that is in the first place, getting access to their means of existence. For that purpose we will investigate which resources they are using (and how) to reach a certain level of economic integration. We will focus the attention on three spheres of integration.

Spheres of integration

The three spheres of economic integration we distinguish are related to participation in the labour market; the relation between the individual and the welfare state; and the position of the individual in social networks. In fact, these three spheres provide the resources that are necessary for full participation in society. They are derived from classic work of Polanyi (1944). The three spheres through which resources can be obtained that contribute to the economic integration of individuals are often referred to as 'market exchange' related resources; resources through 'redistribution' of wealth and rights by the state or other institutions; and resources that can be obtained via territorial social networks in which individuals provide these resources in a 'reciprocal' relationship. We will briefly label these three spheres as 'market exchange', 'redistribution' and 'reciprocity'. It is the position in relation to these spheres, and the way they interact that determines the extent to which households, and perhaps also communities, can be integrated economically – and through that perhaps also socially, culturally and politically – or are excluded from the mainstream of society.

In most cities in the western world, access to resources is dominated by *market exchange* via the formal labour market. Most households try to get a position on the labour market to earn an income. However, the market is not to be regarded as a neutral thing. It generates social stratification and provides unequal access to certain resources based on the strength of the positions people have. Those who have higher skills, those who are better educated, that is, reached higher levels of education, those who have more language skills and perhaps also more other (social) skills; all those people have better opportunities to get resources via the labour market. These inequalities are inherent in market exchange. Some regard this to be a natural thing; according to them people should only know that access to resources requires certain skills; but if they are aware of that opportunities are available. Others regard the inevitable inequality the structural reason why there should be compensation by (state) *redistribution* of goods, services and finances, or they consider that the distribution of some specific resources, like land, labour and money, cannot be adequately regulated by the market and, therefore, needs state intervention. The steady development of the welfare state that provided social housing, social security, minimum income levels, health provision and many other services created massive redistribution in substantial parts of Western Europe, mainly through taxes and social security contributions. The redistribution is mainly taking place via subsidies and benefits. On many occasions these resources can provide sufficient income to survive and to live in a decent place. Redistribution can take various forms. Each welfare state is characterized by some level of redistribution, but some are known as huge redistribution machines (Scandinavian countries), whereas others are seen as small redistribution machines, mainly via strict means-tested mechanisms (UK, USA). Various in-between systems can be thought of. Finally, *reciprocity* helps people to obtain resources through mutual exchange. It implies a capacity to produce some resources for each of the participants in a social network, and it requires the existence of a social network with rather symmetric links between the members and the rest of the network. The most evident networks are the household, the extended family and sometimes neighbourhood networks or networks within ethnic minority communities. Mutual help is one of the most obvious forms of reciprocity relations.

These spheres of integration are not unrelated. However, the type and strength of the relationship is not really understood so far, although some insights have been developed. The confusion may be illustrated by reference to the Wilson–Murray debate. That debate, which is also a political debate, since it is clearly related to different political views – social-democratic versus conservative – addresses the idea that unemployed people, including single mothers, should (the social-democratic view) or should not (the conservative view) receive a fair unemployment or welfare benefit from the state. The first camp defends this idea with the statement that only if people start from a human position, and only if they do not loose the link with society completely, will they be able to regain a stronger position and regain labour market participation. The second camp, which is eager to reduce government expenditure on social programmes, says that the benefit provision will only result in reduced self-reliance. This would mean the receiver only uses the benefit, but does not get the impulse that is required to take the initiative to re-integrate into society (Murray, 1984). This debate reveals different views regarding the relation between the market exchange and the redistribution spheres of integration.

Another idea of a relation between spheres of integration regards the social network. The strength of the social network is not only considered to be relevant as a means for the provision of reciprocal resources, mutual help and small scale mutual services, but may also serve to get access to the resources that are available in the other spheres of integration. Local networks may comprise the knowledge of where to go to in the redistribution arena, for example. The rules and regulations are often so complex, that some support is required to tell people where to get the benefits and facilities that are available, such as individual rent subsidies, income support, or incidental support, for example; but local networks are also considered to be essential to get into a position that leads to the proper routes to a job, that is to resources in the sphere of market exchange (Andersson, 2001; Morris, 1987; Pahl, 1984).

Opportunity structures: Spatial contexts

The opportunity structures that are available to people and that are related to the spheres of integration can be found at different geographical levels. That was an important reason for developing the research programme in the way we did. We covered six European countries, 11 cities, and 22 neighbourhoods (two per city).

Each sphere of integration is – predominantly – related to a different context: redistribution is mainly linked to the state level; market exchange is mainly linked to the urban regional level; and reciprocity is mainly linked to the neighbourhood level. The redistribution sphere thus refers to the welfare state model that is involved. Following the work of Esping-Andersen (1990), Mingione (1991) and others we can – as a minimum – distinguish between four types of welfare states: a social democratic, a corporatist, a liberal, and a family oriented type. The Netherlands comes closest to the social democratic type, but also has corporatist elements; clearly corporatist are Germany, Belgium and France; The UK and Northern Italy represent the liberal welfare state, although it is not the real prototype; and Southern Italy represents the family oriented welfare state. We assume that the level of redistribution via the state is smaller in the order we presented these types. We should, however, be aware of the fact that nation states may have lost position over time, while local authorities may have gained in importance in today's social political arenas. That may also result in the development of a larger role for local welfare provision relative to what will be provided at the state level. In a recent paper, Mingione (2003) has presented original ideas about that shift towards local welfare provision.

The market exchange sphere of integration refers to economic restructuring as a world scale process. Although this is a fairly global process, the outcomes are different at the local metropolitan level. This is mainly due to the cities' different urban economic histories. Some cities are 'marked' by their deeply rooted manufacturing industries history, others are not. These different structures have tremendous impact on the capability of cities to attract new firms. These new firms usually require an attractive non-industrial environment, adequate cultural, social and recreation spaces, and professional workers, rightly skilled to do the jobs in the new economies. The different histories may or may not have led to the required set of conditions. To be able to investigate this effect we selected manufacturing-oriented cities and service-oriented cities in almost all of the participating countries. The first type includes cities with a clear manufacturing profile, which was developed over a longer period of time; they also include large port cities. These cities are: Birmingham, Rotterdam, Antwerp, Hamburg and Naples. The second type includes cities with a much stronger service sector profile: London, Milan, Amsterdam, Brussels, Berlin and Paris.

The reciprocity sphere (social networks) is supposed to operate at the neighbourhood level: the social territory. The neighbourhoods were selected in two different urban settings. One neighbourhood representing a nineteenth-century inner city area mainly consisting of private housing and showing a relatively large functional mix, the other a postwar neighbourhood mainly consisting of social rented housing, showing a much more homogeneous structure and smaller functional mix.

Three target groups: Categories of unemployed

A household's capacity to make use of various opportunities and strategies to cope with the situation and at least partially integrate in the urban society clearly depends on the economic situation and on the character of economic restructuring, on the type and transformation of the welfare state involved, on demographic and on cultural (including lifestyle) characteristics and changes that are affecting social networks and perhaps also on the type and location of the neighbourhood involved. Dependent on the position in these domains, some household categories are at greater risk than others. In our research we focused on three categories of unemployed, three target groups. That focus on the unemployed implies that the labour market is regarded to be the most important sphere of integration in the Western world. A total number of around 600 in-depth interviews with members of the three target groups, and several hundred key person interviews formed the empirical basis of the research programme. The three categories of unemployed are: unemployed immigrants; unemployed single mothers; and long-term unemployed native men.

The first category is one of immigrants who are unable to get a job. Many of them are handicapped in the domain of integration through the market (because of discrimination and/or lack of skills). Unemployment rates tend to be much higher for (low skilled) immigrants than for 'native' citizens. In Amsterdam and Rotterdam the unemployment rate of Moroccan and Turkish inhabitants tended to be approximately four times higher compared to native Dutch (Burgers and Musterd, 2002). Redistribution will not be a viable alternative in some cases, because of a lack of citizen rights or because of the type of welfare state they live in. Therefore, many will have to rely on other ways to get the resources that are required.

Single mothers on benefits are the second category. It is often argued that these households would have relatively weak social ties and run a greater risk of experiencing social isolation and a weakening of local community life. The higher costs that they have because of the children and time devoted to child care prevent them from being fully available for the labour market (Van Kempen, 2002). Their dependency on one income, in the case of unemployment usually provided by the state, and their reduced opportunities to rely on reciprocity via social networks, is considered to contribute to the odds of their becoming classified as a 'risk category'. Whether these assumptions were also found in the respective cases studies, remains to be seen.

The third category refers to the native male long-term unemployed, perhaps the 'classic' example of the socially excluded. We hypothesized that the duration of unemployment they are confronted with may be a factor on its own that might keep them in an excluded situation.

Eleven case studies

The questions that were raised, the hypotheses that were formulated, and the preliminary insights we referred to, are all addressed in the following case studies. It will be no surprise if we state that various clusters of city cases can be made, dependent on the issues we want to highlight most. In this book we chose to organize the city-chapters on the basis of the relevance of the neighbourhoods in enhancing the opportunities to escape from a socially excluded situation. In some cities it was found that the neighbourhood does not play a big role in helping people to escape from poverty, whereas in other cities the neighbourhood in which people lived, made a big difference. However, this is not a unilateral story. Although there is some regularity in terms of the relevance of the neighbourhood, which seems to be associated with the type of welfare regime that affects the cities, this is not without exception.

Besides, we do not intend to focus on this space dimension only. One of the other interesting findings is related to gender. Gender plays a crucial role in the social exclusion process; however, findings in some of our cities deviated somewhat from the hypothesized relationships. We, therefore, also will organize this book along that line. This results in an ordering of the chapters as follows. We start with five cities in which space or neighbourhood does not seem to play a crucial role in affecting the social exclusion situation of representatives of our target groups – Berlin, Antwerp, Amsterdam, Hamburg and Milan. In the latter three cities the gender dimension also receives substantial attention Rotterdam, Paris, London, Birmingham, Naples and Brussels then follow these cases. In these cities space or the neighbourhood does tend to play a role, even though that role is not similar in all of these contexts. The first four cities are predominantly characterized as cities in relatively strong welfare states. Milan, Rotterdam and Paris are somewhat specific cases, as we will illustrate later. The last four cities may be characterized as cities with a relatively weak welfare state involvement, although this is not a uniform cluster either. However, this order functions as a crude multidimensional means to understand the variations we encountered.

Berlin holds a unique position in at least one sense. Since 1990, when Berlin became the capital of a reunited Germany, a tremendous change in the economic situation and the social composition of the neighbourhoods can be observed. This has led to growing social segregation and growing social polarization. However, the analyses of the life chances and coping strategies of groups of inhabitants who are affected by poverty and social exclusion has shown that both neighbourhoods that were studied (Marzahn and Neukoelln-Reuterplatz) can only offer limited resources for their inhabitants. Most respondents are able to use these limited resources for the stabilization of life. However, the neighbourhood did not help to improve their labour market situation. Since many excluded people cannot escape from their neighbourhoods, they tend to identify with their neighbourhood; this seems to stabilize their lives and give shelter against discrimination.

The Antwerp case also revealed only minor area-effects. Strategies of socially excluded residents in the two neighbourhoods that were researched were hardly linked to the area, but seemed to be related to personal characteristics, like age and ethnicity, but predominantly to past-life experiences. In both Dam and Silvertop, the perspectives for socially excluded inhabitants seemed to be highly dependent on whether they were confronted with social exclusion in a very early stage of their life or not. Early deprivation implied lack of opportunities. When these experiences were absent the prospects for improved conditions grew proportionally. As in Berlin (and in other German and Dutch cities) Antwerp's social system played a rather large role in providing the crucial means for a decent existence.

In the Dutch capital, Amsterdam, again few, if any, neighbourhood effects could be found (in Osdorp and Landlust). It is possible that the strong redistributive and universal character of the Dutch welfare state has enabled a fairly similar way of life, irrespective of the location and character of the neighbourhoods involved. This could be a more general explanation for the differences between cities with a well-developed re-distribution of wealth versus cities that do not have these characteristics. Yet, this does not imply that there are no problems of social exclusion anymore. One of the issues that is high on the agenda is the 'feminization of poverty', referring to the gendered character of social exclusion. The position of women and, more especially, single mothers is considered to be the most vulnerable. In the Netherlands, however, they used to get easy access to social benefits. The authors of the Amsterdam chapter expected that the position of single mothers might have become more difficult in the Dutch situation because of a change, in 1996, in the system of the Dutch welfare state, implying more pressure to re-enter the labour market. However, this change did not turn out to affect single mothers too much: they are easily excused for not participating in the labour market. So, un-expectedly the findings point in the direction of a relatively good position for single mothers.

The conclusion drawn in the Hamburg case (St. Pauli and Mümmelmans-berg) also was that neighbourhoods are of only limited importance to their inhabitants when it comes to fighting social exclusion. The authors stated that different neighbourhoods do attract different people, since the neigh-bourhood conditions may be good for some poor and not for others, but after such a sorting process has occurred, no specific neighbourhood effects could be found anymore. As in Antwerp, life experiences and socio-demographic variables were regarded to be most important for the under-standing of different opportunities to escape from social exclusion. As in Amsterdam, gender was also mentioned as a really important variable. However, unlike the situation in Amsterdam, they found that the threat of social exclusion, which people felt, was more severe among women than among men.

The Milan case study (Baggio and Ponte Lambro) is in some respects the first exceptional case study. Milan typically is a city in a state, which cannot be classified as a strong redistributing welfare state. Yet, differences between the impacts of the neighbourhoods could not be found, whereas we tended to expect that these should be found in weaker welfare states. One possible explanation for this is the fact that Milan is a very wealthy city in which some attachment to the labour market is in fact always poss-ible. There is sufficient work available for everyone. The researchers found that life trajectories were more important as an explanatory factor. Especially, the sudden loss of social ties turned out to be of paramount significance. In Milan, just as in Amsterdam, single mothers were most well off in relative terms. They were able to pull resources from the market, but also from social services (they were regarded as the 'deserving poor') and from family and social networks. No other category of socially excluded people could reach their level in all of these domains.

The city of Rotterdam provides another exception, in the sense that this city is embedded in a strong welfare state. Yet, it was found that the space or the neighbourhood was of decisive importance for the activities being undertaken by its residents and for the contacts they were establishing. Especially, the peripherally located neighbourhood Hoogvliet showed strong relationships and more activity among their inhabitants compared to the more centrally located neighbourhood Tarwewijk. One interpretation may be that the Hoogvliet neighbourhood is regarded to be that peripheral, that people are more or less forced to cope with each other. The authors mention transport costs as explaining this, but also the village-like character of the neighbourhood.

Paris is the third somewhat exceptional neighbourhood. Although France is known for its fairly well developed welfare system, that system does not function as an 'equalizer', in the sense that neighbourhood differences would disappear. In fact, it was concluded that neighbourhoods do matter, albeit in a special sense. It was concluded that the historical, urban and social differences between the two neighbourhoods (La Courneuve and Bas-Montreuil) had little impact 'in itself' in the three spheres of integration. Moreover, strategies among the unemployed, aimed at using the neighbourhood's resources are very unusual in both neighbourhoods. However, what did turn out to be important was the difference in experience of poverty. The authors state that the experience of poverty in La Courneuve is one of having a decent home in a deficient environment that has become the symbol of poverty, whereas being poor in Bas-Montreuil implies having a timeworn and small home in a relatively better environment, with a positive collective identity.

Weaker welfare provisions can be found in the four remaining case studies. That seems to be a relevant factor explaining increasing differences between neighbourhoods and larger impacts of neighbourhoods. London is – perhaps – the weakest case to illustrate this relationship, possible again, as in Milan, because the labour market was – during the research – so tight. No core–periphery neighbourhood effect could be found. However, the neighbourhoods appeared to be important resources for the socially excluded. As in Berlin, a strong attachment to place was regarded to reflect sociospatial immobility among the poor and most vulnerable people, and the necessity of having to make do with spatially fixed assets such as housing. Residualization of council housing in London has concentrated many vulnerable and marginalized people in areas where unemployment, deteriorating council housing, petty crime, drugs and prostitution are mounting problems, although historical and institutional specificities rooted in welfare characteristics at national and local levels prevent deprived neighbourhoods assuming the more extreme US 'ghetto' characteristics.

In Birmingham the two neighbourhoods that were included in the research programme were very dissimilar. The neighbourhoods were presented as different kinds of deprived neighbourhoods with different tenure mixes and different histories of development. Sorting processes resulted in different population structures in both neighbourhoods. It was found that the impact of both neighbourhoods was clearly different, which was highly dependent on the paths these neighbourhoods had followed, on their historical trajectories. It was suggested that more diverse areas offer more opportunities to escape from misery than less diverse areas.

This was also a conclusion in the Brussels' case, where it was found that the inner city neighbourhood, which was much more varied in many ways, offered more opportunities in the sphere of reciprocity, in particular. The peripheral neighbourhood did not offer that many opportunities to cope with social exclusion, though.

The experiences of Naples gave way to similar conclusions. Inner city neighbourhoods under Naples' conditions have more perspective than monolithic outer areas, which, in that context, are not very well connected to the city in the first place.

In considering the results from the URBEX project, it is important that we identify the differences emerging between the cities, but the final chapters of this book also reflect upon the implications of the results at a different level. There has been some discussion within the project that by breaking down the factors shaping neighbourhoods and cities into component parts there is an implication that these elements operate independently of one another rather than being interdependent and embedded within the overall social and economic structure of the city. Although we can identify factors that appear to have strong associations with particular cities and explain distinctive patterns of exclusion, these distinctive features are partly the products of other aspects of the city.

One of the strongly emerging themes from the research is that neighbourhoods do provide a distinctive set of resources for households that fall into particular categories. The significance of these different resources for the life chances of households may be open to question, but they undoubtedly do have some impact on the experience of exclusion. The resources associated with particular neighbourhoods change and are themselves the product of previous policies and decisions by households as well as the current organization of communities and the operation of the market, the welfare state and reciprocity at the present time. Neighbourhoods have reputations and built environments that are products at least in part of earlier decisions. Although much of the research indicates that there are strong similarities between the experiences of, for example, lone parents in different places, the context remains important. For example, what kind of housing is available? What kind of opportunities and threats exist is partly affected by the neighbourhood. Some of the chapters conclude that these differences have a largely superficial effect. In other cases there are suggestions that they have a more profound impact on the experience of poverty. All of this suggests different views of the nature of neighbourhood impacts and the final chapters again discuss the different levels at which neighbourhoods may have an impact, whether it is an impact on social mobility and life chances, or simply on the day-to-day experience of living.

The theoretical framework adopted in this research is one that enables these issues to be addressed, but it is important that we point up the importance of changes over time and of historical legacies and do not see the framework as simply of use in providing a snapshot of contemporary social interaction. The debate about neighbourhood effects has to be a dynamic one referring both to changes in the past and the trajectories of change. It needs to reflect upon changing reputations and whether the welfare state is creating stigmatization, reinforcing it or mitigating it. It needs to address the different resources that neighbourhoods offer, but at the same time avoid a series of dualisms. The resources that may be effective for one section of households experiencing processes of social exclusion may be ineffective or even damaging for others. It is not a matter of identifying neighbourhoods with reputations that are good or bad, or resources that are beneficial to those experiencing exclusion or are not beneficial to those experiencing exclusion. The likelihood is that many neighbourhoods have elements of both of these and are in any case undergoing change. There may be positive elements in the reputation for some groups and negative elements for others and there may be resources that are beneficial for some but not for others. The conflicts that are being worked out in neighbourhoods will strengthen the disadvantage experienced by some and weaken it for others.

The overall conclusion emerging is that neighbourhoods matter, but not that there is always a neighbourhood effect that influences fundamental life chances or that neighbourhood effects are either all good or bad. The experience of social exclusion, however, is a lived experience and it is lived in places that differ. Academic and research analyses or policy prognoses that treat categories of the population without any reference to where they live are likely to miss an important dimension of the experience of social exclusion. The implications of this for our approaches to analysis and policy are discussed in the final chapter of this book.

2
Berlin: Opportunities, Constraints and Strategies of the Urban Poor

Andreas Kapphan and Hartmut Häussermann[1]

The questions

Urban neighbourhoods can provide restrictions as well as resources for life chances in general. A neighbourhood can be a source of 'exclusion', but also a source of 'inclusion' or 'integration'. How a neighbourhood works, and in which direction, depends on social, economic and physical characteristics – but also on the life strategy of the private households. There is a complex relation between households and their environment. In this chapter we will try to explore this relationship for different types of households affected by unemployment, in two different neighbourhoods in Berlin. Neighbourhood opportunities can add to the stabilization of life conditions, and so can promote social and economic integration. In this case study we will examine the following questions: Does spatial concentration of poverty affect the coping strategies of people in poverty? Under which circumstances does poverty lead to social exclusion?

Changing Berlin

Berlin holds a unique position because its situation is quite unlike that of any other city within the Federal Republic of Germany. Until 1990, the city was divided in two: the West, which belonged to the political system of the Federal Republic of Germany, and the East which served as the capital of the German Democratic Republic (GDR) or East Germany. Most parts of the housing market in West Berlin were heavily influenced by state subsidies and rent controls; in East Berlin housing was a state affair, and local authorities distributed it. To a certain extent, in both parts of the divided city housing opportunities were not structured by market forces, but by redistribution policies. After the fall of the wall this changed quickly in East and West, and so new patterns of segregation emerged.

Since then, the social compositions of the neighbourhoods have undergone a transformation as a result of recent migratory movements in and out of the city. After 1993, the population started to decline in both parts of the city as a result of the new process of suburbanization, and since 1998 population development has been stagnating (see Häussermann and Kapphan, 2000; Kapphan, 2002).

Migration into Berlin mostly comprises foreigners who came from Eastern European countries, including Russia, Kazakhstan, Poland and countries of the former Yugoslavia, during the 1990s. The number of non-Germans was 443,000 in 2002 or 13.3 per cent of the population, being 17.7 per cent in West Berlin and 5.9 per cent in East Berlin. While the old migrant groups settled in the West before 1990 and have stayed there since, new migrants settle in both halves of the city, so the share of migrants in the East is increasing (see Kapphan, 2001).

Today, the City of Berlin has 3.3 million inhabitants, living in an area of 889 km^2, with 63 per cent of them in the West of the city. Following the political collapse of the GDR in 1989 and the reunification of the city in 1990, there has been continuous economic, social and spatial transformation affecting both parts of the city. 1990 was a year of big expectations for growth and the development of Berlin as a new European centre between East and West. Because of the decision to be the new capital of the united Germany, an enormous increase in population and employment was expected. But it turned out to be very different and the 1990s in Berlin saw a decrease in population, labour force and employment, followed by a rise in unemployment and poverty (see Dorsch *et al.*, 2000; Häussermann and Kapphan, 2000; Kapphan, 2002). The economic change is linked to the global trend towards peripherization of production, while at the same time new jobs are created in the centres of economic development (primarily in the service sector). In Berlin as well as in other European cities, this transition from the industrial to the service city displays clear signs of crisis:

- The overall number of jobs decreased (the newly created jobs could not compensate for the loss in employment stock). Thus, the labour market can less and less provide jobs for the population. Employment declined from 1.69 million in 1991 to 1.48 million in 1998. In East Berlin, the decrease in employment was 9 per cent between 1991 and 1998, where the collapse occurred especially between 1990 and 1992 (and therefore, is not totally included in this figure) stabilizing in the following years. In 1998 one-third of the employed persons of the East commuted to West Berlin. Correspondingly, the decrease in employment in West Berlin may be described as a process that occurred especially after 1995 with a loss of 15 per cent of jobs between 1995 and 1998. These trends can be seen in all the individual districts, but job decline can be said to be considerably high in the inner-city districts of West Berlin. In Neukoelln the number of jobs declined by 22 per cent from 1991 to 1998.

- The share of the unemployed and of welfare recipients is increasing. The state's responsibility to secure income and provision for its citizens grows, and with it its financial burden. In West Berlin, a rise of unemployment occurred between 1980 and 1983, from 4.3 per cent to 10.4 per cent, and then stabilized until 1990. Economic activities and investments in the unification period somewhat reduced the unemployment rate. However, this short-term decline has been followed by a continuous rise in unemployment in West Berlin in the 1990s. In East Berlin, unemployment rose from 6 per cent in 1990 to 13 per cent in 1992, and then increased to 16.5 per cent in June 1997. Since 1994, a higher unemployment rate was observed in the West than in the East. The 2000 unemployment rate for Berlin as a whole was 17 per cent. The rate of welfare-receiving households was still comparatively small in East Berlin (5 per cent) with only small differences between the districts. Among the West Berlin districts, the rate of households on welfare differs enormously. In 2000, the inner-city districts showed the highest rate of welfare recipients: in Kreuzberg it accounted for 17.5 per cent of the population, followed by Wedding with 16.8 per cent and Neukoelln with 13.3 per cent, while in Zehlendorf it was only 3.1 per cent. Overall, in Berlin the rate of welfare recipients among the population was 7.9 per cent.
- The social composition of the city's population and its neighbourhoods, as well as household structures, changes. Suburbanization and selective migration to the urban fringe lead to a concentration of unemployment and welfare dependants in several of the inner city areas and in certain high-rise housing estates at the urban fringe. The selectivity of the mobility deepens social diversity in Berlin's neighbourhoods. This can be shown especially for the big housing estates that were built in the postwar period. In the 1980s, this housing stock had been opened for migrants in the West, but too often discrimination by the 'gate-keepers' stopped such entry. In the 1990s both 'social housing' in the West and the prefabricated housing units in the East became subject to change. The proportions of migrants and unemployed in this segment increased, and in some neighbourhoods migrant households are the only ones to apply for dwellings. Since vacancy became a serious problem for the housing associations, migrants and unemployed were welcomed. This enforced selective mobility exchanges, and some of those neighbourhoods became 'disadvantaged' very rapidly.

The increase in urban poverty is a result of the collective decline of social groups, such as 'the workers'. What previously had been a working-class neighbourhood became a neighbourhood of unemployed, because the dramatic losses of jobs in manufacturing degrade former workers' neighbourhoods ('lift-effect'). But also, there are effects of selective mobility in urban agglomerations – the removal of certain socially and economically integrated groups and the influx of those less integrated – that lead to an intensified concentration of poverty.

Research target groups

As was set out in Chapter 1 the groups researched in this study are exceptionally affected by poverty and unemployment. The selected groups are: long-term unemployed men, aged 25 to 55 years; single mothers depending on welfare benefits; and immigrants affected by poverty and unemployment.

These three groups are unevenly distributed all over Berlin, but they appear in all areas that have seen impoverishment in recent years. In Germany, the unemployed receive unemployment insurance of up to 67 per cent of their former salary, for up to one year; after that period they can get unemployment benefits if there is no family support possible. Unemployment benefits had been continuously up to 2004, but could be reduced to about 50 per cent of former income from dependent employment.

Long-term unemployed men

In 1999, the Berlin unemployment rate totalled 17.5 per cent. About a third had been unemployed for more than one year. Among these long-term unemployed people, men take an over-proportional share. In the eastern part of the city the share of long-term unemployment has so far been lower than in the West. However, the share of long-term unemployment (as a proportion of all unemployment) has been rising in both parts of Berlin during the past few years. All age groups could be found among the unemployed in 1998, but the share of the young aged between 20 and 25 years is a little higher than that of other age groups. In the East, the older unemployed (those above 55 years of age) appear to be over-represented compared to their average share of the population. There, 47 per cent of the unemployed persons are female, compared to 42 per cent in the Western part of the city. Two spatial centres of gravity for unemployment in Berlin have been found: old inner-city housing areas in the West, as well as high-rise housing estates on the fringe of the city. In these areas the share of the unemployed amounts to about 20 per cent of the workforce, which equals an unemployment rate of at least 30 per cent.

Single mothers

Single mothers suffer especially from the worsening conditions in the labour market. As a rule, they need considerable time for their children. Therefore it is harder for them to find work, considering that usually employers prefer other job applicants. If several years go by without employment, their return to the labour market becomes harder. Even without having been officially unemployed for a prolonged period, many single mothers are confronted with a long-term absence from the labour market, because of the period they took off for childcare. There is no statistical data about single parents' unemployment share, but in the statistics of welfare benefits the data show that single parents are overrepresented.

Single parents in the West do not concentrate in specific areas. In the East, besides the old housing, they predominantly dwell in the large housing estates of the outskirts. As a consequence of the stronger integration of women into gainful employment and better access to childcare facilities, the share of single parents of all households was and still is higher in the East than in the West.

Migrants

The share of 'Auslaender' (foreign citizens) in the Berlin population totals 13 per cent. Many of them did not themselves immigrate to Germany, but are 'second generation'. Additionally, there are migrants who are German citizens: they either have been naturalized or they immigrated as 'ethnic Germans', which means, that the family obtained German citizenship at the time of immigration.

The first immigrants of the 1960s and the 1970s, the 'guest-workers', came predominantly from Turkey and Yugoslavia. These people settled in the old housing areas, with a deteriorated housing stock, designated for urban renewal. For this reason, a strong concentration of foreign population in the inner-city districts of West Berlin arose. Immigration in the 1990s on the other hand, originated mostly in Eastern Europe, as Poland and the states of the former Soviet Union sent most of the immigrants. Among them there are a large number of ethnic Germans from Russia and Kazakhstan (altogether 30,000 people). More than one-third of the latter live in the high-rise estates of Marzahn on the fringe of East Berlin and now make up 15 per cent of its population (Kapphan, 2001).

A particularly high proportion of the immigrants of the 1960s and 1970s, as well as the more recent immigrants, are unemployed. The old immigsrants are affected by job cuts in their traditional fields of employment (particularly manufacturing). The new immigrants, on the contrary, are unable to find access to employment in the first place because of the declining number of jobs available for them.

Research concept

Considering unemployment, two area types in Berlin stick out among all areas. First, among the most affected are inner-city areas with a large stock of old housing in private ownership, containing a particularly large share of small flats – the so-called 'Wilhelminian-Style-Blocks'. Here, in turn, many small households, immigrant families and single parents constitute the occupants. Second, there are high-rise housing estates in communal or public housing associations with various types of apartments. They are mainly distributed via 'documents of eligibility' ('Wohnberechtigungs-scheine'), which can be applied for in case of low income. Here too, dwell many single parents and a rising number of migrant households.

Within this spatial context we chose two contrasting neighbourhoods for field research. One is a neighbourhood in northern Neukoelln in West Berlin, with a high share of non-Germans and unemployed – representing the one area type. Private housing in five-storey buildings of the beginning of twentieth century is dominant. The other is a neighbourhood in northern Marzahn on the urban fringe of East-Berlin, which consists of prefabricated houses in six and eleven-storey buildings. It has been the settlement destination for many migrants from the former Soviet Union during the past decade. Compared to other housing estates, it is characterized by a particularly high share of unemployment. The location of both areas is shown in Figure 2.1.

In spring and summer 2000, 56 interviews with persons suffering poverty and unemployment were carried out, half of them in each area. Among the interviewees in each area, ten persons belonged to the migrant group and ten to the single mother group. In each neighbourhood, eight interviews

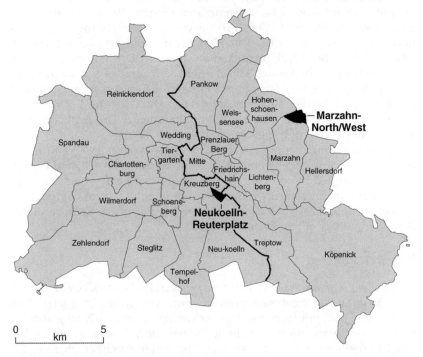

Figure 2.1 Location of research areas in Berlin

were also held with unemployed men aged between 25 and 55 years. The respondents were recruited partly by organizations and associations working in the neighbourhoods, and partly through people who live in the area. Because access to migrants and especially long-term unemployed was difficult, we later decided to ask people on the street to participate in the research.

The target group interviews in those two neighbourhoods had the form of structured talks following a guiding questionnaire, including topics like household dwelling history, education and employment biographies, social contacts, perceptions of their own situation and the neighbourhood, use of public services and opportunities in the neighbourhood. These interviews were accompanied by 32 expert interviews with people working in the fields of social services or in local politics.

The theoretical framework we chose for the project understands social exclusion as a process, in the course of which, goods necessary for the household can no longer be attained to a satisfying degree. Households can attain goods in three levels: in the market, public or community sector. Thus, social integration of a household depends on its capability to acquire resources and services via either market exchange processes (offer of own labour and purchase of services), or transfers of the welfare state (redistribution power of assurance agencies), or personal networks and family structures (in the form of reciprocal exchange relations) (see Musterd *et al.*, 1999b). There are chances of substitution between those three systems. Each of them has specific advantages and disadvantages in quality though, so they cannot become fully and equally substituted (Offe and Heinze, 1986). Apart from those chances, different neighbourhoods offer specific opportunities (opportunity structures) of coping with poverty; in other words, a different resource for poor people who are coping with life (Herlyn *et al.*, 1991).

In the following section, we refer to the opportunity structure and the resources that can be found in the researched neighbourhoods. Then, we summarize our findings across the different research target groups, outlining four main aspects: income and educational background of the interviewees and their chances in the labour market; the time they have been living in the neighbourhood and the networks they are involved in; their perceptions of poverty and exclusion; as well as their strategies to cope with poverty and the role of the neighbourhood for these strategies. Finally we conclude our findings on poverty, social exclusion and the role of the neighbourhood.

Resources in the neighbourhoods

Both researched neighbourhoods have high levels of poverty and unemployment. This leads to a high share of welfare recipients, especially in the case of the Neukoelln neighbourhood. Besides these similarities, the neighbourhoods differ in location and structure, which affects different experiences and paths of development.

The district Neukoelln, as it exists today, was founded in 1920 as a municipality of Greater Berlin. The Northern part of the district was built for the most part right after the turn of the century, when, due to migration induced by the industrial urban development, the need for housing increased extremely. The dwellings were characterized by their cramped conditions, they were over-occupied and only equipped with one ore two rooms, a kitchen, and at the beginning they were even without bathroom facilities. When in 1920, the Southern parts were affiliated to the municipality, the process of urbanization extended to these areas and Neukoelln started to become one of the biggest districts of Berlin.

Our selected neighbourhood 'Reuterplatz' is located at the very North of the district and shows the typical characteristics of an area with old housing stock in private ownership. It is one of the most densely built areas in Berlin with very little public infrastructure and places. 34,000 people live in this area, 31 per cent of them are non-German citizens. Since the 1980s, migrants have settled in the Northern part of Neukoelln; most of them have lived in Kreuzberg before. But unlike Kreuzberg, which neighbours in the West and the North, the Reuterplatz area never became famous for its alternative scene. The neighbourhood kept its character of a poor and run down working-class area.

The East-Berlin district Marzahn has existed since 1979 and is located at the Northeast fringe of the city. It was the first of three new districts that were founded in the GDR-period. The 1973 'programme to solve the housing question in the GDR' initiated the beginning of the prefabricated housing estates. Between 1976 and 1989, about 65,000 apartments in 5 to 20 storey high-rise buildings were built in Marzahn. About 170,000 persons were to live in the new district, which equals more than 10 per cent of the East Berlin population. Marzahn represented the area with the most modern houses in the GDR and attracted people from the run-down inner-city districts and smaller towns. It served as a symbol of demonstrating the ability of the socialist society to secure good and modern housing. Living in Marzahn meant 'living the socialist way of life' and was a privilege. The system of housing distribution in the GDR privileged particular persons or groups of persons following political criteria. This also meant that others (politically unwanted persons) had no chance of getting new apartments in the big housing estates. As a result of this, the district consists of different neighbourhoods with a particular clientele. While in the Southern part (Marzahn I), employees of the administration and the state services and in Marzahn II (central area), employees of the service economies were preferred; the later neighbourhoods (Marzahn-North/West, Marzahn-Ost) were let especially to young families with children (Hannemann, 1996; Niederlaender *et al.*, 1986).

Since 1989, the neighbourhoods have experienced devaluation. Marzahn has lost the high status it held during the GDR-period. The out-migration of the better-off to the nearby suburban areas with smaller, often detached or terraced houses since 1994 has caused a considerable modification of the district's demographic structure. But still, people living in Marzahn identify with their district and believe it is still a middle-class area. Therefore, the formulation and the public discussion about the district's social problems have resulted in a defensive position against the 'unfounded reproaches' on the side of the district's representatives and the inhabitants.

The neighbourhoods differ enormously with regard to the resources and structural conditions that they offer their inhabitants. Although being quite similar in population size, they differ significantly in their population density: in the inner-city neighbourhood the inhabitants have to live in a very confined space with a mixed functional structure, lacking green areas. In Marzahn-North on the other hand, the more open and spacious way of building leaves more open space to the inhabitants but the neighbourhood is mono-functional.

Both neighbourhoods have experienced declines in population, through out-migration, since the beginning of the 1990s. Especially the employed inhabitants move to 'better' neighbourhoods in the inner city or suburban areas which have only just been developed. As a consequence, people begin to concentrate in these neighbourhoods who are in a deprived economic situation and, therefore, cannot afford to move out. The housing market in both neighbourhoods offers a relatively cheap and modernized housing stock. But because the demand for housing in both areas is not as big as the supply, a high share of dwellings are vacant. The estimated vacancy figure for Marzahn is 14 per cent, for the Reuterplatz area about 7 to 10 per cent.

Mostly people also affected by deprivation move to these vacant dwellings. For instance, there has been a high influx of migrants in both neighbourhoods. In Marzahn-North, mainly ethnic Germans from former Soviet Union republics moved to the neighbourhood in the 1990s. In contrast to that, the migration into the Neukoelln-Reuterplatz area consists mainly of Turkish labour migrants and family members joining them, as well as refugees from the Former Yugoslavia and the Middle East. Both neighbourhoods can be said to be in a process of social homogenization and ethnic differentiation of their population structure. The better-off move out and different ethnic groups of lower status move in.

Despite those similarities, there are still remarkable differences in the current composition of population in these areas. People in Marzahn-North are younger and better educated on average than in Neukoelln-Reuterplatz. In addition, unemployment and the processes of impoverishment and exclusion involved are a more recent development in the Marzahn neighbourhood (where they only began after the unification) than in Neukoelln. The Reuterplatz area, as a typical worker and industrial district, was already affected in the 1980s by the processes of economic restructuring, which became even more aggravated in the 1990s.

Both neighbourhoods offer their inhabitants only limited resources to cope with their life situation. First, there is a lack of employment opportunities in the neighbourhoods. Because of the mono-functional structure of Marzahn-North as just an area of housing, little local employment can be found there. In Neukoelln-Reuterplatz the number of jobs has been declining significantly as a result of the de-industrialization of the district's economy and the reduction of retail shops, which has been caused by decreasing purchasing power of the local population. Self-employed start-ups are frequent but seldom successful. Second, the commercial infrastructure can be said to be satisfactory in both neighbourhoods, allowing the inhabitants a cheap supply of daily goods. But, despite an increase in opportunities for consuming in Marzahn-North after the unification, they are still not that differentiated. Specific services and goods for economically deprived people, such as second-hand shops or laundrettes are still missing.

Regarding the supply of social services by the welfare state, the unification of Berlin marked a break in both the researched neighbourhoods. While in Marzahn-North an improvement of the social infrastructure by the establishment of a differentiated system of social services can be observed, the social infrastructure in Neukoelln-Reuterplatz, being in deficit already, have deteriorated even further caused by massive cuts in the welfare budget. Additionally, the quality of social services is getting worse in both areas, because projects have to rely increasingly on financing by public job-creation schemes.

Similarly the conditions for the development of informal social networks in the neighbourhood have deteriorated in both areas in the past few years. The communities that were organized by party organizations in the housing blocks in Marzahn-North during the GDR-period have, for the most part, collapsed and new forms of neighbourly networks have yet to evolve. In Neukoelln-Reuterplatz, the high fluctuation of the population and the lack of space that would support communication, prevent closer relations between neighbours. The exceptions in both neighbourhoods are the social networks of migrants, which are based on stable informal relations in the ethnic communities and on a corresponding infrastructure of formal meeting points. As we will show below, these networks are not inclusive for all migrants.

In summary, one can say that both neighbourhoods face the dilemma of not only having to combat impoverishment, but also having only very limited resources at their disposal, which politics and inhabitants themselves can use for an improvement of the situation. In both areas the establishment of a neighbourhood development programme as a territorial based policy started around the year 2000.

Poverty, social exclusion and strategies

We asked our interviewees about different aspects of their life: their socio-economic situation, their relation to the neighbourhood, their perception of poverty and social exclusion and, finally, about their strategies to cope with their life situation. In the following paragraphs we summarize our findings and present them comparatively.

Education, income and chances in the labour market

The researched groups differ significantly with regard to school and professional education, as well as income. The differences in income, surprising in so far as most of the interviewees live on welfare or unemployment benefits can be explained by the different sources of income people have access to. Incomes are lowest when people have to rely just on welfare benefits. But even then differences can be observed because it is within the discretion of the official in charge of welfare benefits, and depends on the knowledge of the welfare recipients, as to whether they receive one-off payments. To a small extent, welfare benefits can be increased by income gained through casual work; however, it is not allowed to exceed a certain, very small amount. Welfare recipients with small children have higher incomes because they receive special child benefits within the first few years. In addition to that, single parents also get higher welfare benefits for their children in the first six years.

Incomes can be higher when people receive unemployment benefits – up to 67 per cent of the former wages. But payments decrease after a short amount of time, and they can reach a level beyond the welfare benefits charge for the long-term unemployed, and then welfare benefits in addition must be paid. However, some of our interviewees are able to obtain higher incomes by participating in job creation schemes or through regular illicit work.

Within our three researched groups, migrants in both neighbourhoods show the lowest level in education and income, followed by the group of long-term unemployed men. On average the weighted income[2] of migrants in both areas and long-term unemployed in Marzahn-North is below 300 and 340 Euro respectively. However, showing a comparatively lower educational level than the latter, the long-term unemployed interviewees in Neukoelln-Reuterplatz have on average higher incomes because they gain additional money through casual or illicit work.

In trying to estimate the objective chances of the interviewees for re-integration in the labour market, one has to come to the conclusion that the long-term unemployed in Neukoelln-Reuterplatz are worse off. After all, half of them have been without any regular job for the past 15 years. But the long-term unemployed in Marzahn-North also have a comparatively small chance of finding a job again. Migrants seem to face similar difficulties. The ethnic Germans in Marzahn are hindered by their qualifications, which are not recognized in Germany, as well as by their insufficient knowledge of the German language. Likewise, the interviewed migrants in Neukoelln have few chances to find regular work which would secure their subsistence, because half of them did not finish their professional training.

Within the interviewed groups the single mothers appear to be 'better off'. In Neukoelln-Reuterplatz they often graduated or finished professional training, and show a remarkably high income-level, being at the top of all our researched groups in both neighbourhoods with a weighted average income of 434 Euro per month. Their chances of getting a new job are relatively high because they are still in contact with people in the world of work and are committed to finding their way back into the labour market, for instance by continuing their education.

Neighbourhood and networks

The hypothesis is that, to a large extent, social networks and the use of resources in the neighbourhood are related to the length of time that people have been living in the area.

Concerning this duration our interviewed groups show different patterns: single mothers and long-term unemployed men in Marzahn-North, as well as migrants in Neukoelln-Reuterplatz, are the groups that have been living in the neighbourhood for the longest periods. On the other hand, the group of ethnic German migrants in Marzahn shows the shortest duration, having moved to the neighbourhood only during the past five years, followed by the long-term unemployed in Neukoelln, who all have been living there for less than ten years.

It can be observed however that the duration in the neighbourhood has only limited influence on the establishment of networks. Of all interviewees, the ethnic Germans in the Marzahn-North area have the largest circles of acquaintances and the most regular contacts within the neighbourhood. They are also using the diverse services that are offered to them as a group, for example, special meeting points and facilities for counselling. A stable and well-functioning network of support has been established among the ethnic Germans within a short period of time, assisted by services offered by the state. But those networks and social services are ethnically exclusive. Contacts only exist within their own ethnic group, and the services are targeted exclusively at ethnic Germans, the only significant migrant group in Marzahn.

Migrants in Neukoelln-Reuterplatz are the ones best integrated into social networks of all the groups that have been living in the neighbourhood for a longer period of time. These networks however turn out to be ethnically exclusive as well. The use of the social infrastructure by this group is not particularly distinctive, but some meeting points like Turkish cafés exist that are used by some of our interviewees. But not all of the migrants are integrated in ethnic networks and some told us they lost most of their contact through unemployment. Their situation does not differ from German long-term unemployed correspondents.

Half of the single mothers in both neighbourhoods also have a lot of social contacts and are integrated in large support networks of friends. Through their children they have contact with other parents via school or kindergarten, and they also use other opportunities in the neighbourhood. The networks of single mothers in Marzahn-North are more often within the neighbourhood, than those of single mothers in Neukoelln-Reuterplatz.

The group of long-term unemployed men is the one who has the fewest social contacts. Many of them have just one or two friends left, and therefore become isolated. A further and significant difference is that most of the long-term unemployed are living alone. Many of them withdraw from their old circles of friends and meet with other men in the same situation at public places – the places that some of the other interviewees called 'drinker haunts'.

Perception of poverty and exclusion

We also asked our interviewees how they would define poverty and if they would describe themselves as poor. By some additional questions we tried to identify how far they are socially excluded and if they perceive themselves as such. To be able to assess this, it must also be taken into account to what extent these people have realistic chances on the labour market and how far they are integrated in supportive social networks. For the measurement of social exclusion in this section however, we mainly refer to the answers that describe if the interviewees felt 'excluded', defined themselves as poor, had the feeling they can't 'keep-up' with others, experienced stigmatization, and/or had experienced a feeling of uselessness and senselessness. If the respondents agreed to at least three of the items we defined these people as being excluded.

Only a minority of the interviewees describe themselves as poor. Most people dissociate themselves from this term, defining as 'poor' those who have even less than them. Sometimes, the definition – not to be poor – is influenced by earlier experiences. This can be observed, in particular, with regard to the ethnic Germans in Marzahn-North. They deny being poor, comparing their current situation to the situation in the countries they have come from. Living in Germany just for a few years, they still have very clear memories of their impoverished and sometimes life-threatening situations before their emigration, when poverty meant lack of food and starving. Some of the Turkish interviewees in Neukoelln-Reuterplatz define poverty in comparison to the situation in Turkey as well. Most people of the other groups would define poverty as having no roof over one's head – as being homeless.

Some of the interviewees – being asked if they perceive themselves as poor – dissociate themselves from certain groups in the neighbourhood; mostly from people they call 'foreigners' or 'alcoholics'. Even within the Turkish interviewees there is a sharp dissociation from other migrant groups (for example, asylum seekers, gypsies or Arabs). Sometimes these feelings towards other groups serve to affirm a higher status on them. As long as one has not been so far down-at heel as such other groups are seen to be, one can assure oneself of a comparatively high social status despite significant financial problems.

But not all of our interviewees feel this way: a small group, perceiving itself at the lowest end of the social stratum, sees the other inhabitants of the neighbourhood in a similar situation, having the same social status, being unemployed and poor, too. Those who define themselves as poor are regarding the neighbourhood to be as poor as they are.

For some other interviewees it is most painful that they cannot 'keep up' with other people. This feeling is strongest within the migrant group in Neukoelln-Reuterplatz, which can be explained by the relatively integrated position most of the migrants already had before their situation deteriorated significantly in the 1990s. Most of the migrants in Neukoelln lost their jobs only during the last decade. Because of their status as 'foreigners' they feel further excluded. But within the migrants in Marzahn, who are mainly German citizens and did not describe themselves as poor, feelings of uselessness can be observed as well. They are unsatisfied with the fact that they have not been able to work since their migration to Germany and that their qualifications are not recognized in Germany. Even though they have large social networks in Marzahn and like living there, they do not seem to be able to formulate perspectives for their future. They feel helpless in the face of the Labour Office and the conditions of the labour market.

Single mothers are the group with the smallest share of people who define themselves as poor. Often describing their situation as precarious, they were nevertheless able to stabilize their situation, supported by far-reaching social contacts and, in the case of Neukoelln-Reuterplatz, by a higher educational level. Since they feel responsible for their children, they continue to be motivated to try to cope with and to improve their situation. This group often distances itself from conflicts and groups they perceive as aggressive and dangerous (such as skinheads, alcoholics or drug addicts).

Among the long-term unemployed interviewees in both neighbourhoods, three out of four can be seen as excluded, followed by half of the migrants in Neukoelln. Among the other researched groups it is only one out of five. Surprisingly, the perception of poverty in most cases goes along with feeling unable to 'keep up', feeling excluded, useless, and/or stigmatized. Often, these feelings are combined with drug-addiction, alcoholism, health or mental problems. A significant correlation can be found with regard to chances within the labour market. Those persons who have relatively good chances to find a job, only rarely describe themselves as 'useless' or 'excluded'. However, those who have limited chances in the labour market because of their low educational level and who have experienced this when applying for jobs, describe feelings of exclusion, even if they do not define themselves as poor.

Strategies of coping with poverty

The vast majority of the interviewees in both our neighbourhoods are still trying to improve their situation. Predominantly the interviewees try to get access to regular jobs again. It has to be noticed therefore that the interviewees in Marzahn-North have a much stronger fixation on classic standard working conditions (full-time, for an indefinite period, and so on) than those in the Neukoelln-Reuterplatz area. There we found, more often than in Marzahn, 'alternative' improvement strategies besides the search for a job (for example, plans to emigrate or to become self-employed). Single mothers try hardest to improve their situation in both our neighbourhoods. Their motivation to get out of the poor conditions is the largest, because of their responsibility for their children. This holds true for single mothers in both areas, even though they have different strategies for improvement.

Strategies of stabilization play an important role for those who try to improve their situation, as well as for a small group of interviewees who do not see chances for improvement, but who carry on trying to organize life independently. The most important stabilization strategy in both neighbourhoods is the management of scarce resources. The interviewees are able to provide for themselves and their families despite their scarce means through self-restriction and in-depth planning of expenses, the reduction or loss of leisure and cultural expenses, as well as by searching for alternative ways to get resources, such as bartering, charitable aid, or do-it-yourself activities. In the Neukoelln-Reuterplatz neighbourhood a small group of interviewees is additionally doing casual or illicit work to be able to pay for irregular expenses without destabilizing their daily supply and their general financial situation. An interviewee in Marzahn-North has developed a special strategy of stabilization. He tries to prevent his further social decline through taking out insurance plans against different sorts of misfortune.

Besides those material strategies, ways of personal stabilization can be observed in both neighbourhoods as well. People try to achieve social contacts and respect through civil commitment or via alternative role models that are more recognized socially. But just the female interviewees in both neighbourhoods pursue these strategies. As a consequence, women are socially integrated to a higher extent and rarely have feelings of exclusion, uselessness and poverty. These strategies for personal stabilization however are mostly complementary and do not replace the search for jobs.

Only very small shares of interviewees in both our neighbourhoods have a resigned attitude towards their life situation. Having given up any hope for a change in their situation, they just concentrate on activities to provide for their minimal needs. At the same time they are in danger of further social decline, because in most of the cases their social relations have been reduced to a minimum. The majority of resigned interviewees are to be found in the groups of long-term unemployed and migrants in the Neukoelln neighbourhood. Two persons per group have totally resigned – it seems to them to be senseless to look for a job anymore, and alternative roles or activities are also not available. Maybe, resigned people were not eager to be interviewed and, therefore, are not included in our sample. On the other hand, this finding points to a much smaller connection of resignation and feelings of exclusion, senselessness and stigmatization.

Opportunity structures

Both researched neighbourhoods have only limited resources to offer for their deprived inhabitants. But different groups of inhabitants have different access to different resources. It can be said in general, that the neighbourhood plays hardly any role in strategies for improvement of the labour market position, because they cannot offer many regular jobs. Despite many of the interviewees wanting work in the neighbourhood, they see only few chances to do so. That means, for those who want to improve their labour market situation, the neighbourhood is of little help.

On the other hand, for the strategies of stabilization, both neighbourhoods put resources at residents' disposal, and these are used to different extents and in different combinations. Particularly important in this context are facilities for cheap shopping that allow people to live economically. These resources for stabilization have been emphasized by all interviewees, and are seen as most important to get by with a small income.

Social services by the state that can be used for consultation and social care are important in both neighbourhoods, although the service opportunities are better known and more used in Marzahn-North. They play a significant role for the stabilization strategies of the Marzahn interviewees, especially for the ethnic Germans. The differences in use of social services in the two neighbourhoods is also related to the more frequent existence of informal meeting points, such as bars, cafés, etc., in Marzahn-North in comparison to the Neukoelln-Reuterplatz area. This results in a less intensified use of the formal social infrastructure (such as neighbourhood centres) by the Neukoelln inhabitants.

On closer examination, the attitude and behaviour towards the neighbourhood by the interviewees can be split into two groupings: those who are able to use the resources in the neighbourhood to different extents and in different combinations on the one hand, and those who perceive the neighbourhood as a strain and therefore want to leave it on the other hand. In our sample, the ones who are able to use the neighbourhood are the majority in both our neighbourhoods. But in each neighbourhood two different groups – an (established) working class milieu and a migrant milieu – are competing over the scarce resources – employment and welfare – and symbolically fighting for hegemony over the area they both use.

At the same time a small group of interviewees in both areas are not able to use the opportunities of the neighbourhood and want to leave. For those interviewees the social climate in the neighbourhood has become a strain that is keeping them from using the existing resources. Some are mainly bothered about the conflicts in the neighbourhood. It is especially households with children who comprise the group. But their 'flight out of there' is mainly a wish; it is seldom a realistic chance because most of the interviewees lack the financial resources.

To sum up, one can say that the use of the neighbourhood resources requires two things: first, people have to find 'people like them' in the neighbourhood: people who live in similar conditions, with similar attitudes and coping strategies towards their situation. Second, people have to be able and willing to tolerate other social milieus in the neighbourhood besides their own, and ways to communicate with those other milieus have to develop to be able to solve conflicts that might emerge between them.

With regard to resources in the neighbourhood it can be said that inner-city areas with an old housing stock and big housing estates at the periphery differ only slightly. But as a consequence of the differing social composition, both neighbourhoods attract different people who identify with the people and the images of the area.

Conclusion

The conditions of urban development in Berlin changed dramatically in the 1990s. Increasing unemployment and poverty, together with a rising supply of dwellings, has led to growing social segregation and growing social polarization.

In the academic and policy debates about segregation, there is no agreement as to what consequences the concentration of a poor population in a neighbourhood could have for the coping strategies of these populations. One view is that such neighbourhoods are a source of further deprivation because their social homogeneity leads to a deficit of economic, social, cultural and symbolic capital (and there are almost no resources available in the neighbourhood for the inhabitants to cope with their problems). The other view is that such neighbourhoods do have some resources to cope with poverty and exclusion, such as public infrastructure, social contacts, those with similar experiences, as well as a sense of belonging. In this case, the neighbourhood is seen as a shelter against discrimination.

Both positions have in common their emphasis of social networks. Whereas the first one sees their homogeneity as a problem, because a 'culture of poverty' (Lewis, 1966) might develop in such neighbourhoods and reinforce poverty and social exclusion (see Friedrichs, 1998; Wilson, 1987), the second one understands homogeneity in the neighbourhood as protective, because homogeneous social networks allow for collective coping strategies instead of individual suffering (Herlyn *et al.*, 1991).

In our research we have been able to show that neighbourhoods might function in both directions depending on which population groups, with their specific needs and strategies, tries to make use of the resources available. The above-mentioned approaches perceive the population of a neighbourhood as a homogeneous group, as one milieu, for which the neighbourhood structures are either a burden or a support. But if one looks at different population groups separately, it becomes visible that the opportunity structure of a neighbourhood – with its problems and resources – is used differently according to local social milieus (see Keim and Neef, 2000).

This means, that to be able to determine the influence of poor neighbourhoods on their inhabitants it is necessary to answer more complex questions: Which groups of inhabitants are able to use which kind of resources? Why are other groups not successful in using those resources?

Our analyses of the life situation and coping strategies of groups of inhabitants who are affected by unemployment, has shown that both our neighbourhoods can offer limited resources for the stabilization of life of their inhabitants, but cannot help to improve their labour market situation. This can be shown for both our neighbourhoods, for the big housing estate of Marzahn-North in the Eastern part of the city as well as for the old inner-city area of Neukoelln-Reuterplatz in the Western part. There are resources in the neighbourhoods that can be used by the inhabitants, such as cheap dwellings, social infrastructure, rooms for communication, and social networks. But only specific groups, which are established in the neighbourhood, can make use of those resources. This holds true also for the excluded population even if they live in the neighbourhood only for a short time. For other groups however, the neighbourhood can be a strain because they cannot develop their specific coping strategies there. It is therefore not surprising that they are suffering from conflicts and try to leave the neighbourhood.

Notes

1. The authors would like to thank Pamela Dorsch and Ingo Siebert who worked with us on the research project.
2. In the following, income of an interview partner means the weighted income including welfare and unemployment benefits as well as additional payments and salaries. It is calculated for individual household members as follows: the household income (minus costs for rent and secondary rental costs): 1.0 for the interviewee being head of the household, 0.7 for further household members being 15 years of age or over, 0.5 for younger household members.

3
Antwerp: Confronting the Social and Spatial

Inge Van Nieuwenhuyze and Jan Vranken

The focus

This chapter discusses how different groups of socially excluded people in two deprived Antwerp neighbourhoods – Dam and Silvertop – cope with their situation, how they try to participate, or even integrate in urban society, and what the role of neighbourhoods is in their strategies.

We start with a brief description of both neighbourhoods involved, in terms of their history and their resources. Next, we will come to the core question: whether the neighbourhood represents a resource or a constraint in poor people's lives and discuss the importance of the spatial dimension in our population's experiences of poverty, their resources, and their coping strategies. As a general theoretical framework, we will use the three 'modes of economic integration' (see Harvey, 1973; Kesteloot *et al.*, 1997; Mingione, 1991; Polanyi, 1944) through which households and communities may or may not gain access to resources, referring to market exchange, redistribution and reciprocity mechanisms. We will argue, however, that another element should be introduced in the analysis: our population is differentiated according to their trajectories in(to) poverty. Special attention goes to the extent in which past experience – as expressed in the difference between 'generational' poor and 'new' poor – interacts with spatial proximity and neighbourhood site characteristics. This interesting intermediate variable helps to explain the differential use of spatially located resources. Other sources of variation (age, gender and 'human capital') are reflected in the choice of different subgroups: unemployed local households, single mothers and immigrants.

This seems to imply that we are drifting away from the spatial approach towards more 'social' factors; but of course, we are not. It only proves once more that in social reality, very few causal relationships do exist – and this also goes for the relation between the social and spatial dimension, something that is widely assessed by the relevant literature. To take the neighbourhood as the unit of an analysis already implies that we consider the neighbourhood as a relevant unit of analysis. However, in current debates about neighbourhood effects, we are confronted with different points of view on this matter. Musterd and Ostendorf (1998) and Friedrichs (1997) found that some neighbourhood effects could be found, but that they tend to be small in Europe compared to the American experience and hardly add to the explanation on the basis of individual characteristics (see also Atkinson and Kintrea, 2001). Ostendorf *et al.* (2001: 371) state that 'poverty is a personal characteristic and that it is therefore preferable to approach poverty directly instead of hoping for the results of a dubious "neighbourhood effect"' H. T. Andersen (2001), among others, holds another view: 'Without being naive on that matter', he states, 'it can be argued that deprived neighbourhoods ... are also by themselves creating new segregation and inequality. In these neighbourhoods there have been started strong self-perpetuating processes that, by complicated mechanisms, pull them into a downward spiral from which they seldom come up again by themselves' (see among others also De Decker *et al.*, 2001).

These opposing views also explain why we decided on a qualitative analysis of the in-depth interviews. Qualitative analysis is designed to identify processes and meanings, rather than to allow generalizations in a statistical sense. Such a statistical generalization would anyhow be anything but well-founded, since we did not select our respondents at random but very selectively, in order to have a wide array of 'cases' and thus of experiences, trajectories and coping strategies in our 'sample'.[1] We ended up with a total of 39 semi-structured interviews from both neighbourhoods. It can safely be said that the sample of interviewees is sufficiently varied to lead to interesting results about trajectories and coping strategies used by people.

A tale of two neighbourhoods

Common observation and scientific indicators (Kesteloot *et al.*, 1996) suggest the existence of high levels of poverty, unemployment, welfare beneficiaries, immigrants and low housing quality in both neighbourhoods, Dam and Silvertop (see Figure 3.1). In both neighbourhoods, a considerable part of the population is living in poverty. However, the areas differ sufficiently in location and structure to expect a large array of experiences and trajectories. Dam is an inner-city area and has a high share of privately owned housing stock, whereas Silvertop is a public housing neighbourhood on the southern edge of the city. In the following paragraphs we compare the neighbourhoods with regard to the resources and structural conditions they offer their residents in the three afore-mentioned 'modes of economic integration', that is, the market, redistribution and reciprocity.

Both neighbourhoods have followed very different historical pathways. The history of Dam, in the northern part of the city, can be traced back to the Middle Ages. Because it was close to the docks, it gradually developed into a flourishing harbour-related working class area in the nineteenth

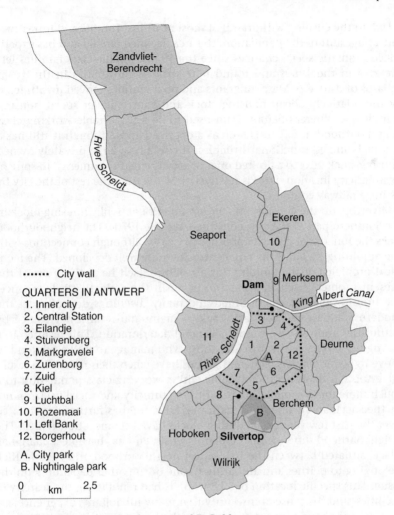

Source: ISEG KU-Leuven, K. Pelemans and F. Guldentops

Figure 3.1 Selection of deprived neighbourhoods in Antwerp city

century. A railway yard and a railway station were constructed. The City Slaughterhouse paved the way for further growth of this working class area. Many companies and tradesmen settled in the area, particularly in the northern part. Next to this business function, the neighbourhood had an important housing function. The beautiful mansions of managers and industrialists built in the first half of the twentieth century remain a sign of the wealthy past of the area. In the second half of the twentieth century, the port and the related industrial activities moved further north.

Due to the ensuing withdrawal of most of its institutions and infrastructure and a shift of the population, the area declined rapidly and has experienced dramatic social changes since the 1960s. Middle-class families left the area in the 1960s and found new attractive dwellings in the green suburbs of Antwerp. Many migrants and poor families moved in, attracted by the relatively cheap housing stock and some smaller social housing complexes. Whereas before, Dam used to be a respectable working class neighbourhood, today, it is seen as a deprived area although it still has a relatively mixed functional structure. It contains a large privately owned housing stock next to a limited offer of social rented apartments. In spite of its inner-city location, Dam is relatively isolated from the rest of the city by its huge railway complex.

Silvertop, on the contrary, is a mono-functional public housing block in the Southern part of the city, constructed in the 1970s. The neighbourhood lacks the functional diversity of other city parts, although connections with the adjoining Kiel and the city centre are quite well developed. The technical problems of the building infrastructure itself lie at the roots of the present problems, which started to occur in the early 1970s. Ever since, the housing quality has declined and many dwellings do not meet the modern standards of comfort. Lack of maintenance and negligence by authorities and tenants, caused a general deterioration. This resulted in a strong urge to leave the area and those who manage to find a job tend to move to better districts. Different groups have taken their place. As a result, Silvertop has evolved from a stable white, working class population to a much more mixed population in terms of ethnicity and social background. As the social and economic situation of Silvertop has further deteriorated over the past few years, the housing blocks have become a transit area. The neighbourhood suffers from an identity crisis, and has become a 'marginal' place, situated between the Exhibition neighbourhood and the old Kiel, belonging to neither and affiliating to one or the other depending on the issue. This specific location of Silvertop, its bad reputation, the scarcity of facilities, and the sense of insecurity that many inhabitants experience, are reasons for abandoning the area in both the sense of leaving it and of leaving it to itself.

This different background may be important for future developments. In Dam, a number of big projects, which are expected to add economic and social value to the neighbourhood, are being launched or realized. Dam Station has become a public meeting place and information site, the railway yard will become a combination of 'city park' and business site, the old slaughterhouse is being redeveloped. Entrepreneurs are expected to jump at the offer of growth potential, creating employment for low-skilled people and resulting in the increased well-being of the local population. Already today, the area around the slaughterhouse with its up-market restaurants has become a completely different world. In Silvertop, on the contrary, there is little in the way of investment in the area. The inhabitants face uncertainty about future renovations, since around the time of the interviews, the Flemish Minister for Housing threatened to tear down the apartment blocks, officially because renovation would be too expensive. However, a number of initiatives have been taken to ameliorate the atmosphere, such as a thorough renovation of the high-rise buildings. These diverging prospects show the path-dependency of both neighbourhoods: their future is very much linked to the past. Thus, in spite of it not being better-off at the time of our research, Dam has more of a future than Silvertop.

What kind of opportunities and restrictions do these neighbourhoods offer to their inhabitants? In the next section, we will describe the kind of arrangements people make to cope with their situation. This presentation will again be structured around the three spheres of integration: market, redistribution, and reciprocity.

The spatial dimension of integration and coping behaviour

The market

Both neighbourhoods lack employment opportunities. In Dam, the number of jobs has declined significantly as a result of the withdrawal of the port, the de-industrialization of the area's economy, and the emigration of retail shops. Because of the mono-functional structure of Silvertop as a housing area, few jobs are available locally. Unemployment leads to less spending power and to difficulties with the social housing company, as the tenants are often unable to pay their rent. This sometimes results in court summons and even evictions, which rarely solve the problems. The larger area around Silvertop – the so-called Kiel – provides some employment facilities, but it does not attract the unemployed people of Silvertop. This seems not so much the result of a neighbourhood stigma but of a skill mismatch: Silvertop is only able to provide unskilled people while the jobs at offer in the Kiel area often require some degree of skill. State benefits constitute an important source of income for all households.

The relation between the sphere of the market and that of state redistribution is a most important political item. 'Active labour market policies' are about the explicit desire of policy-makers from almost all parties to 'activate' social beneficiaries who are considered as 'available for the labour market' to get off social benefits and take up a job – of any kind – or attend training of some sort. 'Activation policies' are, however, handicapped by the existence of a 'poverty trap': people on benefits tend to refuse job offers because they would not be better off, and in fact, sometimes worse off. The groups most likely to be trapped into poverty because of this 'poverty trap' are single mothers. Several respondents pointed out that their replacement income is almost as high as the wage they would receive for the kind of job they could obtain. Moreover, they would lose the right to some extra provisions for the unemployed, like increased child benefits. This explains why part-time or low-paid jobs are not attractive; they would lead to less income and would often increase costs, having to provide for childcare or for transport.

Because of the lack of spending power, a most important survival strategy in both neighbourhoods is the management of scarce resources. Most interviewees are able to provide for themselves and their families through self-restriction and in-depth planning, the reduction or quitting of leisure activities, or through alternative ways to obtain resources, such as bartering, charity, or do-it-yourself activities. Both Dam and Silvertop house specific services and goods for economically deprived people (second-hand shops or laundrettes). Especially in Dam, cheap shops provide the residents with a daily supply of cheap goods, which also enables them to make ends meet. It is strange, however, that no ethnic entrepreneurship has developed within the local ethnic community, perhaps because the core of their communities is situated at the other side of the railway yard. As for shopping outside the area, restricted mobility handicaps both lone mothers (socially) and disabled people (physically) from both neighbourhoods. This is most acutely the case for Silvertop, where shopping opportunities are virtually absent.

The housing market is a third element to be considered. Both neighbourhoods offer a relatively cheap housing stock. In Dam the private rental sector provides run-down, very basic rooms or apartments, whereas in Silvertop the social housing company rents out all dwellings. In spite of the physical deterioration of the flats, almost all residents in Silvertop seem to be happy with them. This could be explained by the residents' relative 'upward mobility' from former privately rented dwellings into the relatively comfortable apartments of the Silvertop. Generally, the quality of the housing in the social rented sector seems to be better than in Dam, which still has a lot of low quality run-down houses. In this inner-city neighbourhood, people are living in a very confined space that lacks green areas. Silvertop has a lower building density (compared to the inner-city), parks and greenery, and 'rooms with a view'. Some interviewees also mention improvements in the quality of the living environment. However, like so many estates from this period, negative aspects seem abundant: the housing lacks identity, there is noise from the neighbours, dirt, lack of services, and a general perception of decline. On the other hand, social housing has a stabilizing effect, because the contracts offer security. In the private rented sector, the housing situation is far more precarious and uncertain.

The residents of Dam moved to the neighbourhood not only because of its relatively cheap rents (basically meaning very bad housing at a normal price), but also through the mediation of friends and acquaintances and because some interviewees had already lived in or near the neighbourhood.

They consciously choose to move back into the area because they are familiar with it and felt comfortable there. Moving to Silvertop is rather more the result of a market mechanism, because people are free to accept or refuse the apartment offered by the housing company. In both cases, however, all population groups under review have in common that they have privately rented in Antwerp at some time in their 'housing career'. These dwellings were mostly unsatisfactory: usually the rent was excessively high for an apartment lacking basic comfort. Access to social housing certainly meant an improvement in the housing trajectories for all respondents, but more so in Silvertop.

Redistribution

With regard to state redistribution, all our respondents are, and have been for several years, on social benefits. This is not exceptional since all legal residents – but not undocumented people – are entitled to them. The absolute bottom-line is the in-kind help that is provided by the Public Centre for Social Welfare, PCSW. This is the local public institution that is legally responsible for 'guaranteeing an acceptable level of welfare for all citizens', in practice taking care of providing a minimum income and other forms of assistance, sometimes in-kind.

Whether these benefits are sufficient to secure a decent standard of living is a different question that is usually answered negatively (Vranken *et al.*, 2000, 2004). As for the important housing dimension of state redistribution, we have shown before that the relatively comfortable and secure social housing removes an important concern for the households in Silvertop.

In both areas, the social infrastructure – here referring to a system of social services – has improved as a result of the establishment of a differentiated system of social services. Their quality is rather high, in spite of a heavy workload for the social workers and the complexity of the problems. Despite ongoing processes of impoverishment and social exclusion, Dam had to wait until the late 1980s to receive special attention and Silvertop until the 1990s. A series of electoral victories by the extreme rightwing 'Vlaams Blok' (now the 'Vlaams Belang') triggered the first urban programmes: VFIK (1992–6), which was followed by the Sociaal Impulsfonds (Social Impulse Fund) SIF (1996–2002) (De Decker *et al.*, 2003). The VFIK stands for Vlaams Fonds voor de Integratie van Kansarmen (Flemish Fund for the Integration of the Poor). Although not an 'urban development programme' in the strict sense, it was very much focused on combating poverty in areas of selected cities. These programmes were expected to promote social cohesion in deprived areas. However, there are many needs to be covered by the limited resources, which politicians and inhabitants want to spend differently. The main concern of the inhabitants is (in)security and cleanliness in the neighbourhood and they criticize the insufficient engagement of the city and the police when it comes to these items. Since many services did depend on subsidies from these urban development programmes, the end of the SIF programme in 2002 rendered the situation even more precarious than before.

Market exchange opportunities and the possibilities of benefiting from state redistribution are generally equal in each neighbourhood; opportunities for *private redistribution*, on the contrary, clearly differ. In Dam, private redistribution is abundant and easily accessible. Single mothers and other local households benefit from food parcels, cheap clothing and related goods from different organizations, such as the parish. Many households include the opportunities offered into their coping strategies and so charity has become an accepted resource in Dam. For some, these opportunities even constitute a form of shopping or meeting other people as they frequent different places, three or four times a week. Others, on the contrary, only go there after a breakdown event, when no other possibility is left. For them, asking for help, the feeling of dependency, queuing and shame constitute serious thresholds. They approach social services only in specific conditions. This shows that the inclusion of charity into a coping strategy depends very much upon specific characteristics of the group in question. Turkish and Moroccan people do not usually rely on these resources. Not only have Turkish and Moroccan people different norms and attitudes towards work, state help and securing an income; they also can fall back on proper forms of solidarity they did not mention in the interviews. On the other hand, some programmes attract large numbers of (mostly undocumented) migrants. In Silvertop, no organizations are active, which makes private charity a less obvious choice than in Dam.

Reciprocity

Both neighbourhoods were of the working class type until the 1970s. Since then, their population has changed through emigration and immigration. The employed residents moved to 'better' neighbourhoods, mostly in the green suburban areas. Economically deprived groups – migrants, refugees and Belgian outsiders – took over. This resulted in Dam and Silvertop becoming 'deprived neighbourhoods'. There was also a change in the composition of the foreign population. In the 1960s and 1970s, Moroccan and Turkish 'guest workers' took over from their Italian, Spanish and Greek predecessors. In recent years, they are in their turn replaced by an influx of immigrants from all over the world. Both neighbourhoods can be said to have gone through a process of social homogenization and ethnic differentiation of their population structure.

Silvertop is, more clearly so than Dam, characterized by both a social and ethnic mix of its population and at the same time social homogeneity: there is not the slightest hint of poor and less poor living together. Initially some white, working class people, mostly from Antwerp, often couples with young children and some older people lived in the apartments. Since then, the social composition has changed greatly. The significant turnover of residents is due to several factors, such as the ageing of the original population and the increasingly negative reputation of the buildings, which is in its turn promoted by the very low rent and the relatively short waiting list that attracts a different kind of people. The result is a mixed but poor population, most of them on some kind of social benefit. A relatively large group of older people, often widowed, has lived there since the 1970s. This more stable part of the population is very much in the minority now. Poor 'natives' and many ethnic minority groups, often people with problems, have moved into the area. The considerable range of languages increases the communication problems.

Living together in the Silvertop Complex turns out to be difficult and creates a lot of irritation and conflicts. Older inhabitants blame the newcomers, and in particular the refugees, for the pauperization of their neighbourhood. Very few inhabitants looked forward to a transfer to the Silvertop Complex, but they had to accept accommodation because they were urgently in need of housing or did not have a choice. Inhabitants who succeed in getting a job do not wish to remain in the neighbourhood any longer, although they often cannot leave the neighbourhood immediately because of financial reasons.

In Dam, the population is slightly more socially mixed. A limited number of residents are more affluent and their orientation is towards the inner city and its cultural capital. The bulk of the population in Dam however is not prosperous. One part is transitory, very mobile and is not closely connected to the neighbourhood; they tend to be urban nomads, undocumented immigrants, or people without a fixed residence. The other group has been living in Dam longer, often for many years. Part of the attraction seems to be the village mentality: some people are born in the area, others come to live there because of the presence of friends and family; and some may even return after having left the area for a while. This second group consists mainly of local elderly, and of some families of blue-collar workers living in the area. It is yet unclear what will result from the major changes the neighbourhood is heading for, but gentrification is not a real option at this point in time.

As a result, living together in Dam is very different from Silvertop. The majority of the inhabitants participate in informal local social networks, which consist mostly of family-based or proximity-based acquaintanceships and constitute an important support in coping with problems. Most people have a very positive view of these networks because they assist people in knowing and helping each other with shopping, cleaning or gardening. One street organizes barbecues or parties. A group of residents participates in parish or neighbourhood activities. The potential for developing networks in Dam is sustained by private redistribution structures and by local associations. They provide meeting places for people with common concerns, and have already led to organizing for political power (for example, 'Recht-op').

As a result, the sense of belonging, of being part, of a shared identity and commitment is fairly strong; it borders on neighbourhood chauvinism. Negative features, however, are the gossip, conflicts between different groups and difficulties for newcomers to integrate. Complaints about noise of children and pets, or other discomforts causing feelings of resentment are frequent. Particular are the tensions between ethnic groups. The older migrant groups (Moroccan, Turkish) are being accepted, perhaps because both they and the native population now have a common 'enemy', the most recent wave of newcomers: black people and gypsies in particular.

In both areas, the possibility to meet – the 'social infrastructure', but in a different sense than that under 'redistribution' – is considered of great importance. There is, however, a lack of public meeting places. Children's playgrounds are often claimed by informal groups of youngsters, accused of hanging around, creating a sense of insecurity, making other people feel uncomfortable. Some people do not use the scarce neighbourhood meeting resources at all. They spend most of the time inside their apartment, which represents for them an important factor of stability in their otherwise precarious situation, and at other times use the cheap shopping opportunities in the area. Their social life predominantly takes place in private mutual visits.

In Silvertop, reciprocal exchanges only exist between close neighbours, since there are no meeting places, associations or even formal networks in the neighbourhood. Community building in the blocks is very difficult, if not impossible. The success of the reciprocal exchanges depends on the type of neighbours. As only very few people were born or raised in the area, residents mainly have the bulk of their contacts (family and friends) outside the area, and do not feel related to the neighbourhood.

In the past few years, conditions for the development of informal local social networks in both areas have deteriorated. The strong influx of ethnic minorities produces feelings of insecurity with both Belgian and settled migrants. High immigration and emigration rates in the neighbourhood and the lack of facilities for communication hamper closer relations between residents. A negative perception of the neighbourhood contributes to a deteriorating quality of living. Residents fear that the area will become a ghetto. However, as financial resources to move out are missing, people are forced to put up with the conditions in the neighbourhood, a situation that increases stress.

Other variations in integration and coping behaviour

The focus of this contribution so far has been on the spatial dimension, the neighbourhood. However, the research also had a transversal focus: it was aimed at different target groups with a low to very low income – single mothers, long-term unemployed and ethnic minorities.[2] Differences between these groups' resources for, and paths of, integration could not be attributed to social background, family histories or restricted labour opportunities; they often showed more similarities than dissimilarities in these respects. Both 'single mothers' and 'long-term unemployed' may have switched from one group to the other shortly before the interviews. Even migrants, who do have a different background, share a number of experiences with the other groups; the reason may be that we mainly interviewed third generation immigrants. They rely on the same resources and possess a similar attitude towards the neighbourhood. The variation between the interviewees needs to be attributed to other factors.

Some of the differences in strategies might be explained by demographic factors. One of them is age, which has an important impact on labour market opportunities. Indeed, several people told us their chances to find any form of employment were restricted due to their being 'too old' – sometimes already at 35. Their chances for additional training are limited, particularly if they do not have any previous experience. Younger respondents, mainly migrants, had not yet given up hope and were actively engaged in all kinds of training or temporary work, hoping it might lead to a full-time, steady and rewarding job. Another important factor is household composition and, in particular, the presence of children. The age and children variables are nested with the gender one. Men particularly mention the argument of age, whereas the presence of children is a determining factor for women. Women give priority to the raising of children, even above employment, a decision based on financial considerations and a traditional role pattern. For them, the household represents the only chance to obtain a certain status when other possibilities (education, job, income) have proved to be unrealistic. Even though the circumstances may be difficult and might have persuaded other couples to split up, they stick by their partner and children with great persistence. The age and the number of children, and being a single mother, also made a difference. Lone mothers with small children were restricted in their strategies. Additionally, the labour market itself is gendered. Poorly educated women are employed in the external secondary labour market such as in cleaning jobs, while men had blue-collar industrial jobs (the internal secondary labour market). This is also the area where moonlighting strategies are sometimes developed.

A fourth variable is the number and degree of handicaps or illnesses, which can leave people with no other option than to accept permanent exclusion from the labour market. The educational capital of the respondents is another factor to be taken into account. Indeed, poor education strongly limits labour market opportunities, and low educational achievement is a common factor for a majority of respondents. Often encouragement or assistance was lacking as the parents themselves had limited experience with education. The household's precarious financial situation sometimes prompted the children to finish school early in order to provide extra income for the family. This is the start of a precarious labour market career. Migrants often have to cope with racism as well. In short, their chances of finding an official job, let alone a well-remunerated one, are marginal.

In addition, interviewees made us understand that there are many degrees and forms of poverty and that their impact on people living in poverty can be very different. Although our interviews were not meant to relate life histories, we came across many different trajectories. Poverty as a result of major fraud and swindle is seen as different from poverty due to early school leaving. Exclusion because of serious illnesses is expected to offer other possibilities and to impose other limitations than exclusion linked to loss of confidence in oneself and others. Regarding previous life experiences, people living in a situation of exclusion or poverty today might be 'classified' along a line describing their life history. The determining variable might preliminary and roughly be defined as 'early confrontation with exclusion', resulting in a difference between 'generational' poor and 'new' poor.

On the one end of the continuum, we find people born and raised in poor and deprived families, the so-called generational poor. Their life history is an illustration of early vulnerability in different areas, where a single event or a combination of negative experiences ignites a downward trajectory towards exclusion and poverty. Early deprivation is marked by a lack of opportunities. Placement in a home, difficult family relationships, and unpleasant contacts with a range of professionals; all have been part of their social world and lives since childhood. This has of course major consequences: both personality and basic skills are marked by these experiences (Thys *et al.*, 2004; Vranken and Steenssens, 1996) and by a constant struggle to deal with this 'inherited' vulnerability. The generational poor do of course encounter opportunities and take initiatives in different areas of life (market, redistribution and reciprocity), but in general they do not succeed in reversing their situation permanently because problems that try their coping capacities keep popping up. Periods of harmony and balance are but temporary and one single negative event can easily disturb the precarious equilibrium. It is clear that growing up in poverty seriously limits the opportunities of individuals, and clouds their future.

At the other end of the continuum, we find people who grew up in a relatively stable and problem-free context. This is not to say, of course, that in their family trajectories no single trace of bad luck can be found. However, one way or another they managed to cope with it. They possess some strength and self-confidence, a power to deal with the difficulties of their lives. One single setback would generally not bring them into a situation of need, or only temporarily so. The fact that they have ultimately reached a point of deprivation has to be attributed to an accumulation of events. The situation of exclusion was mostly linked to exclusion from the labour market. Since most were poorly educated, they were engaged in manual labour. After some time, they developed health problems and have been forced to survive on disablement benefits. Others were dismissed and were unable to find a new job. These are mostly skilled workers: gainful employment played and plays a major role in the construction of their identity, which makes finding themselves unemployed much harder.

Past experience seems to be an important element when considering life histories and poverty; we can, of course, distinguish between worse off and better off cases, marked by longer or shorter periods of stability and comfortable living conditions, but at some point we seem to encounter a fault line which can not be overcome by the individuals on their own (Vranken, 2000). What could this 'fault line' be?

Is it because some of the poor possess a 'culture of poverty', which enables them to survive in poverty but at the same time prevents them from using the resources if and when they become available? The most plausible hypothesis is that of an 'adaptation' approach such as developed by Rodman (1963) in what he termed the 'lower class value stretch', expressing a dynamic relation between general values, specific living conditions and scarce resources. People who grew up in poverty do not seem to have different hopes and dreams about the future than those who grew up with more opportunities; indeed, they adhere to common values and want to realize them. Because of the lack of resources, however, these values must be temporarily 'stretched' – that is adapted to particular circumstances – so as to enable the poor to survive without loosing contact with the dominant culture. It is in this framework that 'coping strategies' have to be understood and we will provide illustrations from our research.

Market strategy

Employment in low-quality and short-term jobs in the secondary or informal labour market alternated with longer periods of unemployment. Periods during which they tried very hard to find a job alternated with points in time when work was not a priority. But, during most of their active life our respondents saw having a job as important, thus subscribing to mainstream values. Nonetheless, they had to 'stretch' these values and rules so that they became better adapted to the inadequate and insufficient means they possessed (Vranken and Steenssens, 1996). Young migrants seem most eager to find a job. Their fathers used to work, and they have been socialized into this work ethic: men are supposed to earn an income to support the family. Some respondents engage in moonlighting, but this is mainly a strategy of the higher educated, the ones with the necessary skills. The moonlighting sector reflects the segmentation of the 'regular labour market'.

Respondents proved very creative in finding ways of coping; some of them have a full-time job in looking for the cheapest options and in exchanging goods and services. Generally, however, it seems that people adapt to very limited amounts of money, and they do not think too much about it. Some of them have been saving on food and electricity for years. Some interviewees, however, do not seem to have the most rational consumption patterns, which often leads people to blame them for their poverty. One explanation could be found in a lesser known form of 'coping strategies' – that of a preference for consumption goods with a high 'symbolic' or 'token' value which links them to 'normal' society (Vranken and Steenssens, 1996). As poor people do not derive status from their position in the labour market, their educational achievements, or income, they have to turn to another socially highly valued domain, that of consumption. The absence of a 'deferred gratification pattern' ('sow now, harvest later'), resulting from socialization processes and from a lack of positive experiences, will lead to spending an occasional extra bit of money, particularly when children are involved. There is also the need to overcome stress, which for most of them is not an event but a permanent state, a way of living. Stress does, indeed, not only result from loosing a job, lacking money to pay a bill, the breaking up of a relationship, but also from recurring events. This helps to explain the high bills for cigarettes, alcohol and drugs – and ensuing debts, which in their turn lead to even more stress.

Redistribution strategy

The income differences we noticed can be explained by people's different income sources. A clear hierarchy exists, according to the economic market position and the related social status and political power of these sources. Guaranteed minimum income schemes stand at the lowest rung of this ladder and that also means that they produce minimal incomes. Differences are observed because extra benefits are within the discretion of local administration (the PCSW), and depend on the knowledge and bargaining power of the welfare recipients. To a small extent, benefits can be increased by income from work, which however is not allowed to exceed a certain, very small amount. Incomes will be higher for people receiving regular social security benefits, such as unemployment benefits. However, the amount of unemployment benefits depends on the last wage and decreases after a certain period for those who are not a head of household.

Reciprocity strategy

Possibilities for building social networks depend on many factors. Which of these factors did we encounter in our interviews? Household composition seems to be a prominent variable and this is so for clear reasons. The opportunity to start relations and to keep them going depends very much on the number of members in the household and their occupation; which means that significant differences will occur between the networks of single parents, single persons, couples or couples with children. Another factor to take into account is life history or more in particular the type of life events; whether serious crises have occurred. Families who have been subjected to periods of serious conflict do not provide a stable supporting network, a major disadvantage for individuals in times of need. As we suggested earlier, single mothers and their children seem to obtain much support from their own parents. However, since these parents are not very wealthy themselves the level and diversity of this support will not be very high. Poor people's networks usually consist of strong links and weak links are fairly rare – and, therefore, they are unable to experience 'the strength of weak links'.

Relationships with neighbours tend to be frequent but superficial. In general, help will be mainly of an emotional and practical nature, as the financial means in the potential network are limited for almost all inhabitants of the neighbourhood. People with a better-off background seem more able to prevent this process of gradual isolation through voluntary work in charities or in visiting people. They point out that these commitments are very important in structuring time, feeling useful and important for other people, and in providing themselves with a social network of supportive, understanding friends.

Conclusions

The central question in our research was 'what resources or constraints do neighbourhoods present to their residents'? Literature generally emphasized processes carrying on within families and kinship and friendship groups, but had not addressed the impact of the neighbourhood's resources. We found only small differences between people's strategies in the inner-city area with its old housing stock and in the big social housing estate in the Southern periphery. This may be due to the fact that the latter neighbourhood is only peripheral to a limited extent. Inhabitants in both neighbourhoods use the neighbourhood's resources for their coping strategies, they identify strongly with their area, and they perceive positive changes in their living environment and the built infrastructure, if such changes occur. Those who want to stabilize their situation do find resources in the area.

On the other hand, it is not clear whether a long stay in the neighbourhood should be interpreted as an indicator for a positive attitude towards the area. Few attractive features can be found in either of the neighbourhoods. Decisive might be the availability of cheap housing, either in the privately rented or in the social sector. They do not have the financial means to move, or have already given up hope of ever being able to do so. Rather, it is the place where people at the margin of society find a place to live and cope. Both neighbourhoods offer limited resources for the stabilization of life of their residents, but these are physically, economically, socially, culturally and politically unable to improve their situation.

The most important difference regarding the subject of our contribution is the higher security that is provided by social housing. Another is the better opportunities that Dam offers in the reciprocity sphere and the implication that there is a future for Dam but not for Silvertop.

Dam has a clear identity, a distinct location, a specific atmosphere and a village mentality. It houses many social organizations. Moreover, a number of big projects are being launched and the city government intends to seize the opportunity to give a positive push to the development of the neighbourhood and its inhabitants. In Silvertop less positive dynamics can be noticed.

URBEX was about the spatial dimension, as this had often been overlooked by previous literature. However, when looking at coping strategies, it turned out that important differences occurred that were not linked to the area: age and ethnicity, but mainly past experiences. The distinction between the poor who were excluded early in their life and the ones raised in stable families turned out to be useful: in general we may say that people from the second group generally make better use of the resources that are offered by long-term help (like social housing, moonlighting or budget training), where as those who were deprived early are often condemned to charity. This may also be a major point to make when discussing policy choices. Maintaining and further developing a general social security system is necessary to prevent people sliding into poverty after a series of negative experiences. But it is clear that providing these opportunities is not enough to lead the generational poor away from the path they seem destined to follow; more is needed. The most skilled and self-confident groups will benefit from benefits and support, and they may manage themselves to get out of deprivation or at least reach an acceptable standard of living. This may not be the case for everybody. Most generational poor seem to have developed strategies and capacities that are fit for coping in situations of hardship. They are, however, clearly not designed for escaping exclusion, which seems to require a different set of capacities: including a feeling of control and the general knowledge to combine and create a successful mix of strategies. This is where a more attentive educational system and self-help organizations could play a major role.

We, therefore, may conclude that the resources that the neighbourhood offers are one influence on the way that family and kinship networks do function. Indeed, the neighbourhood is several things simultaneously: an organized collection of houses, public spaces, traffic, private businesses and public services, a collection of persons and groups sharing an area for living and working, and a complex set of relations between both the spatial and social dimension.

Notes

1. Respondents were selected through a variety of methods: formal channels of social assistance institutions; posters in local shops and services in the area; lifts and corridors of the estate; they were asked whether they knew other possible interviewees as well (snowball method); and a fourth way was to address people when walking in the streets or the corridors. All of these methods have certain biases, advantages and disadvantages intrinsic to the approach, but we hope to have spread the risks of systematic and one-sided distortion by combining them.
2. This means that important groups constituting the poor population such as elderly people and undocumented immigrants were not considered in this research.

4

Amsterdam: Gender and Poverty

Wim Ostendorf and Joos Droogleever Fortuijn[1]

Social exclusion in the European Union

Many words are used to point to poverty. Marginality and social exclusion are relatively new ones. Social exclusion is a contested concept. Generally unemployment is seen to be the most important element. However, social exclusion also relates to generalized disadvantage in terms of education, training, housing and financial resources. Social exclusion also relates to the extent and quality of social networks people are included in.

The multidimensionality of the concept was clearly expressed in the Commission of the European Communities 1992 paper *The Community's Battle Against Social Exclusion*:

> Poverty is a complex, heterogeneous phenomenon and cannot be defined solely in terms of low income levels. As many studies have shown, the deprivation suffered by the poorest classes extends to many fields – employment, housing, health, education, social life, etc. The European Community and several of its Member States now consequently tend to define poverty in terms of 'social exclusion', a definition that encompasses both the processes of exclusion and the resultant situations. It also serves to emphasize the multifaceted nature of the phenomenon and the multiplicity and diversity of the factors that combine to exclude individuals, groups or even regions from those exchanges, activities and social rights, which are an inherent part of social integration.

Many of these problems appear to be most manifest in large metropolitan areas. Problems of social exclusion are not new, but some argue that in the past two decades they have become more severe in many cities. Many researchers and politicians have pointed to the increase of social polarization between well-educated people included in the labour market and society and under-educated people often excluded from that market and society; or between people with and people without a well-paid job; between men with jobs and women without jobs; or between people with voting rights and political power and those without. Several studies appeared in which dual or divided cities, polarized societies and the urban 'underclass' were the central themes (Fainstein *et al.*, 1992; Sassen, 1991; Wilson, 1987).

The cumulative process of social exclusion may be at its worst where the place of residence or quality of the neighbourhood adds to other factors involved. This kind of perspective is widely accepted. However the impact of the different factors has not been explored sufficiently.

This chapter deals with the interconnection between gender and urban poverty in The Netherlands and more in particular in Amsterdam and focuses on the position of single mothers in the labour market and in the social security system. First, we elaborate on the relation between gender and poverty and on the changing character of the Dutch welfare state. Next, we present an overview of the changes in the labour market participation of men and women in The Netherlands in general and of single mothers in particular. Next, we introduce the two low-income neighbourhoods in Amsterdam, Landlust and Osdorp-Midden, where the fieldwork was conducted. Then, we compare the coping strategies of unemployed single mothers with those of unemployed men in these two neighbourhoods. In the conclusion we challenge the idea of vulnerability of single mothers by demonstrating the relatively successful social integration of this category and we judge the role of the opportunities the two neighbourhoods offer.

The gendered nature of social exclusion

Although problems of poverty and social exclusion concern both men and women, they are not gender neutral. Literature on urban poverty and literature on gender issues both refer to the gendered character of social exclusion. Unskilled persons, immigrants, single mothers and single older women are considered to be vulnerable categories (SCP/CBS, 2001). Women are over represented in low-income groups and in groups with long-term low incomes (Portegeijs *et al.*, 2004). Single mothers in particular are indicated as high-risk categories in terms of poverty and social exclusion (Jehoel-Gijsbers, 2004; Kodras and Jones, 1991; Rose and le Bourdais, 1986). This is caused by the combination of several poverty-increasing characteristics of single mothers: their household income is generally lower than that of other households, in particular two earner households without children; by definition single mothers do not have a partner adding to the income of the households; and finally, in many cases single mothers are unemployed and dependent on social benefits. Traditionally, the gender positions of men and women in European societies were clearly defined. Society used to be constituted with families with a male breadwinner and a female housekeeper. Men were dependent on their wives for the unpaid household tasks and the care for their children; women were dependent on their husbands for their incomes. In this respect single mothers have a problematic position: they are mothers without the financial support of a male breadwinner and they are breadwinners but they have less access to the labour market because of time–space constraints regarding their tasks in their households and the raising of their children as well as because of gender segmentation and discrimination on the labour market.

Recent developments, however, might have relieved this problematic position to some extent. As women are more dependent on part-time employment, the shift away from male-dominated Fordist employment based around full-time, unionized workforces towards more 'flexible' and casual forms of non-unionized service employment, might have improved the chances on the labour market for working women (Watt, 2003). For working mothers, and in particular for single mothers, it is extremely important that they can combine the task of raising children with a job. Therefore, having a 'flexible' and part-time job nearby the place of residence is indispensable. Various parts of the city or metropolitan area can be very different in offering local jobs and as such can be very divergent in offering chances to single mothers (Vijgen and Engelsdorp Gastelaars, 1992).

The Dutch welfare state and marginality

'Work, work, work!' was the slogan of the socialist party leader who became Prime Minister after the elections in The Netherlands in 1994. Gradually the social security system changed from the provision of an income for people who are not able or willing to work into a system with the emphasis on labour participation. This priority is related to a policy of reducing state expenditures and a state withdrawal, but at the same time motivated by a changing perspective on poverty and citizenship.

Esping-Andersen (1990) makes a distinction between liberal welfare states with an emphasis on market exchange – social democratic welfare states with an emphasis on redistribution, and corporatist welfare states with an emphasis on reciprocity. The Dutch welfare state is characterized as a mixture of the social democratic and corporatist types, but since 1990 the Dutch state is in a process of reconstructing the welfare state gradually in a more liberal direction. Ten years ago redistribution of income and reduction in the levels of income inequality formed the fundaments of the Dutch social security system. Two parts of that system are especially important. First, unemployment insurances, disability insurances and social security payments guarantee a minimum income level for people who are not able or willing to work. Second, individual rent subsidies in combination with a high share of social housing in the total housing stock guarantee decent housing for low-income households. In the past ten years, the government reduced the expenditures on social security and rent subsidies. Nowadays reintegration and participation form the main themes in social policy. Social security institutions are more now, than in the past, focused on reintegration of unemployed and disabled persons in the labour market.

Within the social security system the change of the Social Security Act in 1996 has been especially important for single mothers (Knijn, 2002). In general, people are entitled to benefit payments based on the condition that they are available for labour market participation. They must actively apply for a job, are forced to accept a job mediated by a job centre or to enter a training programme. Before 1996, single mothers were released from these duties. In the former Act the gender position of single mothers was defined in terms of motherhood. They used to derive their citizenship rights from the female gender role as mothers. Motherhood was seen as a full-time job; single mothers were not expected to provide for their income by participation in the labour market.

This perspective changed in the new Social Security Act. All persons, including single mothers, are nowadays defined in terms of the (traditionally male) position of the breadwinner. The law makes an exception for single mothers with pre-school children, but as soon as the children are 5 years old, mothers are expected to participate actively in the labour market. In practice, however, most mothers with children between 5 and 18 years old are released from the compulsory labour market participation. The local 'Centres for Work and Income', which are responsible for the awarding of social security payments, and the single mothers still operate in accordance with the female gender position. In particular in the large cities the social security institutions are primarily engaged in the provision of an income for people who are not able or willing to work rather than in the reintegration of non-working persons in the labour market. These institutions are heavily loaded with work resulting from the concentrations of unemployed persons in these cities. The low educational level and the need for childcare provision in combination with the lack of day care facilities in particular complicate reintegration of single mothers. As a result, the entitlements of single mothers on benefit payments have been reduced only slightly after the introduction of the new Social Security Act.

Summarizing, since 1996 the system can be characterized as ambiguous. Officially, single mothers with children over 5 years of age have to be available for the labour market, to look for a job and to earn an income in order to make a living. In practice, many people, both single mothers and the social security institutions, especially in the cities, behave according to the situation before 1996: single mothers give priority to their task of raising their children and are excused for not participating in the labour market.

The changing picture of Dutch labour market participation

Increasing female participation

For a long period the labour market participation of women in The Netherlands was low compared with other European countries (Table 4.1).

Table 4.1   Male and female labour market participation in eight countries of the European Union 1970–2000

	Men				Women			
	1970	*1980*	*1990*	*2000*	*1970*	*1980*	*1990*	*2000*
Belgium	86	72	71	74	40	48	46	57
Denmark	92	89	87	84	58	71	78	76
France	88	83	75	74	48	53	57	62
Germany	93	82	80	81	48	49	56	63
Ireland	97	89	78	79	34	35	43	56
Italy	87	83	77	74	34	41	43	46
The Netherlands	87	78	80	84	31	35	52	66
United Kingdom	94	89	88	84	51	58	67	69
European Union	90	82	80	79	44	50	54	60

Source: SCP 1983: 234; OECD 2001: 210/211

In 1970 only 31 per cent of Dutch women participated in the labour market, compared to 87 per cent of the men. Only in Ireland was the gender difference higher. The female participation rate remained low during the 1970s. During the 1980s and the 1990s the rate increased tremendously. In 2000, the rate was more than twice the 1970 rate and is now above the mean rate of the European Union. Only in the Scandinavian countries and the UK are the participation levels higher. During the same period male participation in The Netherlands changed barely. In 2000 the rate was slightly above the mean participation rate in the European Union.

Table 4.2   Part-time work (less than 30 hours per week) of men and women in eight countries of the European Union 1990–2000 as percentage of total employment

	Men		Women	
	1990	*2000*	*1990*	*2000*
Belgium	5	7	30	35
Denmark	10	9	30	24
France	4	5	22	24
Germany	2	5	30	34
Ireland	4	8	21	32
Italy	4	6	18	23
The Netherlands	13	13	53	57
United Kingdom	5	8	40	41
European Union	4	6	27	30

Source: OECD 2001: 224

Specific for the Dutch labour market is the prominence of part-time work. In The Netherlands both men and women work twice as often part-time compared with the other countries of the European Union (Table 4.2). The level of part-time employment of Dutch women is exceptionally high in the European Union. The Netherlands is the only EU country where the majority of the women work part-time. Unlike other European countries, full-time working mothers are exceptional, in particular when they have pre-school children. Notwithstanding the relatively high position on part-time work for Dutch men, working part-time at 13 per cent is still rather exceptional for Dutch men.

Participation of single mothers

In 2000 6 per cent of all households and 16 per cent of all households with children are one-parent families (CBS, 2002: 29). Ninety per cent of all single parents are single mothers. Thirty years ago for both men and women widowhood was the main cause of single parenthood. In 2000 too most single fathers are widowers; most single mothers, however, are either divorced or have never been married. The labour market participation of single parents is lower than in other household types (Table 4.3). Unemployment rates are substantially higher among single parents than in other household types. The participation rate of single mothers is lower than of mothers in two-parent families; working single mothers, however, work more hours per week than working mothers with a partner (SCP, 1997).

The increase in the female labour force has broken down the dominance of the traditional breadwinner–housewife family and resulted in more financial independence for mothers with and without a husband. Nowadays most women are no longer primarily housewives, but they are women with a job and an income of their own. Most women, however, work part-time; many of them work a limited number of hours in a low paid job. Most women with children are at least partly dependent on the income of their (former) husband or on social security.

Table 4.3 Labour market participation and unemployment of people in different household types in The Netherlands 1999

	Participation	*Unemployment*
Single persons	69	5
Persons with partner, without children	67	2
Persons in two-parent families	73	3
Single parents	57	14

Source: CBS 2000: 31

The case of urban marginality in two Amsterdam neighbour-hoods

The spectacular increase in the female labour market participation, the recent changes in the social security system and the resulting consequences for single mothers in particular, form the context of the URBEX-study on processes of social exclusion in Amsterdam (Blok *et al.*, 2000; 2001). The study aims at studying the different so-called 'modes of integration' people may 'use' as strategies that help them to escape from poverty: the labour market, the welfare state, and their social networks. Based on a statistical analysis two neighbourhoods, Landlust and Osdorp-Midden, identified as having clear concentrations of poverty, were selected (Figure 4.1). Both neighbourhoods belong to the category containing the 14 poorest neigh-bourhoods of Amsterdam. In these neighbourhoods in-depth interviews with local residents and other key actors were held in order to develop an understanding of how neighbourhood features, opportunity-structures and social networks as well as economic restructuring, changing welfare states and changing housing systems affect processes of social exclusion and inte-gration. By comparing men and women in these two neighbourhoods it

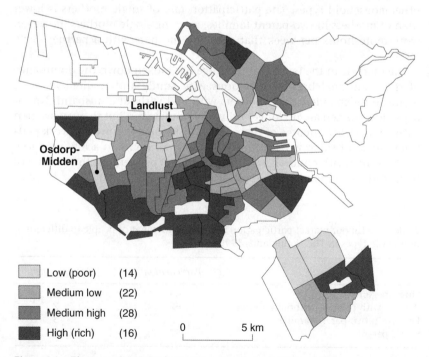

Figure 4.1   The spatial distribution of poverty in Amsterdam, 1998

can become clear to what extent women and more in particular single mothers have to be considered as urban poor and to what extent this is influenced by the opportunities the neighbourhoods offer.

A profile of Landlust

Landlust is situated in the west part of Amsterdam – close to the centre – and belongs to the so-called '20–'40 belt. This means that the biggest part of the neighbourhood was built just before World War II, during crisis years. As a result, this part of the neighbourhood is characterized by a tight and economical design, with high densities. It was built according to the architectural style of the *Amsterdamse School* and originally was meant for housing blue-collar workers. This area mainly consists of private rented housing. A smaller part of the neighbourhood was built after World War II, during the 1960s. Mainly housing associations constructed these recent dwellings (social housing). In the absence of owner occupied housing, this resulted in an almost 50/50 share of private and social rented housing in Landlust. Rental prices are rather low in Landlust; nevertheless 22 per cent of the households received rent subsidies in 1996. Although many houses have 3 or 4 rooms, the average floor plan of the houses is rather small: 35 per cent of the dwellings have 40 to 50 m^2 and 37 per cent 50 to 60 m^2. The building type of most housing blocks is 3 to 4 storey flats or apartments. Landlust shows a mixture of functions: some parts are very lively with offices, a marketplace, (ethnic) shops and services. Other parts have a residential function only.

In the early 1980s Landlust became an immigration area. Many immigrant families, mostly from Turkish or Moroccan origin, settled in the neighbourhood. This was stimulated by an out migration of – mainly – Dutch people to suburbs and new towns outside the city. Ethnic immigration in Landlust depends highly on the characteristics of the housing stock: dwellings are relatively cheap and, although they are small, they have relatively many rooms, attractive for the large ethnic families with low incomes.

In Landlust, policies have started to decrease dependency on benefits and to increase labour market participation. The goal is very ambitious: offering 40 per cent of the some 1,000 unemployed a job or at least a training programme.

A profile of Osdorp-Midden

Almost the entire neighbourhood of Osdorp-Midden was built in the 1960s. The neighbourhood is part of the *Algemeen Uitbreidingsplan voor Amsterdam* (AUP, General Amsterdam Extension Plan) that dates from 1935. The AUP is a well-known town-building plan, which contained global directives for the future extension of the Amsterdam city up to the year 2000, such as a spacious design, green areas and a clear separation of different functions such as housing, transport and shops. Osdorp-Midden is a so-called garden city, situated in the *westelijke tuinsteden* (western garden cities). In order to reduce the cost, the construction of housing blocks is based on repetition, that is, the different types of housing blocks are 'copied' several times, resulting in a rather monotonous design. Due to this design Osdorp-Midden is a rather monofunctional (residential) neighbourhood. There are only a few streets with some shops and services. For daily products, inhabitants are dependent on a shopping centre outside the neighbourhood. As a result, the neighbourhood is not lively at all.

The housing stock comprises for almost 100 per cent social housing. Rents are rather low, but 35 per cent of the households received rent subsidies in 1996. In general dwellings have 3 to 4 rooms. The average floor plan of the dwellings is larger than in Landlust: 30 per cent of the dwellings have 50 to 60 m² and 40 per cent 60 to 70 m².

Like Landlust, Osdorp-Midden experienced a strong inflow of ethnic minorities in the 1980s and 1990s, stimulated by the aging of the population and by an outflow of more affluent people – mostly young families with children – leaving the neighbourhood for new and more comfortable suburban dwellings outside the city. In only 20 years the rate of ethnic minority people developed as in Landlust from about 10 to more than 50 per cent; mainly Moroccans.

Based on the national *Grote Steden Beleid* (Big Cities Policy), an extensive urban renewal programme is in process in Osdorp-Midden. The physical structure of the southern part of our research neighbourhood gets a real face-lift; dwellings are renewed and some will be enlarged. Next to this, the policy also aims to increase labour market participation.

Comparative perspective on the two neighbourhoods

Both neighbourhoods are characterized by a low income level, high unemployment rates, a high share of residents living on benefits, many households receiving rent subsidies, an increasing share of immigrants, a high percentage of single parents and low participation in elections. However, this situation has to be understood in the context of the Dutch welfare state. The neighbourhoods are poor, but not hopeless. Although the debate sometimes uses strong words, there is absolutely no reason to describe the neighbourhoods as ghettos. Foreign visitors often find it very difficult to understand that this kind of neighbourhoods is described as disadvantaged or problematic: they do not observe real poverty and see a description of middleclass as more appropriate. Nevertheless, within Amsterdam these neighbourhoods are problematic. Not only regarding the position of the residents, but also regarding the amenities or infrastructure and the residential quality that they offer. Table 4.4 shows the satisfaction of the residents with their own neighbourhood on several criteria, compared to their benchmark-neighbourhoods (neighbourhoods offering a similar housing stock) and to the city's average in 2001. The two neighbourhoods score systematically lower than their benchmark-neighbourhoods and the Amsterdam neigh-

Table 4.4 Residential quality of Landlust and Osdorp-Midden based on judgements of the residents as compared to their benchmark-neighbourhoods and to Amsterdam in 2001 (1 is a low score, 10 a high score)

Indicator of residential quality	Landlust	Compared to benchmark	Osdorp-Midden	Compared to benchmark	Amsterdam
Maintenance of public space	5.4	–0.6	6.0	0.0	5.8
Maintenance of dwellings	5.7	–0.8	5.7	–0.5	6.7
Residential environment	5.5	–1.1	5.8	–0.6	6.9
Nuisance of neighbours	6.2	–0.5	6.6	–0.3	6.8
Nuisance of other persons	6.1	–0.9	6.4	–0.1	6.8
Clean neighbourhood	5.2	–0.6	5.6	–0.2	5.7
Commitment to neighbourhood	4.5	–1.2	5.1	–0.4	5.6
Social cohesion	5.7	–0.8	6.0	–0.3	6.4
Criminality	5.3	–1.1	5.8	–0.1	6.2
Safety during the day	7.3	–0.7	7.3	–0.2	7.9
Safety during the night	5.8	–1.1	5.6	–0.4	6.6
Amenities	6.5	–0.5	6.8	0.0	6.8
Total judgement	5.5	–1.6	5.8	–0.7	6.9

Source: RIGO Leefbaarheidsmonitor, Lemon leefbaarheidsonderzoek, Veer 2004.

bourhoods in general. The satisfaction in Osdorp-Midden is somewhat higher than in Landlust.

The provision of medical and childcare services and local employment forms important neighbourhood qualities for single mothers. Childcare provision is somewhat better in Osdorp-Midden (192 places for children per 10,000 inhabitants) than in Landlust (125 places per 10,000 inhabitants). The availability of local jobs is different in the two neighbourhoods. In the city district of Landlust some 476 jobs are available per 1,000 people between 15 and 65, while in that of Osdorp-Midden only some 273 jobs are offered. The comparative figure for Amsterdam is much higher: 788 jobs (O and S, 2002).

The fieldwork

In both neighbourhoods, households were selected for further analysis with the help of in-depth interviews in early 2000. All types were households of long-term unemployed (at least two years) with low education and known for their high-risk position in the restructuring economy and welfare system in The Netherlands. Here we concentrate on single mothers and on Dutch unemployed men, 25 in total. Single mothers are supposed to have weak social ties and a great risk of experiencing social isolation and weakening of local community life and, therefore, less reciprocity opportunities. Their dependency on one income provided by the state, and their supposed reduced opportunities to rely on reciprocity via social networks, contribute to the classification as a 'risk category'.

The interviewed persons were selected in various ways: through neighbourhood channels (self-organizations, health centres, neighbourhood centres, public and private welfare workers), via the municipality, and by responses to notices posted in local shops and services. Single mothers were most willing to participate. Unemployed men were more difficult to find, as their numbers are very small. It is assumed that the favourable economic situation in The Netherlands and in Amsterdam in the 1990s promoted a return to the labour market for many of this category, resulting in the most problematic people still left behind. They also had the most 'hostile' attitude. One reaction at 11.30 am was 'You wake me up for such nonsense!?'. The duration of the interviews varied from 1.5 to 3 hours. The central question to be answered with the help of these interviews is: 'To what extent can we understand the differences in strategies of unemployed single mothers compared to the unemployed men as moulded by the opportunity-structures that are available for these people in each neighbourhood?'

Single mothers in Landlust

Most of the six interviewed single mothers are low educated, young and divorced. They have one or two young children, some of them pre-school children. Some single mothers never married. Two of the single mothers grew up in the neighbourhood, whereas the others settled there later; the first group is much more rooted in the neighbourhood compared to the other women.

All single mothers, except one, are currently dependent on welfare benefits. As most of them are very young they are not on welfare benefits for a very long period. One woman currently has a full-time job but was on benefits at the time of selection. Two other women will be active in the labour market very soon.

Ms A. is a single mother with two children in primary school. At a very young age she left school without certificate because of the illness of her mother, the divorce of her parents and a constant moving between the houses of her parents with 50 km in between. At this moment she does voluntary work in the school of her children. She tells:

> It is very important. In the first place because I like it, in the second place because you are among people and you have something to do. Yes, for me it is very important, otherwise I sit at home and I really want to get to work ... I have been offered a job at another school. They need a teaching assistant and they want me

to come to work and in between I can try to get my certificate ... To be honest, I have applied before for a police job. I did several tests and stood them well and I could start immediately. But I didn't realize that this job had one problem: shift work. Sometimes you start at 6 am and I don't know any childcare centre opening at 6 o'clock in the morning. So, I had to cancel it and I did keep on benefits. Thank God those days are soon over; I can leave it and get to work ... Yes, and when you come home, mmm, lovely, you deserve it to flump on the sofa, you know.

Some other women postpone their labour market participation until their children are in primary school. In other words: they make use of the opportunity to bring up their children. So, although single mothers are on benefits currently, they are active in job searching or in improving their capabilities for a job, while they will be active in job searching as soon as their children go to primary school.

Ms B. used her time when her children were under the age of five, to become a teacher for young children. She also followed the obliged internship during these years and now she is ready for a job when the youngest will go to school. She says:

Now I do have a future, I can go to find work. I will not any longer be all day at home. And although my education is not the real top, it is a start and I enjoyed doing it. Compared to the social benefits that I receive now, I will earn only 45 Euro more during the first year in my job, but it is a start ... And there are many jobs on offer for me, especially in day-care centres. No problem whatsoever. My first choice would be to work in a day-care centre that is nice, with lots of contacts with the parents of the children.

Most women get a lot of support from their social network and have stable social relations, not only with neighbours, but also with family and friends. Especially the women who grew up in Landlust have many supportive relations in their own neighbourhood. Some women are active in voluntary work in their own neighbourhood, for example in their children's school or day care centre. Although job opportunities are scarce in Landlust, several single mothers use these opportunities successfully. There is a growing shortage of teachers and employees in day care centres over the past years. In particular single mothers seem to fill in these vacancies.

In general, single mothers could be labelled as active and socially integrated. Most of them have a well-structured life, related to the school schedules of their children. They are oriented on and integrated in their own neighbourhood. Single mothers combine strategies in different spheres and they have fairly good chances to change their situation. The strategies of all single mothers can be labelled as strategies in line with the present regulations, as they try to get ahead in society by either improving their skills or active job searching. Only one – recently divorced – woman had feelings of exclusion.

Single mothers in Osdorp-Midden

In Osdorp-Midden seven single mothers were interviewed. Most have a Dutch or Surinamese background. They are around the age of 30. Most of them have one child. All interviewed single mothers are low educated. Most single mothers are unemployed for a short period of time. Only two of them are without work for a longer period (more than 10 years). These persons show greatest distance from the labour market. Probably, one of them will never work again, as she prefers to bring up her four children. The other, however, still has some chances, as she is busy with re-education. The reasons why the single mothers became unemployed are diverse. For example, some of them could or would not combine work with bringing up their children, whereas others became redundant or partly disabled. Nevertheless, three women are currently active in the labour market, one of them part-time and two of them full-time. The women who work part-time deliberately choose such a job: one of them wants to be at home when her son comes from school for lunch, whereas the other prefers a full-time job, but has no after school care for her daughter.

Ms B. is a single mother with one child at school. She says: 'I am absolutely against the new law, that you must work when your child is 5 years or older. I think as a mother you deliberately choose to bring up your child and part of the upbringing has been cut of because you have to work.' Nevertheless, she started working shortly before the interview. She tells about her work: 'It is in the kitchen of a home for the elderly. I got this job via the Insurance Administration Office, because I am 25 per cent incapacitated because of back troubles. I cannot do certain types of work. This job is adapted to my condition and I really like not being dependent on benefits anymore.'

For most single mothers, social network support is very important, for both financial and emotional reasons. Only one of them does not have a strong social network. They are clearly neighbourhood oriented in their social networks and the use of facilities like shops and community centres for their children. At the same time, however, they experience a neighbourhood stigma: they feel dumped in the area together with other poor people as cheap housing is allocated to people with low incomes. In other words, they point to the institutional dimension of spatial segregation of poor and rich people, which in their view is unjust.

In summary, as in Landlust, most single mothers in Osdorp-Midden are labour market oriented and their strategies conform to the present regulations. In this respect they are very critical of the Employment Exchange, as one single mother tells:

> I was called [by the Employment Exchange] and I went to the interview, because I wanted to enter one of their projects. Yes, for mothers who re-enter the labour market, because my daughter just became five years old and then you must go to

work. That was okay for me, although I was pregnant, but I just wanted to do something. I can arrange childcare and I am ready to get to work. They just told me to go home for another five years. Come on, at least they should motivate you!

Dutch unemployed men in Landlust

In the Landlust neighbourhood, six Dutch unemployed men were interviewed. The majority of them are single-person households; only one has a family with two children. They are between 30 and 50 years of age and have a low educational level. In general, their focus on the labour market is not strong and social network support is weak. The neighbourhood has no meaning for them and is just a place to live. Two respondents know they won't get employed again and do not actively look for a job. This can be understood by their mental and physical health problems. These men experience social exclusion.

Mr. P. is now 47 years of age and has been on social benefits for almost 25 years. He suffers from mental problems and is under medical and psychiatric treatment. He says:

> My childhood was not good. We had many conflicts at home. My mother was also manic-depressive; it is in the family, probably genetic. During the last years I have found the right medication. It is getting better now. Now that I feel better, I hope to find a job, because being always at home makes a person crazy ... I think I will not get a job because of my psychiatric problems; and also because of my age. That is how the system works. They prefer young people. And if I will find a job it will be very difficult to keep it because of my medication; my medication is very heavy. So, I think I will not find a job in the coming five years.

One person does not want to work and is finding all kind of ways to stay out of the hands of the employment- and benefit-agencies, especially by constantly starting a new education. He says:

> I am used to my freedom now and, therefore, I stopped looking for a job. In order to get a social benefit I had to work or to start an education. I have chosen for the last option and I have started an education. I have done all kind of things, over and over again. I remained positive and that works! The civil servants select on motivation, not on quality. And they are happy with me, because that is how the system works. They protect their own position too. In this way they make a professional unemployed out of you.

Three other persons are active with working and earning money; not officially, but 'black', in addition to their social benefits and without informing the social security agencies. They generate additional income via informal activities (hustling) outside the neighbourhood, try to maximize their benefits from the state without looking for a job (although they are obliged to) and use the safety net as a hammock as long as they are not offered a well-paid job; they refuse a job with a low income, a job that is demanding or asking for flexible working hours. Only the man with a family can be characterized as a person acting according to the official rules. He followed the formal route to employment and currently works 20 hours per week, but is paid by the welfare bureau for the time being, as he first has to show whether his business is viable. This person is also best integrated into society: he has good chances to become independent from benefits and is also best embedded in social networks.

Dutch unemployed men in Osdorp-Midden

Six Dutch long-term unemployed men were interviewed in Osdorp-Midden. They are younger than the interviewed native-born men in Landlust. Their educational level is low. Most of them are single.

The interviews show that most unemployed men in Osdorp-Midden have limited chances of being active in the labour market. This makes them heavily dependent on benefits. Some of them cannot work because of mental problems or drugs addiction. Mr R. says:

> I have had a very difficult childhood. Manic-depressive. It does not change, it even gets worse. I have tried to commit suicide three times. Now I have promised to my mother not to try it again as long as she is alive. I have a very good relationship with my mother. But she is the only one to withhold me ... The employment agency does not make any problem. They have labelled me as psychiatric, they know that I have never had a job.

Others could work but have problems in getting a job. One of them, for example, spent 10 years in prison and is still confronted with his criminal record. Another is a restless person: he stayed in orphanages, experienced a period of homelessness, was in prison for one year, and whenever he has a job he does not show up after one day or one week.

Two persons can work, but do not want to, because they are active in informal activities outside their neighbourhoods. Mr T. says:

> I have never done my homework at school. So, I left school early. Then things went wrong: criminal things, a lot. I was convinced that I could make it this way ... I have been dealing drugs in the house of my mother. She did not like this. Neither did the neighbours. They kicked me out ... But I have earned a lot of money, with some good deals sometimes 5,000 Euro in a month. But this did not give me complete satisfaction ... When you are addicted to drugs you do not want to work ... The biggest problem of not having a job is that you do not have a regular life, nothing is important.

The single father is the only person acting in line with the official regulations. He has had his present job for 4 years and works 23 hours per week. Social benefits supplement his wage to the official minimum family income. In contrast to the other men, he did not experience problems in his life that make him unable to work or form a barrier to labour market participation. He has also the most structured daily life as he has to take care of his daughter. He has an extensive and stable social network.

In summary, the strategies of most Dutch unemployed men in Osdorp-Midden are focused at using the benefits of the welfare state and/or at informal or illegal paid work. They are not oriented on or integrated in the neighbourhood and, in general, live in isolation.

The meaning of the two neighbourhoods

Single mothers have their activities and social contacts mainly in the neighbourhood. Therefore, they can be labelled as typical neighbourhood users. Single mothers also have most of their social and supportive relations close by. In addition, half of them are active in voluntary work. In contrast, Dutch unemployed men do not interact with the neighbourhood. They only do their shopping in the neighbourhood and for the rest do not mix with other people. Single mothers are more bound to the neighbourhood as they have children in primary school there. The single mothers also experience no serious difficulties in accessing childcare facilities in their neighbourhood.

A few single mothers succeeded in finding work within their neighbourhood. They were not dissatisfied with the neighbourhood and the local services and they had no strong wish to leave the neighbourhood. Many interviewed people wanted to improve their housing situation within the neighbourhood. The Dutch unemployed men are content with their present dwelling and have no plans to move to another dwelling or neighbourhood. The people indicating that they want to move to another dwelling are often searching in their own neighbourhood. Some single mothers prefer to move to another neighbourhood. One might expect that for them their present neighbourhood functions as a push-factor, as they live in a deprived area. However, the interviews do not support this view. Some prefer to move to another area because of pull-factors. Others wait for the moment that their dwelling will be renovated or demolished as part of the urban renewal programme. In Amsterdam, people who are forced to move to another dwelling for the reason of urban renewal, get a financial compensation for such a move. So, for them this programme is also appealing in terms of money.

Job opportunities are relatively scarce in Landlust, while Osdorp-Midden hardly offers any job opportunities to the respondents, mainly as the neighbourhood is a monofunctional, residential area. In line with these differences, single mothers in Landlust have found a job more often in their own neighbourhood than single mothers in Osdorp-Midden. So, for single mothers the neighbourhood appears to play a role, in particular for offering part-time jobs in schools. This does not apply to the Dutch unemployed men; if they work it is outside the neighbourhood. This difference is sharp and remarkable. Watt (2003) points to the same configuration in his study on marginality in the borough of Camden in London. Women do use the opportunities of the local labour market, in particular in shops, health centres and schools. Unemployed men are not interested in these jobs, because they have difficulties in adapting to the more 'flexible' labour market circumstances. They consider the wages as too low and see only full-time jobs as offering sufficient 'respect'.

Gender and poverty: Conclusion

This study tries to reveal how single mothers and Dutch unemployed men cope with the problem of social exclusion in two Amsterdam neighbourhoods: Landlust with a more central location and a mix of functions and Osdorp-Midden with a more peripheral location and with a pure residential function.

It appears that the rather low unemployment rate that characterized Amsterdam early in the twenty-first century does not cause exclusion from the labour market for those who are able and willing to work. For those unable or unwilling to work, the Dutch welfare state offers the chance to have an alternative way of life as some sort of compensation. The state bureaucracy appears unable to reintegrate unwilling people in the labour market. Nevertheless, life on social benefits is not easy and often results in a shortage of money. A shortage of money, in many cases not helped by a strong and effective social network, results in forms of social exclusion. It is remarkable that single mothers do not show the clearest forms of social exclusion: they show good prospects on integration in the labour market, have strong rights on social assistance and have a supportive social network.

So, regarding the three modes of integration, the Dutch welfare state appears to be very important for both groups. The labour market is important, but for single mothers only. Social networks appeared to be important for single mothers, while the Dutch unemployed men were clearly isolated.

The analysis of the interviews has not revealed clear differences between the two neighbourhoods. The neighbourhoods may show different characteristics regarding location and mixture of functions, but the single mothers and unemployed men in these neighbourhoods show similar lives. Moreover, none of the interviewed people point to their neighbourhood as a cause of their problems or lack of social integration. In many cases the respondents point to personal circumstances as cause of their problems. Maybe 'this lack of negative influences of the neighbourhood' is connected to the role of the Dutch welfare state in preventing the poverty of the residents and in preventing clearly disadvantaged neighbourhoods as well. That is to say: the two neighbourhoods clearly belong to the category of poor neighbourhoods in Amsterdam, but this position is only relative; very sharp differences, as might exist in cities of countries with less pronounced welfare states, do not exist.

As indicated, the analysis of the interviews did reveal clear gender differences. The unemployed men, who were unable to find a job even in the present favourable job market, apparently have serious problems. In some cases personal, mental or physical health problems result in weak social networks and bad perspectives on labour market entry. Others do not want to work for a modest income, but prefer the higher sum of social benefits and additional income out of informal or illegal activities outside their own neighbourhood. It has been suggested that men have bigger problems in adapting to a more 'flexible' labour market than women, as they still refer to 'proper wages' and full-time jobs.

The ambivalent gender position – the ambivalence between the female gender role as mother and the male gender role as breadwinner – provides single mothers with better perspectives on integration than unemployed men. Motherhood results in social integration: they have a regular day schedule, work as volunteers in child-related activities, follow courses, have strong supportive networks, and are integrated in their neighbourhood. This social integration resulting from motherhood provides them at the same time with opportunities to fulfil their role as breadwinner. So, unlike the expectation of many observers the new idea of social security that was introduced in The Netherlands in 1996 and that asks for labour participation of all persons – men and women, parents and non-parents – older than 18 years, does not appear to increase the social exclusion of single mothers. On the contrary, it seems to support the social integration of women, especially with respect to the labour market.

Although single mothers are over represented in the categories of people on benefits and in low-income groups, they cope successfully with the problems of poverty and have good perspectives on social and economic integration. The unemployed men in this study are more subjects of concern. These men 'integrate' outside the regular labour market or they are socially excluded.

Note

1. The authors gratefully acknowledge the assistance and collaboration of Hans Blok and Jorrit Visser in the data collection and analysis.

5
Hamburg: Contradicting Neighbourhood Effects on Poverty

Martin Kronauer, Peter Noller and Berthold Vogel

Social exclusion and the neighbourhood: Some basic assumptions

The 1980s were a crucial turning point in the postwar history of German cities. The federal government changed its policies and departed from the tradition of providing public housing at a time when most cities, struggling with economic and social restructuring, became confronted with rapidly increasing numbers of unemployed and welfare recipients. Labour and housing markets, which before had been separated in their effects to a considerable extent by state intervention, have, since then, interacted much more closely. The result is growing socio-spatial segregation: the clustering of poor and unemployed populations in particular urban districts and neighbourhoods.

Neighbourhoods with high shares of unemployed and poor people are nothing new in the history of cities. In the first decades after World War II, however, in Germany as in most European countries economic growth, employment growth, the extension of welfare state provisions and services, and demand-oriented policies had worked together and almost eradicated unemployment, decreased income inequality, and considerably lowered the poverty rate. Viewed against this particular historic background, the return of poverty-stricken neighbourhoods takes on a new quality indeed. It calls into question the capacity of highly developed capitalist societies to provide all citizens with a decent, culturally adequate standard of living and means to participate in the life of society – a definition of welfare which after World War II has become a widely accepted criterion for a democratic society. But we must also assume that the period of unprecedented social 'integration' by means of increasing living standards, almost full employment and welfare state intervention which now seems to have come to an end shapes in particular ways the experiences of poor people and their efforts to cope with precarious living conditions.

How do people with high risks on the labour market – long-term un-employed men and single mothers on welfare – perceive and cope with the threat of social exclusion? And how do the neighbourhoods in which they live influence their perception and their coping? These were the questions that we tried to answer by empirical research in two urban quarters of the city of Hamburg. Stating the questions in these ways already has two important implications.

The first implication is that being long-term unemployed and being a single mother on welfare indeed poses a threat of social exclusion. The term 'social exclusion' became prominent first in France and had then been adopted by the European Union in the late 1980s (see Paugam, 1996; Room, 1998). It is now widely used (though still contested) by European scholars in order to grasp the new qualities of urban poverty. The concept can only be properly understood in the above outlined context of notions of welfare and social participation as they have emerged after World War II. Since there is not enough space here to go into the details of the concept and the international debates about it, we only briefly outline how we use the term (for an extended discussion see Kronauer, 2002). In our under-standing, it refers to the interplay of several modes of social belonging and participation in the life of society. Particularly significant among them are access to employment or to another recognized position within the social division of labour; involvement in social networks based on family, friend-ship, acquaintanceship; and finally, access to institutional (state) protec-tion, services, and participation based on citizenship and (political, social) rights. Holding a recognized position in the social division of labour means access to the 'organic solidarity' (Durkheim) of formally (often unequally) structured interdependence; being involved into social net-works of kinship and acquaintanceship means access to social reciprocity on an informal basis of interdependence; having access to institutional (welfare state) support and services means participating in society as a citizen with entitlements to 'social rights' (Marshall), i.e. to a culturally defined living standard. The various modes of social belonging relate to each other but at the same time follow different 'logics'. There is no social right to employment in most countries, and on the other hand not every kind of employment provides a decent standard of living. The social composition of personal networks depends to a certain extent on employ-ment status, but there is no such thing as a social right to friendship. The current debate in Europe about 'inclusion' and 'social cohesion' in times of high structural unemployment is very much a debate about the relationship between employment and social rights, and how they can be combined in new ways. For a more detailed analysis of the modes of social belonging see Kronauer (2002).

Social exclusion, in turn, implies a combination of various kinds of deprivation: marginalization on the labour market and in employment, up to total exclusion from gainful employment (without, at the same time, holding an alternative social status such as student or retirement); a weakening of social ties up to social isolation or a confinement of social networks to people in similar disadvantaged position (and therefore with very limited resources to help out of poverty and unemployment); and exclusion from institutional (welfare state) support or a stigmatizing treatment by such institutions, with a substandard level of provision. The idea behind the concept of social exclusion is that in highly developed capitalist societies employment still plays – directly and indirectly – a pivotal role in the distribution of income and social recognition.

Long-term unemployment considerably increases the risk of definite exclusion from employment, particularly if it lasts for more than two years. In Germany during the 1990s, only 15 per cent of the people with unemployment spells of more than two years found gainful work again (Gilberg *et al.*, 1999: 284). But long-term unemployment also involves the other dimensions of social exclusion. It puts a heavy stress on personal social networks, which are important potential resources of material and emotional support. In many cases it induces income poverty, which not only often means financial hardship but also the inability to keep up with others and to live up to common social expectations. Welfare state support for the long-term unemployed, after insurance benefits have expired, is in Germany means tested and, therefore, subject to discriminating administrative controls and has a poor reputation.[1] Single mothers, on the other hand, do not fit into the social ideal of the complete family as it is favoured by welfare state regulations. Their obligations at home make it difficult for them to find employment, and state support is again based on means testing. When we speak in the following about a threat of social exclusion for these two categories of people, however, we not only refer to particular living conditions and their consequences for social relations. If 'social exclusion' is a meaningful concept for empirical research, it should also have its subjective expression. It should show in the ways in which people perceive themselves *vis-à-vis* others and society at large.

The second implication in our starting questions is that the neighbourhoods in which the poor and unemployed live actually have an impact on people's experiences of and coping with the threat of social exclusion. For urban scholars, this seems almost to be self-evident. Poor and unemployed people are less mobile than the employed and better off and, therefore, depend more on resources in their close urban environment. Neighbourhoods can have positive or negative effects on the various dimensions of social belonging. They can be the basis of social connections, which might or might not lead to jobs, material and emotional help. But they also influence the living standard by the condition of housing and infrastructure, by the availability or lack of institutional support, by the density of administrative and social controls. However, it is still not clear, *how* neighbourhoods and social conditions interact. In particular, this is not clear with regard to neighbourhoods with high (above average) rates of poor and unemployed inhabitants. There are two widely held views about it.

The first view can be summarized as the 'concentration-effect' hypothesis. It holds that the more poor people live in a particular neighbourhood, the more they are additionally disadvantaged. The argument has most thoroughly been elaborated and based on empirical research in Chicago by William Julius Wilson in the context of the American debate about the emergence of a new urban underclass (see Wilson, 1987; 1996). In this view, social isolation is the crucial link between neighbourhood and labour market. The more the poor live among themselves, the less they have contacts to working people who can provide help in the search for jobs and act as 'role models' for the young. It has been questioned that the 'concentration-effect' hypothesis can be applied without modifications to European urban quarters. Differences in the level of concentrated poverty, in the extent of racial segregation, and in the extent and quality of state welfare provision have to be taken into account. Recent research in Germany has indicated, though, that even there (with a much lower welfare-density rate than in American inner-city quarters) the spatial concentration of poverty leads to an extension of poverty spells (see Farwick, 2001). However, there is, as yet, no convincing interpretation of those findings. Farwick considers as one possible explanation the stigmatization attached to the areas of concentrated poverty. Friedrichs and Blasius (2000), also argue in the vein of the concentration-effect hypothesis. Their evidence from four neighbourhoods of Cologne remains inconclusive, however, and it is not clear whether in fact the variation in poverty density or other neighbourhood characteristics account for the differences in deprivation effects of the neighbourhoods.[2]

The second view can be characterized as the 'neighbourhood-type effect' hypothesis. The share of poor people in this view is less important than the functional and social composition of the neighbourhood. Mixed use, inner-city neighbourhoods are more supportive for poor people than monofunctional, purely residential housing projects at the fringes. They provide more formal and informal job opportunities, more supportive networks, and a less stigmatizing urban environment. This hypothesis is prominent among European scholars and was taken as a starting point for the European research project on the spatial dimensions of urban social exclusion and integration (URBEX). We had also used it in our prior research about neighbourhood effects on social exclusion.

Looking for empirical answers to our starting assumptions, we had to further specify them. The following four questions, each linked to specific hypothetical expectations, guided our research:

1. Do people on welfare and the long-term unemployed perceive themselves at all as facing a threat of social exclusion? We expected that
   people with high risks on the labour market indeed see themselves
   exposed to a threat of social exclusion – long-term unemployed men
   more than single mothers on welfare, because the latter at least had to
   perform the socially accepted role of caring for their children.
2. What impact does the neighbourhood (or, more broadly, the urban
   quarter) have on the perception of a threat of social exclusion? Here we
   expected that the neighbourhoods play an important role, with the
   inner-city quarter being more protective, the housing projects on
   the other hand increasing feelings of exclusion.
3. How do people on welfare and the long-term unemployed view and evaluate their living quarters? What are the reasons for their judgments? How
   people speak about their neighbourhoods and whether they wanted to
   stay or to leave, we took as an important indicator of resources (or the
   lack of resources) in the neighbourhood for coping with difficult circumstances of life. According to our 'neighbourhood-type effect' hypothesis,
   we expected that the inner-city quarter gets much better ratings from its
   poor inhabitants than the housing estate at the fringe of the city.
4. Who can draw upon financial resources from the neighbourhood, who
   cannot, and why? With regard to the actual coping strategies, we again
   expected a neighbourhood difference: the housing estate provides fewer
   opportunities than the inner-city quarter.

Before turning to our findings, a few words about Hamburg and the two
neighbourhoods in which we did our research are necessary.

Hamburg: City of new economic growth, city of new poverty

Hamburg, Germany's second largest city with 1.7 million inhabitants, more
than any other big city in the country, epitomizes the two sides of the coin
in the current socio-economic transformation. It is one of the richest cities
in Europe. The northward extension of the European Union and the
unification of Germany gave, in the 1990s, a strong boost to its position as
a central hub of European trade. In addition, beginning in the 1980s
Hamburg was able to restructure its economy successfully. While the
harbour-related industries lost much of their importance for employment
(even though the harbour itself is still a strong economic factor as the
second largest in Europe), the city expanded in advanced services – media
and communication, corporate services. But also in manufacturing,
Hamburg attracted new high-tech industries such as aircraft production
and biotech firms. It has already accomplished what many cities in the
international competition are still striving for. The new service economy
and selected, high-tech industries are the propelling forces of economic

growth (see Gornig *et al.*, 1999). Shifts in the political emphasis of the local government away from concentrating its support on the 'old industries' – shipyards, oil and steel – had contributed to this effect. In many respects, Hamburg's recent history is a success story. Employment grew in the 1990s, in contrast to the overall German development. The per-capita income is far above the West German average.

At the same time, however, welfare expenditures also steadily increased. In 1970, 17,650 people received welfare benefits, in 1997 the number had risen to 159,681. Even more significant is the fact that, in the 1990s, Hamburg ranked second among the big German cities with regard to the share of population on welfare. Only Bremen's record was worse in this respect (see Alisch and Dangschat, 1998: 101). Long-term unemployment also posed a severe problem. Hamburg's restructuring, then, shows all the signs of an uneven development. Economic growth in some sectors goes along with decline in others, and the former does not naturally heal the wounds of the latter. Läpple speaks with regard to Hamburg about a 'decoupling of employment growth from unemployment' (Läpple, 2003: 196). People who had lost their jobs in the old industrial economy have great difficulty in finding work in the new one. The expanding service sector offers more opportunities for women than for men, particularly redundant male workers. As in Germany in general, low and unskilled workers and people in their mid-forties and older are the main victims of unemployment. Women, however, are against the trend and less afflicted in Hamburg (see Dorsch *et al.*, 2000). But it is not only the combination of growth and decline that leaves its mark on the Hamburg labour market. The problematic side of the new service economy also shows clearly. The number of jobs with reduced social protection and employment security, among them prominently temporary work, increases steadily

St. Pauli and Mümmelmannsberg: Poverty in different neighbourhood contexts

The uneven development in Hamburg finds its spatial expression in a highly unequal spatial distribution of welfare recipients in the city (see Alisch and Dangschat, 1998). The concentration of poor people is highest in the central district (Hamburg Mitte). From this district we chose our two urban quarters for research. Since we wanted to study 'neighbourhood-type effects', we included a prewar, mixed-use, inner-city area (St. Pauli) and a postwar housing estate at the fringe of the inner city (Mümmelmannsberg).

St. Pauli has a long tradition as a popular lower-class working and residential area. Historically its social life had been shaped by the harbour on which it borders. Housing small businesses, shopkeepers and craftsmen, and offering casual work to day labourers, it functioned in the past as a 'zone of transition' in the sense of the Chicago School of urban studies, providing all kinds of opportunities to survive for the poor and the 'little people'. Due to container shipment and other forms of rationalization, the harbour today has no longer its pre-eminent employment and economic significance for the area. But it still informs the tourist image of St. Pauli. 'Reeperbahn', the quarter's famous red-light district, is a worldwide attraction. The history of the area also constitutes a particular local identity, characterized by a reputation of social tolerance despite occasional conflicts, and grassroots involvement in local politics. Young people looking for niches for an 'alternative' lifestyle like to live in St. Pauli, but so do increasingly members of the new middle class. As a prime location at the centre of Hamburg, St. Pauli faces considerable pressures of 'gentrification', with many of its small local businesses already being pushed out and replaced by advertisement agencies and software developers of the new economy. Trendy restaurants as well as pawnshops and second-hand stores are meanwhile equally characteristic of the area.

With 17 per cent of its 31,000 inhabitants on welfare in 1998, St. Pauli is statistically the poorest quarter of Hamburg. Almost 40 per cent of the population are migrants, the majority of Turkish descent. Typically 'urban' is the quarter in still another respect. Single households account for more than 72 per cent of all households in St. Pauli, as compared to 48 per cent in Hamburg as a whole. Public, semi-public and private institutions address particular disadvantaged groups. St. Pauli has its own local welfare office. The quarter was included in the city's programme to fight poverty on the neighbourhood level. Several initiatives care for children and youngsters, for Turkish girls and young women. Social workers provide help for vagrant Punks.

St. Pauli, then, provides a good example of an inner-city quarter with a high share of poor inhabitants but also a considerable functional and social mix. It has always been an urban area in which the not-so-well-off had a place. But it is now confronted with the double effects of urban restructuring: social invasion by representatives of the new service economy and decline of even casual job opportunities for the unskilled.

Mümmelmannsberg is situated at the eastern fringe of the central district. It was built in the 1970s as the single largest public-housing project of the city at the time. Today about 21,000 people live there, mainly in moderate high-rise apartment buildings. At the time of its planning and construction, Mümmelmannsberg was a pet project of the Social Democratic local government, a symbol of progress. It was to alleviate the housing shortage in the inner city and to provide families of moderate income with comfortable and affordable housing in a quasi-suburban environment. A reform school combining different educational levels was established and is still a central institution in the quarter. Health centre, kindergarten and shopping mall made Mümmelmansberg a fairly independent living quarter. Work was to be reached by automobile via the highway. Since 1990, a subway line connects the quarter to the city centre.

The population mix of Mümmelmannsberg changed in the 1980s. Vacancies increased and were filled by the city with the allocation of welfare recipients. In the meantime, the concept of large-scale housing estates itself had been considered more critically in urban planning. The perception of Mümmelmannsberg changed from 'model' to 'problem quarter'. The first official report of the city on poverty, published in 1993, painted for the area a picture of misery and despair (see BAGS, 1993). After German unification, a new housing shortage reversed the middle-class exodus. But long-term unemployment remained above Hamburg average, as did the share of welfare recipients. 'Welfare density' in the mid 1990s in Mümmelmannsberg was at about 15 per cent. In 1997, 24 per cent of the population were migrants. The outside perception of the area also changed little – despite considerable efforts on the part of the city to refurbish the area with trees and shrubs, despite investments in the reform school, and despite the quite proper appearance of most buildings. Also in contrast to the outside perception, Mümmelmannsberg has a considerable community life. Various institutions sponsored by churches and the city offer services to single mothers and youngsters. Like St. Pauli, the quarter has its own local welfare office. Complaints often raised by women in our interviews concern the still limited opportunities for shopping in the area.

Experiencing the threat of exclusion: Do neighbourhoods matter?

In two separate, but strongly related research projects conducted in the second half of the 1990s, we interviewed local and city experts and 150 long-term unemployed men and women on welfare (mainly single mothers) in both quarters.[3] To get an answer to our first two questions – do people with high risks on the labour market perceive a threat of social exclusion? and what impact does the neighbourhood have on such a perception? – we had asked four questions (introduced and prepared for by the context of previous questions), which addressed various dimensions of a possible experience of social exclusion:

1. Do you sometimes feel useless (referring to the dimension: having a recognized social position in society)?
2. Do you feel sometimes looked down upon by others (referring to the experience or expectation of stigmatization in face-to-face contacts)?
3. Is it difficult for you to keep up with others (referring to social, relational aspects of financial situation and living standard)?
4. Do you feel as an unemployed person 'left out' (referring to an overall sense of not being able to participate in the life of society)?

Three or four positive answers we took as an indication of a strong perception of a threat of social exclusion, two positive answers as indication of a partial experience of such a threat, one or no positive answer as indicating no perceived threat.

Given the selection of our interview partners, it might be no surprise that a great majority, of about three-quarters, of our respondents expressed strong or partial feelings of social exclusion. However, what we had not expected was a gender difference that directly runs counter to our hypothetical assumption. While the answering pattern of men was distributed fairly equally among our three categories 'strong', 'partial' and 'no' stated feelings of a threat of social exclusion, women by more than 60 per cent ended up in the category 'strong', while only 13 per cent did not report any such feelings (or only in one dimension).[4] Family support helped somewhat to mitigate against an experienced threat of social exclusion for both sexes; marital status, however, did not make any difference. Not living alone had some positive effects on men, but not on women. Having children also was of no or only little help for them. Most strongly was the feeling of a threat of social exclusion linked to the length of unemployment, the duration of welfare dependence, and the perception of one's chances on the labour market. However, while this held true for both men and women, women expressed feelings of exclusion more strongly than men during shorter periods of unemployment and welfare receipt. Our assumption that women depended less on employment and financial independence for defining their social status, based on findings in a prior research project on unemployment in two small towns (see Kronauer *et al.*, 1993), did not at all bear out in our Hamburg research. It might well be that the high share of single mothers (with their particular, ambivalent social position, carrying a high burden of responsibility, being at the same time discriminated against at the labour market; getting state support but mixed with administrative controls) in our sample and the urban lifestyle to which the women were used influenced our findings.

What impact does the neighbourhood (or rather: the urban quarter) have on the experiences of a threat of social exclusion? We approached this question by linking our categories of feelings of exclusion to the answers to another question – whether or not people wanted to stay in the neighbourhood or rather wanted to live somewhere else. Here again we were up for another surprise. Only in one of the two quarters (St. Pauli) and here only for specific subgroups of the poor we found a neighbourhood effect on the experience of social exclusion. All in all such effects were weak or, as in Mümmelmannsberg, did not show.

For women in St. Pauli who strongly felt a threat of social exclusion, we found the expected link to the neighbourhood. They also strongly expressed their wish to leave. For two categories of our male respondents, the quarter worked in the opposite direction, as a buffer against feelings of exclusion. Men who were already out of employment for five years or longer reported fewer experiences of exclusion than the long-term unemployed with shorter unemployment spells. Some of them had adapted to their situation and felt less social pressure. St. Pauli more than Mümmelmannsberg offered social niches in which such an adaptation could occur. Also people who did not adhere to the pre-eminent norms of the 'work society' (and therefore did not feel excluded from it), but wanted to share with others an 'alternative' lifestyle found opportunities to do so in St. Pauli. However, both groups represented only a minority of the men we interviewed in this quarter. For the others, feelings of social exclusion and feelings about the neighbourhood were fairly disconnected.

In Mümmelmannsberg, this was even more striking. The male respondents who wanted to leave the quarter were also the ones who expressed the least feelings of exclusion. And on the other hand, people who strongly felt excluded in most cases did not feel uncomfortable in the quarter where they lived. This held true for men and women alike.

From our findings follows an important conclusion. Obviously, for the majority of our respondents feelings of exclusion and perception of living conditions in their immediate urban environment refer to different aspects of people's lives with little overlap. The frame of reference for feelings of exclusion goes far beyond the neighbourhood and relates to institutions of society at large (such as gainful employment, welfare). Only in very specific circumstances, could the quarter enhance or protect against experiencing a threat of exclusion. But this in turn also implies that the neighbourhoods, as much as they might matter in other respects, are of only limited importance for the people when it comes to fighting social exclusion.

Experiencing the neighbourhood: Are there typical differences?

This does not mean, however, that neighbourhood conditions cannot make a difference with regard to other aspects of the daily coping with unemployment and poverty. To find out more about neighbourhood effects in this respect, we started out again from our question whether people preferred to stay in the quarter or wanted to leave (wished to live somewhere else). We took this as a first indicator of living conditions to be found in the urban environment, which in the view of our interview partners, could either make life even more miserable for them, or on the other hand, provide important resources in their daily struggles.

From the 'neighbourhood-type effect' hypothesis it was to be expected that St. Pauli would be considered far more positively than Mümmelmannsberg. However, even this assumption did not hold. While two-thirds of the interviewees in St. Pauli wanted to stay, the share in Mümmelmannsberg was only a little bit lower (60 per cent).[5] Even more interesting than the similarities in the overall rating of both quarters, however, are the underlying differences in the reasons given.

For residents of both quarters, the rent level is an important reason for living in the area. But in almost all other respects the positive and negative judgements could barely be based on more different criteria. Social characteristics of the quarter play a decisive role in the evaluation of St. Pauli: good contacts among neighbours, a shared understanding of difficult circumstances in life which would be hard to find in other places, a shared local identity ('we-feeling'), and the social diversity rank high in the positive judgments. But social characteristics are also most prominent and controversial issues in the critique of the neighbourhood: drugs, prostitution, alcoholism, an urban environment which does not suit the raising of children.

Social qualities of the neighbourhood, in contrast, have no positive appeal at all in Mümmelmannsberg, but this does not matter much. Instead, the quality of housing and physical infrastructure, and the closeness to green space are important – aspects that are totally missing in the evaluation of St. Pauli. In social terms, living together with or near family members is particularly relevant for inhabitants of Mümmelmannsberg – and not at all for our interview participants in St. Pauli. When asked whether the high share of unemployed and poor people in the quarter is of any help for one's own living situation, at least a relevant minority of the respondents in St. Pauli agreed – but no one in Mümmelmannsberg. Here an interesting gender difference came to bear. While the women responded mainly with indifference, the men viewed the high share of poor people in Mümmelmannsberg much more as a disadvantage and a source of insecurity – an indication of greatly different social meanings of the quarter for both sexes.

How can we explain our findings: the similarity in the overall judgements, with very different reasons given for those judgments? The first and most important reason is the different social composition of the poor populations in both quarters. As already mentioned, St. Pauli has a far above average share of single households, mainly men living alone. Mümmelmannsberg and the larger area of Billstedt of which it is a part, in contrast, have a much higher share of families living in it than St. Pauli. The differences in household situations and in the quantitative representations of the subgroups in our interview samples of both quarters reflect this sociodemographic difference. The variation in the social composition of the poor populations in St. Pauli and Mümmelmannsberg is not the result of a random selection, but at least in part also of migration choices. Asked about why our interview partners lived in St. Pauli, they indicated again social characteristics of the area as the second most important reason after rent level. In Mümmelmannsberg, closeness to the family was very important, after rent level and quality of housing. Also more respondents in Mümmelmannsberg than in St. Pauli had grown up in the area and decided to stay close to their family.

Different people and household situations mean different needs and expectations with regard to the urban environment. Mümmelmannsberg had been built for families with children. The quality of housing was a much more important consideration than any social neighbourhood quality. Home and work were spatially separated to enhance the quality of the home. Social life was meant to be foremost family life and was to take place in the evening hours, when the husband came back from work. Such a physical arrangement and social destination of urban space still makes sense for women with children, even when they are single mothers and out of work. This holds particularly true if family members live nearby who can be helpful in caring for the children. Kinship networks are the most important source of support for the interviewed poor in Mümmelmannsberg, much more than friends. A precondition for the appreciation of living in a housing estate is, of course, that the buildings and public infrastructure are well kept and safe, that family-related services (schools and medical services in particular) are available and of decent quality. All this is more or less the case in Mümmelmannsberg, at least since recent years. The quarter is by no means an abandoned area such as an American inner-city ghetto – in contrast to the stigmatizing outside perceptions. By far, the majority of people we asked told us that the quarter was improving and that they expected it to further improve in the future (while people in St. Pauli expected the opposite – a further deterioration of an already declining environment). Even the welfare office in Mümmelmannsberg has a far better reputation among the poor than the welfare office in St. Pauli. No wonder that 15 out of 20 women whom we interviewed in our first study in Mümmelmannsberg, almost all with children, wanted to stay in the quarter – not being enthusiastic about it, but appreciating the living conditions. In our smaller URBEX sample, the reactions among the women were more mixed compared to the more positive views of the men. But here again the influence of local family ties came into focus. About half of the long-term unemployed men with whom we talked had children and/or lived with a partner in the household.

St. Pauli is not a social environment of and for families. Most people live alone (at least in German households), men and women alike. But it is also, in the social stratum of the poor, a much more male- than female-oriented environment. In both surveys, the great majority of our male respondents stated that they wanted to stay in the quarter, and many did so with a considerable amount of local identification. The women, in contrast, were divided in their opinions and much more ambivalent. St. Pauli offers social niches particularly for people with a longer lasting biography of living at the fringes of the 'work society' – with broken work histories, recurrent unemployment, a social decline stretched over an extended period. But it also sometimes allows people to hide from the critical views of former acquaintances when life has taken a sad and sudden turn downwards. For the poor in St. Pauli, friends are much more important as a source of help than kinship.

Our finding forces us to reconsider critically the basic, underlying assumption of the 'neighbourhood-type effect' hypothesis. By comparing neighbourhoods, we do not only compare 'typical' differences in land uses and built environments and how they affect a particular population (in this case unemployed and poor people). Instead, we compare 'typically' different neighbourhoods with 'typically' different populations. Different neighbourhoods attract different people, and this holds true to a considerable extent also for the poor. Many of them end up in a particular neighbourhood by chance, some by administrative allocation. But many also make a choice, even though they are poor and the alternatives are very limited. Different poor neighbourhoods, therefore, also address different needs of the poor.

But there is another important side to this pattern as well. Both quarters make life more difficult for poor people who cannot or do not want to take advantage of the particular resources provided by the neighbourhood, or whose needs are not, or are too little, met by the specific neighbourhood conditions. The men and women who, as a minority, did not like to stay in St. Pauli had in most cases two characteristics in common. They once had been employed in stable positions and then experienced a rather sharp biographical break and social decline. And they had come to St. Pauli not voluntarily but because they did not see any alternative for themselves. For both reasons they could not, or did not want to become part of the St. Pauli milieus of the poor. They easily ended up as outsiders among outsiders. So it is not just gender, but also biography that makes an important difference for liking or disliking living in St. Pauli. Gender is of particular relevance when it comes to issues of security in the area and of raising children. In Mümmelmannsberg, on the other hand, the family-oriented infrastructure that helps women with children (but also men with family ties) to cope with the difficult circumstances of their lives further aggravates life for men who are without a family and out of work. For them, the built-in purpose of the housing estate as a place of family life, physically detached from work but depending on employment at a distant workplace as its supplement, is utterly meaningless. In contrast to the large majority of women in Mümmelmannsberg who told us in the first survey that they wanted to stay, a small majority of men would have preferred to leave.

In short: urban quarters are not uniform in their effects on people within the same income bracket. Even more, they often produce contradictory results. The same social and physical conditions that might be supportive for some categories of the poor can, at the same time, be of no use or even detrimental for others.

Who can mobilize financial resources in the neighbourhood, who cannot?

In principle, there are three sources from which poor people can mobilize financial means: the welfare state or private charities (redistribution), kin or acquaintances (reciprocity), the market via formal or informal employment.

Support from the welfare state is based on and limited by entitlement; charities depend on good will; kin or acquaintances help, as a rule, on the basis of reciprocity with the expectation that they will get back what they have given; formal employment is more the problem than the solution if unemployment is the reason for impoverishment; informal employment depends on attitudes, skills, opportunities and the strictness of administrative and social controls.

Neighbourhoods have little impact on welfare state regulations, except in the rare cases that the welfare state intervenes on the neighbourhood level (with specific social services for instance) and gives its population an opportunity to participate in the decision-making process. Formal labour markets also operate largely on principles that reach beyond neighbourhoods or particular urban quarters. Charitable institutions, however, are often neighbourhood based. The social networks of the poor, too, depend – for reasons mentioned before – more than the networks of the well to do, on spatial proximity. Informal work requires trust – something that neighbourhoods can provide but also undermine (by the social control of mischievous neighbours for instance).

It was one of the major goals of the URBEX project to find out for each country how different categories of poor people (long-term unemployed indigenous men, single mothers, unemployed migrants) manage to survive by drawing upon resources from redistribution, reciprocity, and the market, and what impact different neighbourhood settings have on their efforts. In this respect, the Hamburg case provides only limited results, for one simple reason. We had approached our interview partners at the welfare offices in both quarters. All of them, therefore, were not only entitled to but also actually received welfare benefits. In fact, by choosing this approach for pragmatic reasons, we also captured an important feature of the German welfare state. Welfare as a financial support of last resort is in principle granted to everybody in need. However, not everybody takes it up – because of shame, of lack of information, of fear of administrative control, or for whatever reason else. Poor people beyond the reach of the welfare state are not represented in our sample. Our material from the URBEX survey, therefore, only allows to draw some conclusions with regard to the two most contrasting groups *inside* the welfare system: people who are able to mobilize financial resources from the three sources market (informal or regular, low level employment), personal networks (friends and family), and the state (welfare, unemployment assistance) on the one hand, and people who depend on the state only on the other.

The ones who have, get more – this old popular wisdom holds true, to some extent, even for the poor. Poor people with access not only to welfare cash benefits but also to formal or informal work in the market and to financial support from friends or relatives also more often than others get help in kind from friends and family members.[6] In addition, they are particularly able to mobilize the welfare office for extra material support (such

as a special one-time allowances for furniture). In most cases the beneficiaries of all three sources of financial help are tied in large networks of
friends and keep regularly in touch with them, the majority also report
good contacts to neighbours. Partial feelings of exclusion dominate in this
category, while strong and no experiences of a threat of social exclusion are
about equally represented. In other words: access to financial means from
the market and reciprocity goes along with a whole array of additional
material and emotional resources that help in coping with the difficult conditions of living in poverty. But it is also linked to particular options and
strategies in the labour market. The majority in this category consider the
chances in the labour market as good, most of them having specific plans
for retraining or already concrete, possible jobs in mind for the future.
They apply for work by still making choices, or withdraw from the labour
market only temporarily, for particular reasons. Only one person in this
category has definitely given up any hope of finding a regular job and
stopped searching. All in all, the people who can tap all three resources for
financial support can combine particularly well coping strategies *within* the
current, distressing circumstances of life with promising labour market
strategies to *lead out* of those circumstances. There is no indication in our
material of a 'culture of poverty' trap in this category – people remaining
dependent on welfare because they prefer to live on benefits and additional
incomes from informal work.

In the contrasting category, people who have to rely only on the welfare
state for their income, more than others resort to self-provisioning and
second-hand clothes from charitable organizations. As a rule, they are
attached to only a small circle of friends and about half live rather isolated
lives. Most experience the threat of social exclusion strongly; only two
report no such feelings. Prospects on the labour market are considered
much bleaker than in the case of the resource-combining category. Only a
small minority has an optimistic outlook. Most describe their chances as
precarious or bad. Asked about specific actions on the labour market which
they want to take in the near future, there is barely any other answer than
the generally expressed will to go on with job applications. Choices are no
longer to be made on the labour market.

There is no obvious pattern in the distribution of social characteristics
between the two categories. Long-term unemployed German men more
than single mothers and unemployed migrants seem to be able to draw
upon all three sources of financial support. A spatial effect, however, shows
more clearly. People of the first category we found in our sample twice as
often in St. Pauli, and people of the second category equally more often in
Mümmelmannsberg. Access to informal work makes the decisive difference.
Here at least the 'neighbourhood-type effect' hypothesis seems to bear out.
As we have seen, however, having access to informal work or not is but one
aspect of relevance for people coping with poverty in particular urban
settings.

Conclusions

At the beginning we asked what different neighbourhood contexts mean for people struggling with poverty, long-term unemployment and the threat of social exclusion. At the end, we had learned a lot about the complex relationships between gender, biographies and households on the one hand, and the housing and social conditions in particular urban quarters on the other. Neither the 'concentration-effect' hypothesis nor the 'neighbourhood-type effect' hypothesis was able to express and explain in a satisfying way those complex interrelations. By discussing the material, we reached three conclusions. They have, in our opinion, consequences for poverty-oriented policies, and equally for neighbourhood-oriented policies.

First, different urban quarters (different in terms of housing stock, land uses, infrastructure and history) attract different poor populations and address different needs. Even poor people often make choices in their selection of neighbourhoods – though limited ones, and by no means all of them. Policy intervention should accept that there is no particular neighbourhood type which is most helpful for all poor people. But it can also take the choices of the poor as a starting point for targeted support. 'Choice' of a neighbourhood is only a meaningful term (for the poor as much as for others) as long as the neighbourhood provides decent housing and infrastructure and a safe place to live. It requires private and even more public investments to make or keep it that way.

Second, living conditions in a 'poor quarter' are often contradictory in their effects. Conditions that provide opportunities for some categories of the poor can at the same time enhance the problems of others, particularly of those who are neighbourhood-bound with little or no chance to leave (single, long-term unemployed men in Mümmelmannsberg, confronted with a family-centred social and built environment, were a case in point). Policy intervention should always be aware of possible unintended effects of its actions and try to give such unaddressed needs a voice, however difficult this might be.

Third, the characteristics of a particular urban quarter can make life for the poor easier or more distressing. In the latter case, they may well further decrease people's opportunities and increase their feelings of misery and exclusion. This is reason enough for political intervention in support of the neighbourhood. But neighbourhood intervention is not enough to combat social exclusion. Even neighbourhoods that are described by the poor in mainly positive terms do not compensate for the social effects of long-term unemployment and poverty, and as the interviews showed, barely compensate for feelings of exclusion. The relative detachment of feelings of exclusion from the neighbourhood setting is just another indication that the causes of social exclusion originate beyond the borders of any urban quarter, and beyond those borders they must be tackled.

Notes

1. For a European comparative study on unemployment and social exclusion, taking into account the effects of different welfare-state arrangements, see Gallie and Paugam (2000).

2. Friedrichs and Blasius strove to test Wilsons argument about negative socialization effects of neighbourhoods with concentrated poverty. However, what they actually did in their survey was to inquire into links between poverty and attitudes towards deviant behaviour rather than to demonstrate actual effects of behavioural patterns learned in the neighbourhoods on labour-market performance. The study nevertheless produced interesting results. It showed that the Turkish populations in the neighbourhoods were more 'conformist' and inclined to subscribe to stricter rules than the Germans.

3. The German 'Volkswagen Stiftung' funded the first study. In 1997 and 1998 we interviewed 97 long-term unemployed men and women on welfare in the two quarters, 60 per cent of the interviewees were men, 90 per cent were of German descent. About half of the interview partners were in the age group between 35 and 49 years, only 15 per cent were older than 50. Eighty-eight per cent received welfare benefits, 84 per cent were long-term (more than one year) unemployed. About half had no specific occupational qualification. We used a highly structured questionnaire with open questions (allowing the respondents to give their own answers). Subjects covered were work histories, experiences with work, unemployment and welfare, financial consequences and coping with them, social contacts, use of time, perception of chances on the labour market, labour-market behaviour, perception of the neighbourhood and the living quarter, reasons for moving, self-perception *vis-à-vis* society. In addition, we asked in a standardized way for personal data and household characteristics. We approached our interview partners via the labour office and the welfare offices in both quarters. For analysing the material, we prepared a code sheet with various categories in which for each interview all the relevant information on single questions but also on more complex combinations of questions were recorded. This allowed for a statistical overview of the material and some cross tabulations which helped to detect relevant and typical relations and to guide qualitative interpretations. For the second study, in the framework of the URBEX research, funded by the European Union, in 2000, we interviewed additionally 53 people, this time concentrating on single mothers on welfare, long-term unemployed German men, and unemployed migrants. To make the two studies compatible, we used in part some of the questions of the prior study again, but also shifted the emphasis in the URBEX research more on the common issue of the resources that the people are able to mobilize from the state, the (labour) market and social networks. Again we approached our interviewees via the welfare offices. For the analysis of the material we used the above outlined procedure.

4. We refer here to the findings of our first study, but the picture was very similar in the URBEX study as well.

5. Again the numbers refer to findings of the first study. Here we had asked: Do you like to live in St.Pauli/Mümmelmannsberg or would you rather live somewhere else? The URBEX interviews lead to a similar distribution: Sixteen people in St. Pauli declared that they wanted to stay, 15 in Mümmelmannsberg; five people wanted to leave St. Pauli, seven Mümmelmannsberg. Five persons in both quarters emphasized their ambivalences about it.

6. In our URBEX sample these were 13 people. Fifteen people belonged to the opposite category, depending on public welfare only.

6
Milan: Urban Poverty in a Wealthy City

Alberta Andreotti[1]

The neighbourhood effect

At the beginning of the 1990s, the review of Jenks and Mayer (1990) on neighbourhood effects concluded that 'no general pattern of neighbourhood effects could yet be found. The empirical evidence [wrote the authors] is contradictory and sometimes thin in the areas of educational attainment, cognitive skills, crime, labour market outcomes.' Since that review however, much research has been completed that provides some evidence for neighbourhood effects in those fields, using statistical data and sophisticated statistical models, even though it is not always clear which mechanisms are at work (see Brooks-Gunn *et al.*, 1993; Case and Katz, 1991; Leventhal and Brooks-Gunn, 2003). Also important to note, is that many researchers found that in comparison with family characteristics, neighbourhood effects have a negligible impact. Nevertheless, it is nowadays widely accepted that neighbourhood effects exist, and more generally, that living in a specific place makes a difference in terms of social opportunities, and feelings of social exclusion. Most researchers in this field would probably agree that living in a disadvantaged neighbourhood enhances the conditions of exclusion.

These effects are perceived to be much more relevant for people at risk of social exclusion, and welfare recipients who often have fewer chances to get out of the neighbourhood and to get in touch with positive behavioural models and socio-economic resources outside the neighbourhood.

One of the mechanisms identified in the literature with regard to the way in which the neighbourhood can affect survival and coping strategies of residents (how people accomplish their daily life activities, the tasks of acquiring the material means of existence, the social support for existence (social networks, social care, emotional support)) and can enhance their exclusion, is the presence and access to institutional (Jenks and Mayer, 1990), economic and social resources (Friedrichs *et al.*, 2003). The presence (or absence) of social services, public institutions, shops (which also provide job opportunities), youth gangs, parks, social associations and common narratives about the neighbourhood, can provide variations in the quality of life and can contribute to structuring differently the coping strategies of residents.

In this contribution, I will address this point by trying to depict *how* the neighbourhood can affect the survival and coping strategies of three categories of welfare recipients in two disadvantaged neighbourhoods of the city of Milan, located in northern Italy. The three categories of welfare recipients are: single mothers with minors; long-term unemployed males; and foreign immigrants coming from developing countries. I will concentrate on the mechanisms and on the reasons why neighbourhoods are important, and on the concrete strategies people deploy in the neighbourhood. In this sense, the chapter does not provide a statistical analysis proving the existence of the neighbourhood effect. Though, it intends to show, through a qualitative approach, how the structure and the characteristics of the neighbourhood can affect the survival and coping strategies of welfare recipients.

I argue that the opportunities available in the neighbourhood are the results of the specific historical trajectory of the area, of the local political decisions, and more generally, of the conditions of embeddedness of the neighbourhood. Paying attention to the conditions of embeddedness means drawing attention to how the logics of integration have been constructed in the neighbourhood, and how the survival and coping strategies of welfare recipients are related to them (see Mingione, 2004).

In order to carry out this type of analysis and to consider the complex interaction between the different integration patterns, the analysis will be structured in two steps. In the first step I will refer to the historical trajectory of the two neighbourhoods selected for the analysis – Ponte Lambro and Baggio – to show similarities and differences in their development and integration patterns. In the second part, I will refer to the empirical material gathered from in-depth interviews with the three categories of welfare recipients in the two neighbourhoods, focusing on their strategies.

Before starting with the neighbourhoods, it is important to frame the analysis into its socio-geographic context, so that the relevance of the Milanese case can be highlighted.

The city of Milan and its spatial concentration

The municipality of Milan, with its 1,300,000 inhabitants, is the core area of one of the most important and populated metropolitan regions of Southern Europe. Milan is the centre of the great majority of financial and executive activities in the private sector of the Italian economy, performing a crucial economic role for the Southern European market. It is the Italian city that best represents the main features of the so-called postindustrial economies, both from a socio-demographic and from a socio-economic point of view: a growing foreign resident population, low birth rates, relatively high divorce and separation rates in comparison to the rest of the country, a very developed tertiary service sector, a very low unemployment rate, and the highest level of per capita income in the country.

Several ecological analyses carried out in Milan (Benassi, 2005) show that differences among neighbourhoods are not very pronounced. This is particularly true for the unemployment rates, which do not differ greatly within the city. The labour market in Milan is not geographically divided, so that a person living in any neighbourhood can find a job in any other area of the city, especially in the centre where activities concentrate. This

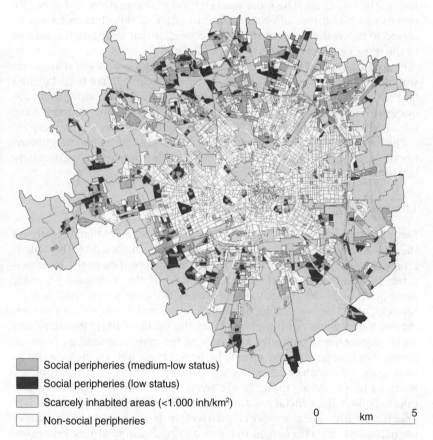

◼ Social peripheries (medium-low status)
◼ Social peripheries (low status)
▢ Scarcely inhabited areas (<1.000 inh/km²)
▢ Non-social peripheries

0 km 5

Source: Comune di Milano and Dipartimento Sociologia e Ricerca Sociale, Milano Bicocca

Figure 6.1 The social status of Milan neighbourhoods, 2000

feature of the Milanese case is particularly relevant and will come across again in this text.

From a spatial point of view, the city of Milan can be thought of as a concentric circle model with three main circles (Figure 6.1).[2] The first and smallest one represents the city-centre where higher educational levels and job positions concentrate. The second one represents the residential districts, and the third one represents the outlying neighbourhoods with lower income households. Some of these latter neighbourhoods developed mainly after World War II under the pressure of migration, and it is precisely there that social problems concentrate. However, these neighbourhoods are not entirely monofunctional – they are the location of some strategic urban functions such as universities, as well as new parks and new residential buildings. The most marked form of segregation, as Preteceille remarks in his studies of other European cities (2000), does not seem to regard so much the lower as the upper classes, which segregate themselves in the more central and exclusive areas of the city.

Ponte Lambro and Baggio, the two selected neighbourhoods, share some similar qualities – both are located in the third circle, have been labelled 'at risk', have experienced a strong presence of drug-dealing, and are quoted in newspapers as 'hot neighbourhoods'. Both neighbourhoods have been included in the municipal project of 'Re-qualification of periphery'.

The fact that Milan is not a segregated city, and that the two neighbourhoods have some similar features, makes this comparison particularly interesting.

The two neighbourhoods: Baggio and Ponte Lambro

Ponte Lambro is situated on the extreme eastern edge of Milan, exactly on the other side of the city with respect to Baggio, bordered by the Milan-Linate airport, the countryside, and the river Lambro (one of the most polluted in Lombardy). Ponte Lambro is one of the very few Milanese neighbourhoods that is spatially isolated – the only access road being a tunnel. Ponte Lambro developed mainly in the mid 1970s, under the pressure of a new wave of immigrants from the south of Italy. Its urban and social physiognomy radically changed with the massive building of council housing in that period. The criteria by which these new council dwellings were assigned privileged families in hardship (mainly coming from the south of Italy), people under house arrest, and other problematic households. Besides the official assignments, a successful migratory chain was operating with official residents' relatives, or friends squatting in empty council dwellings. This helped to create a district comparatively homogeneous in terms of social composition, but quite problematic. Serious problems of squatting and unpaid rents were present, which have still not been completely solved.

Baggio was close to some large industrial areas in the 1970s, which have now been replaced by some main tertiary companies (Vodafone, St-Microelectronics, Banca Intesa, Decathlon). In terms of the city layout, the neighbourhood is located on the extreme western edge of Milan. It is crossed by two important highways, which constitute the main axes along which traffic moves. It is fully integrated in the urban built environment and contrary to Ponte Lambro, it does not evoke a feeling of separation from the city.

Immigration in Baggio took place at a different time than Ponte Lambro. The neighbourhood had already become the object of massive migratory flows shortly before World War II. The first migrants came from other northern Italian regions, while a growing number started to arrive from the south in the postwar period (in particular from Puglia, Sardinia, Campania, Sicily). Migration to Baggio took place at a time of exceptional industrial growth, during which there were practically no problems in finding a job in one of the big factories around Milan. This certainly facilitated settlement, something that did not happen in Ponte Lambro. This has had important consequences on the social structure of the neighbourhood.

The population of Baggio consists mainly of families from southern Italian regions, but who have been living in Milan for several decades, and whose children were born and have grown up in Milan. These children have higher educational levels and higher job positions, and have settled next to their parents. The evolution of employment in Baggio clearly shows this shift: from an almost exclusively working-class area to a white-collar area. In 1991 white-collar inhabitants represented 45.4 per cent of the inhabitants, and blue collar 34.6 per cent. The latter percentage is higher than the city average (26.6 per cent), but lower than in Ponte Lambro.

The different timing of migration has consequences also on the age structure of the residents (despite the fact that in both cases the age average is higher than the city one, in Baggio residents are, on average, older than in Ponte Lambro) and on the role of social housing, which comprised two-thirds of the housing stock both in Baggio and Ponte Lambro before the widespread sales took place.[3] In Baggio it was an important element of upward mobility (low rents equal greater savings and higher consumption levels). In Ponte Lambro it was part of a household survival strategy – squatting.

Of course, even the integration of Baggio's population did not occur without social problems; experiences of deviance, dropping out, and squatting were present too, to such an extent that the outside perception of the neighbourhood, up to a few years ago, was not at all good. In a survey carried out at the beginning of the 1990s, the inhabitants of another neighbourhood located in the third circle of the city and with the same features as Baggio – Quarto Oggiaro – answered the following question 'In which neighbourhood do you think inhabitants are worst off?'; they declared 'in Baggio' (Guiducci, 1993).

Nevertheless, from the 1990s onward, the social divide between the two neighbourhoods has increased. Baggio has undergone a deep upgrading, with the construction of new, high-quality private dwellings, the physical renewal of many council estates, which have now been privatized, the physical renewal of several public places, and the drainage of the nearby park which is the biggest in the city. All these changes involved the local administration as well as a great number of local associations which actively promoted, and participated in the projects.

These structural changes, together with the increased heterogeneity of the population have contributed to modifying the outside perception of the neighbourhood that has now almost entirely lost its negative stigma.

In Ponte Lambro, the situation is more complex. The population is still rather homogeneous. Ponte Lambro is still an area with a clear majority of blue-collar workers: almost 60 per cent of people in employment are workers (in industry or in the service sector). The attempts at upgrading set in motion by the public administration failed dramatically[4] and the few new social services set up in the area were forced to close due to repeated vandalism. Problems of deviance and specifically youth deviance (youth gangs) are still present.

Finally, as far as infrastructure and services are concerned, the two areas also appear slightly different. Both neighbourhoods are relatively well connected to the rest of the city as far as transportation is concerned, but shops and social services are not equally present in the two areas. In Baggio there are still some craftsmen (a glazier, a shoemaker), open markets, and diverse small shops. Social services, both private and public, are at the core of the neighbourhood and can be reached on foot. In Ponte Lambro there is the municipal market, but no other shops; and while there is one private Catholic social service organization inside the neighbourhood, the public ones are outside and can only be reached by bus or car.

This qualitative analysis, considering the different historical and social development of Ponte Lambro and Baggio, reveals fairly clearly two different configurations with different opportunities for the residents. Two different patterns of social and economic integration were at work in the two contexts. These patterns were – and still are – intermingled with the socio-economic conditions (and development) of the city as a whole. Indeed, the different capacity of the city to integrate immigrants in different historical periods played a major role in shaping these two patterns. Residential policies carried out by the Municipality of Milan further contributed to distinguish the two neighbourhoods' trajectories.

Given these findings, some explorative questions and some hypothesis can be put forward.

- Do strategies of residents change in the two contexts, and how?
- Do strategies change according to the different categories of welfare recipients?

- Do welfare recipients housed in Baggio feel more integrated and use the services more than the welfare recipients in Ponte Lambro?
- Can we speak of a 'concentration effect' in Ponte Lambro, implying the fact that residents are more bounded to their neighbourhood?

In the following paragraphs, some evidence will be presented to answer these questions.

Survival and coping strategies

Analysing the actors' coping strategies means investigating the interaction between the actual conditions of the actor and the specific resources available to him/her. Two types of resources can be considered: 1) personal resources, and 2) material and social resources (opportunities).

Personal resources are shaped by the individual's cultural context (ethnicity, gender, age), as well as by education and personal attitudes. Material and social resources have been identified in this research as: 1) labour market; 2) family and social networks; and 3) social assistance services. In this perspective, the individual is an active subject who makes choices and actions, even if bounded by the given context.

In order to explore the survival and coping strategies of the three categories of welfare recipients, 61 in depth interviews (32 in Baggio and 29 in Ponte Lambro) were carried out with single mothers,[5] unemployed males, and immigrants living in the neighbourhoods for at least three years.[6] Interviewees were contacted through public social services, charity associations, and the local church. All interviewees had received or were receiving economic support at the moment of the interview.

The strategies observed are quite heterogeneous and highly affected by the individual's previous trajectories, nevertheless some specific features related to the structure of the two neighbourhoods and their outside perception can be highlighted.

Getting resources from where? The labour market

As we have seen, the city of Milan has a very low unemployment rate and no large differences can be found among the different neighbourhoods. Finding a job is not difficult, even for those people who are on welfare benefits and who live in neighbourhoods considered at risk of disadvantage. No cases of discrimination on the basis of place of residence have been noted among the interviewees. This emphasizes the fact that the relatively negative stigma attached to a neighbourhood (which is however very low in the city of Milan) is not pervasive and does not define its residents. However the three categories of welfare recipients display some differences in their relation to the labour market.

The young single mothers interviewed, both in Ponte Lambro and Baggio, are active in the labour market, and none of them has ever really been unemployed.[7] In this respect, the Milanese single mothers are not excluded from the labour market. It is more a case, as Morris (1995) suggests, of exclusion *in* the labour market, since these women systematically not only occupy the lowest positions on the employment ladder – a fact that is related more to inequality (scarce access to education and therefore lower educational qualifications) – but are concentrated in a specific sector, cleaning work, which offers little or no job security (being laid off without warning, no holidays, no temporary unemployment measures). The high employment rate of single mothers reflects the national situation, in which they are generally more active than the average female population (Pedersen *et al.*, 2000; Saraceno, 1998). This can be explained by referring to the Italian welfare system. Indeed, even though single mothers with minors are one of the groups considered 'deserving' and entitled to some welfare benefits, both at national and local levels these benefits are not at all generous and certainly do not allow them to live without any other income or economic support. The Italian benefits vary individually and geographically; there is no overall national scheme, rather, there are regional and local, and often private, initiatives. This means that there is no guarantee of obtaining the same benefits – even if suffering from an equal condition of need – in different local contexts (see Fargion, 1997). In this sense, young Italian single mothers are indirectly forced to enter the labour market and to find a job – even unstable or under-paid (Saraceno, 1998). These same mothers make good use of public education services such as the public nurseries or all-day school attendance for children, so that they can have more time to work. In Milan, the high rate of female employment is therefore the result of two elements: 1) the need of women to work as they do not have other sufficient forms of subsistence; and 2) the dynamic local labour market which provides opportunities for all social groups.

The labour market situation for foreign immigrants, whether male or female, is rather similar to that of young single mothers. All immigrants interviewed, regardless of their place of residence, are working full time with a regular or non-regular contract. When they are not working it is because of health problems.

The worst situation appears to be that of Italian unemployed males, who are, in many of the cases analysed in this research, the most dependent on local public social assistance. They often cumulate a series of problems, whether they are single men, or household heads. Saraceno (2002) found similar results. However, this does not mean that unemployed men are more entitled to benefits than others, or that benefits are more generous for them. Yet, it means that when they become entitled to these benefits their life history has already experienced a dangerous downwards trajectory, which is difficult to reverse. For our interviewees the inability to find or to maintain a job adds to other problems, often of a relational nature, aggravating a situation that is already difficult, as in the following example:

I started having some minor contact with the world of work while I was studying. A few little jobs to make a bit of money, like selling things ... then I did my civil service, and then I was at home for a while with my mother. Then there was this period when I chose to go and live in a little place where I did a bit of agricultural work. Then one fine day I found myself looking for a home ... it might have been here, it might have been in another town ... I found myself here in Milan ... and just by chance, without even trying particularly hard I mean, by means of an ad in the paper this bed-sitter came up, where I'm still living. I've done jobs, from pony express messenger work to odd jobs in one of those cooperatives with different services ... but after a while I get fed up ... I'd like to do something like being an artist (unemployed male, 42 years old, Ponte Lambro)

In these cases job instability has little to do with the structure and dynamics of the local labour market which do, in fact, allow the interviewees to survive thanks to the availability of odd jobs. In a rich context such as Milan, exclusion from the labour market or the impossibility of remaining on it steadily seems the result mainly of individual (fragmented) situations. These are cases of people who have not succeeded in developing effective strategies of integration, partly conditioned by cognitive or relational limits, or the 'inability to see' forms of behaviour that are different to those they practise. This inability is the result of a mixture of factors which involve: education, upbringing in the broad sense of the term, cognitive and social abilities, and skills. G. is a 42 year old long-term unemployed man from Baggio who for several years was self-employed collecting papers and iron in the street. Several years ago, he had to stop because he did not manage to earn enough money, but he could not even imagine working as a wage-earner with a fixed time-table in a firm. He went on doing some odd jobs and from time to time he goes back to collecting what he finds in the street, even if it is not profitable.

This does not mean that if someone does not find a job it is because he/she does not want to, but to emphasize the fact that the lack of a job is the symptom of a deeper and more serious form of ill-being which mainly involves the sphere of the individual life, specifically health and sociability. The lack of a job is not the cause of a situation of need, but rather the consequence of it.

Thus, as far as labour market is concerned, the empirical results reveal that no differences between neighbourhoods exist. Interviewees, when working, do it outside the neighbourhood, and they are quite mobile within the whole city. Differences can be found among the three categories of welfare recipients.

Social networks and use of services

Social networks

All interviewees in both neighbourhoods have rather strict social support networks. On average, the number of persons named by the interviewees as support-givers is three. The support is mainly given by kinship, and more specifically by parents. The literature on social support highlights that greater physical proximity facilitates exchange and mutual support – it is more likely to have support in caring for grandchildren, or some material help, when relatives live nearby (Fisher, 1982). These situations are more common in Baggio than in Ponte Lambro, and the reasons can be found in the different migration times. In Baggio we frequently find examples of *non co-habiting multigenerational* families (Barbagli, 1997), that is to say individuals with kinship ties living separately but who can be reached in a short time – a phenomenon amply documented in Italy (ISSP, 1986), and less so in Ponte Lambro. From this point of view, the interviewees living in Baggio have more frequent contacts and exchange with their relatives who mainly live nearby, and they receive more support. Interviewees in Ponte Lambro appear to be more isolated and, in many cases, to have weaker social support networks to rely on. These considerations are applicable to national single mothers and unemployed males, but not to foreign immigrants. The latter have an even stricter social support network compared to Italians, and no family support. These features relate to Italy only recently being an immigration country. Information is the main resource circulating within the social networks.[8]

Relations with neighbours do not appear of great relevance in either of the two neighbourhoods. For all the interviewees, daily life with neighbours is characterized only by basic exchanges such as 'good morning', 'good evening', and nothing more. Interviewees seem to carry out protective strategies, avoiding any kind of relations. The length of time they have lived in the neighbourhood does not encourage inclusion in the pattern of local community relations, so that even some people who have been living in the same place for 15–20 years feel like strangers.

Almost none of the interviewees join, or have ever joined, any neighbourhood associations, or community activities either in Baggio or in Ponte Lambro, except for two women. In both cases it was only for mere utilitarian reasons, as these associations represented their interests with the municipality and complained about the level of rents and the conditions of the council flats.

In this sense, the presence of a wider range of associations in Baggio does not affect the strategies of the interviewees. It is not the presence of the associations *per se* which makes the difference, but the access to them, and the capacity of people to access them and to consider this participation as a one of the possible options (*functioning*) the person has for improving his/her well being (Sen, 1999). The fact of including this *functioning* – joining an association – as one of the possible alternatives depends on the personal, social and cultural characteristics (education, professional skills, personal abilities), and on the social conditions of the contexts (the fact that the associations exist). The great majority of the interviewees do not have these personal, social and cultural characteristics, so they are not even able to make a real choice of joining or not. Therefore, despite the fact that there are more associations in Baggio, there is no difference among the strategies of the interviewees and their way of doing or conceiving things. The greater presence of associations can have good externalities for the residents as well as for the interviewees, but it is a by-product effect,[9] and does not affect their strategies.

Use of social services

The use of public social services appears to be slightly different in the two contexts. As already seen, in Ponte Lambro residents often have conflictual relationships with public services and this antagonism emerges quite clearly with respect to social services.

All categories of welfare recipients in Ponte Lambro make less use of the local public social services – which are authorized to provide economic benefits – than those in Baggio. This is partly linked to a vicious circle in the collective image both of social workers and of residents. The public social workers – who are based outside the neighbourhood – perceive it as a relatively disadvantaged and 'criminal' environment. On the other hand, the residents perceive the social workers as people who should be kept as far away as possible from their households, as they do not know their situation, and for fear that they might 'take the children away'. This negative perception is fuelled by events that have actually taken place. Rather than submit to the social services control, the interviewees prefer to renounce any claim to benefits (including those of an economic nature), partly in view of the fact that they cannot be certain of obtaining them, since there are no universal criteria governing the awarding of them. In Milan, everything depends on the municipal budget and not even conditions of proven need guarantee that benefits will be obtained. The public social services thus remain a resource to turn to in extreme cases in Ponte Lambro.

In this situation, the Catholic charity association – the Centro Vincenziano – located in the neighbourhood assumes greater importance. Together with the church, it is the reference point for the population in economic need in Ponte Lambro.

In Baggio, the Centro Vincenziano, also located in the neighbourhood, seems to be an important reference point for foreigners, but far less so for Italians, especially for younger ones:

Q. 'Have you ever made use of the Centro Vincenziano in Baggio?'
A. 'The priests' centre? Where the Moroccans go? (Derisive tone of voice) I'm certainly not going there, no, I'm not done for yet, you mean I should go and act like a stray dog that has nothing, too, really ... personally ... they go there because they don't pay and they have no other place to go and no one to rely on.' (Single mother, 34 years old, Baggio)

In Ponte Lambro, where the public social services are little used and do not make much of an impression on the area, the private charity association is the main source of institutional support, while in Baggio there is the opposite trend. There seems to be a sort of necessary alternative.

The school system marks another important distinction between the two neighbourhoods in terms of future perspectives. In both neighbourhoods there is no secondary school. In Ponte Lambro there is one primary and lower secondary school, while in Baggio, which has many more inhabitants, there are three schools – primary and lower secondary. In Baggio, out of the three schools located in the neighbourhood, only one has a negative reputation, while the others are widely appreciated and also have experimental programmes that are positively mentioned in the municipal newspapers. In Ponte Lambro, the situation is more complex. Several interviewees – those who are better off – prefer to send their children to schools outside the neighbourhood so that 'the child gets a change of environment' (single mother, 34, Ponte Lambro). This is how negative selection is set in motion: those who attend the local schools are prevalently children with problematic families (not only for economic reasons). The same goes for the other services of the area: the use of local facilities is left to those who do not have alternative resources, triggering a dangerous and vicious circle.

Finally two further elements must be mentioned before concluding: the desire to move from the neighbourhood, and the feeling of exclusion. The information collected thus far would seem to suggest that there should be a greater presence of people who would wish to live in Ponte Lambro than in Baggio. Despite the fact that this research project is not statistically representative, and that no conclusive results can be put forward in this regard, it is quite interesting to note that the number of people who declared a wish to move is the same in the two neighbourhoods. In both neighbourhoods, there are interviewees who feel satisfied with the higher presence of green spaces with respect to the rest of the city, and in both neighbourhoods there are interviewees – mainly living in highly degraded estates – who wish to move, but not necessarily outside the neighbourhood.

In the same way, feelings of exclusion and uselessness are not related to the place of residence, but to personal experiences and individual trajectories. Differences in this case are more related to the three categories of welfare recipients. Unemployed males are the ones who feel worst. In several situations a feeling of resignation and lack of confidence in personal potential prevails. There is a strong fear of gradually exhausting resources that have been laboriously accumulated, with the risk of entering a spiral in which various possibilities (odd jobs, benefits and assistance, help from relatives and friends), which tend to be inadequate and temporary, gradually start to disappear. These feelings are less present among single mothers, who can probably find a major source of identity and utility in their role as mother, and among foreign immigrants.

Ponte Lambro: A concentration effect?

The features described for the neighbourhood of Ponte Lambro, and the interviews carried out in this neighbourhood approximately recall some of the conditions highlighted by the literature as typical of a 'concentration effect': a greater concentration of difficult and deviant situations compared to the rest of the city and weak or non-existent social support networks. The literature, however, points out another condition related to social networks that suggests a concentration effect: the fact that social networks are restricted almost entirely to the neighbourhood (Friedrichs, 1998: 85).

This condition is not satisfied in Ponte Lambro. The few social ties interviewees have are in this case mainly located outside the neighbourhood and spread all over the city, even if concentrated in the third circle of the city. In this sense, conditions of strong closeness inside the neighbourhood – which means fewer chances to access information and exchange (see Wacquant, 1996; Wilson, 1987) – do not exist.

On the contrary, a spatial concentration of activities is found in Baggio, where interviewees seem to be more drawn into their own neighbourhood. As a matter of fact, the presence of all services within the neighbourhood, and the location of most of their social ties in the neighbourhood prevent people from going outside it.

There is, therefore, openness on the part of all the interviewees towards the rest of the city, which is much more pronounced for the interviewees of Ponte Lambro. These features prevent us from speaking of social closure or of a 'concentration effect', even though this does not mean that coping strategies are not affected by the place of residence. In this sense the distinction between 'neighbourhood effect' and 'concentration effect' – which are rather often used as synonymous – is quite relevant (see Kronauer *et al.* in Chapter 5 of this book). Despite the fact that no concentration effect can be seen in the two neighbourhoods, their social structure produces different effects on the life strategies of the interviewees, as we have seen. However, the direction of the causal relationship between neighbourhood and strategies must not be conceived of as a linear and monodirectional one. Indeed, the structure of the neighbourhood is not decided by an external superior entity (even though the developing period of the two contexts has been mainly driven by the city council, which highly shaped the social structure of the areas). Rather, it is the result of an ongoing interaction with the residents and their strategies.

Conclusions

This chapter focuses on the importance of the neighbourhood in affecting survival and coping strategies of three categories of welfare recipients in two disadvantaged neighbourhoods on the periphery of the city of Milan. The chapter tried to see *how* this happens, and the mechanisms that lay behind this process. Explicit references have been made to the neighbourhood as a micro-system and to the concrete opportunities it offers in terms of job opportunities, services available and social support networks.

The different historical trajectories of the two neighbourhoods has brought about diverse social configurations and different patterns of social integration, as far as residential and working patterns are concerned.

In studying the individual strategies of the interviewees, the empirical findings suggest that differences related to the place of residence and its configuration exist, and are mainly in relation to social networks and social services. However, this is not the case as far as labour market and job opportunities are concerned. The importance and dynamism of the Milanese labour market, in some way, slackens the role of the neighbourhood. The relatively wide demand for labour throughout the city and its nearest suburbs offers good prospects for those inhabitants of neighbourhoods, whose main problem is the lack of an income. In this respect, the analysis of the neighbourhood as a micro-system definitely cannot be separated from an analysis of the urban local system and its characteristics, mainly the market. Indeed, the fact that job opportunities are spread all over the city and that inhabitants are relatively mobile – even the most deprived ones – prevents people from being stuck in the place where they live, and not having information or resources from outside. In this respect, people's strategies are only partly affected by the neighbourhood of residence, as the whole city, and its opportunities are the reference point for the youngest and most active people.

Empirical findings further suggest that strategies can widely vary, even within the same neighbourhood, depending on the category of welfare recipients that one is considering. Single mothers and foreign immigrants in the city of Milan are the categories which manage to get most of their resources from the labour market, but while members of the first can also rely on their kinship support, the latter do not. Unemployed males are the ones least able to profit from the resources offered by the local contexts.

The different uses of neighbourhood resources that each category of people make must be taken into account when analysing the neighbourhood effects. This highlights that survival and coping strategies of actors are not affected in a linear way by the resources available within the neighbourhood, but rather that there is a bi-directional process going on. The use of some resources, and not of some others on behalf of a certain category of residents, in turn shapes the feature of the resources available in the neighbourhood.

Notes

1. The Italian scientific research team of the URBEX project was co-ordinated by Yuri Kazepov. Paragraph 2 of this contribution is based on chapters 1 and 3 written by David Benassi in 'Spatial Dimension of Urban Social Exclusion and Integration, the Case of Milan' in A. Andreotti and Y. Kazepov (eds) 2002, URBEX series no 16. I would like to thank the author for permission to use this material.
2. Many thanks to Guido Martinotti who let me use some of the maps of the LABSMA laboratory. Many thanks also to Marianna d'Ovidio who elaborated these maps. The index status has been elaborated by the LABSMA. It has been calculated using the following variables: residential density, presence of managers and entrepreneurs versus presence of blue collarworkers, presence of graduates versus presence of residents with primary education only.
3. Milan is the Italian city with the highest percentage of public housing (about 20 per cent of the city's housing stock and even more than 30 per cent if housing from building co-operatives is considered (Source: 1991 Census data).
4. The well-known architect Renzo Piano planned the re-qualification project. The project consisted in moving the residents from the so-called 'white houses' and to restructure these buildings into office space for high tertiary functions of the public administration. The residents would have obtained another council house in another neighbourhood. The project was not discussed with the residents, at least at the very beginning, and residents were highly against its implementation. The plan did not receive the support of the residents.
5. It is important to specify that single mothers were separated, divorced or widowed, both in Ponte Lambro and in Baggio. There is only one case of an unmarried mother in Baggio.
6. Another 60 in-depth interviews have been carried out in Milan with welfare recipients, investigating life trajectories and life strategies in previous researches (see IARD, 1995; Saraceno 2002). Although these interviews were not all conducted in the same neighbourhoods, we also rely on them to construct our argument.
7. Some of them are working part time (as they have young children to care for), so they do not have a sufficient income. Others are working full time but they still are in public assistance schemes as they had previous problems of deviance mainly concerning the ex-partner, and the social services are obliged by the law to take care of them until the situation of danger for the children is completely overcome.
8. Information is a resource that in the cases analysed does not imply an economic loss for the givers. For this reason there is no problem in its circulation. Information mainly concerns information on social services, where to buy things or having material support.
9. See the rich literature on social capital as a collective good and the possible positive consequences for the collectivity, e.g. Putnam (2000). However, social capital can also have negative externalities (see among others Portes, 1997).

7
Rotterdam: Social Contacts in Poor Neighbourhoods

Ronald van Kempen[1]

Life and the neighbourhood

A large amount of literature exists on the topic of the physical and social development of neighbourhoods. It seems that no firm generalizations can be made about the relation between physical and social characteristics of neighbourhoods. Of course, some standard works are known, such as Oscar Newman's *Defensible Space* (Newman, 1972), and Jane Jacobs' *The Death and Life of Great American Cities* (Jacobs, 1961), but these books mainly focus on details of neighbourhoods, such as sidewalks and corridors. A more general question such as: 'Does an area built in the 1960s offer better life chances than an area built at the end of the nineteenth or beginning of the twentieth century?' has not been answered adequately in the literature. Probably, this is because the question is too difficult, mainly because differential spatial contexts always lead to different answers.

Not much is known about the life in neighbourhoods that are characterized by large numbers of specific groups of people, such as minority ethnic groups or low-income households. In this chapter we want to try to fill this gap – at least partially. The focus is on the question of how people live in some selected urban areas in Rotterdam and how their lives are affected by neighbourhood structures and opportunities. More specifically, we will focus on the question of whether there are differences between neighbourhoods with more or less similar concentrations of poverty with respect to the opportunities these neighbourhoods offer for their inhabitants.

In this chapter we will compare two neighbourhoods in Rotterdam: one of them is located in a rather peripheral area (Hoogvliet-Noord) and one in a more central area (Tarwewijk). The selected areas are known for their relatively large concentrations of minority ethnic households and low-income households. It is hypothesized that low-income households in the more central area have more possibilities than those living in the more peripheral area. This is because the more central area offers more opportunities than the peripheral area, not only in the neighbourhood itself, but also in the immediate vicinity.

After a brief literature review, we will give a description of the areas, which will give an indication of the opportunity structure in both areas. Then we will focus on the three investigated groups in each area: single mothers, long-term unemployed and ethnic minorities. For all groups we will apply the Polanyi-scheme (see Chapter 1 of this book) to try to find out how they cope with their poverty in terms of market exchange, redistribution and reciprocity. In the conclusion we will focus on the differences and similarities between the two areas.

Literature review

Which problems are attached to spatial concentrations of poverty? And which advantages can be discerned? A brief overview of the literature is useful here (see Boal, 1976; Bolt *et al.*, 1998; and Van Kempen and Priemus, 1999 for more detailed overviews).

It is sometimes considered important that employment should be found in the neighbourhood where the potential employees live. Put negatively, when employment moves away, low-educated persons especially might end in a situation of unemployment or even long-term unemployment (Wilson, 1987). It might however also be argued that employment does not necessarily have to be located around the corner. As long as people can reach the job within a limited amount of time and as long as the trip does not cost too much, problems might not be too big. In the Netherlands, for example, people usually ride bikes, which means that a job located some five kilometres away is for most people accessible in terms of travel time and travel costs. Also, one can use public transport, which in Dutch cities is rather well developed. Central areas might have a more advantaged position than peripheral areas in this respect.

A main drawback of poverty concentrations seems to be found in 'wrong' contacts between people. A spatial concentration of unemployed, for example, may hamper contacts with those who have a job. Information on job openings is thus not exchanged. A spatial concentration of ethnic minority groups may lead to an over-representation of contacts between people coming from the same ethnic background, which might lead to a bad command of the majority language. This is likely to decrease the possibilities on the labour market. A concentration of many unemployed people might not motivate the unemployed to look for a job (Friedrichs, 1998; Wilson, 1991). A negative consequence of concentrations of poverty is thus that only contacts with specific individuals exist. This might lead to specific behaviour. Criminal individuals might for example influence others to show criminal behaviour too. In a more general sense, it is argued that concentrations of poor people might lead to much 'bonding capital', but to not so much 'bridging capital'. Bonding capital refers to strong ties between people that lead to a low amount of new information (for example, on job openings or alternatives on the housing market), while bridging capital refers to so-called weak ties that do give information about the opportunities in the wider world (Granovetter, 1973). Especially in poor areas, contacts in many cases belong to the category of bonding capital (see Burns *et al.*, 2001; Lewis, 1965; Morris, 1993; Suttles, 1974).

There is however also a positive aspect to be mentioned. Physical proximity of like-minded people may lead to social patterns in which people feel safe (see Botman and Van Kempen, 2001; Ellen and Turner, 1997; Henning and Lieberg, 1996). A spatial concentration of immigrants may attract more immigrants, because it is here where they will find social, economic and emotional support (Dahya, 1974; Enchautegui, 1997).

In the Netherlands, the influence of poverty concentrations on people's lives in neighbourhoods is not yet fully determined. The influence of the neighbourhood on the behaviour of people does exist, but has a minor influence in comparison to individual and household characteristics (Musterd *et al.*, 1999a; Van Beckhoven and Van Kempen, 2002). However, it has also become clear that low-income households have more activities within their direct living environment that those with higher incomes (Botman and Kempen, 2001; Musterd *et al.*, 1999b). We will try to find out in the rest of the chapter if low-income groups indeed make use of the neighbourhood and if differences between the two neighbourhoods in our research can be discerned.

Rotterdam and its neighbourhoods

Rotterdam is now the second largest city in the Netherlands, following Amsterdam. The city itself has over 590,000 inhabitants and approximately 282,000 dwellings. Since about 15 years ago, the city of Rotterdam has been considered one of the main engines of the Dutch economy. This is a result of Rotterdam's port activities. Rotterdam is still the largest port in the world in terms of throughput (Kreukels and Wever, 1996). Almost 300,000 jobs are related to port activities, some 6 per cent of all jobs in the Netherlands. Between 1988 and 1995, while total employment in the Netherlands increased by 7 per cent, employment in the Rotterdam port declined by 16 per cent (Centraal Planbureau, 1997).

The river Maas divides Rotterdam into a northern and a southern part. This division is not just physical; it is also present in the minds of the city's inhabitants. People residing in the north of Rotterdam do not usually engage in activities in the southern part of the city, and vice versa. Both parts of Rotterdam contain pre-World War II, early postwar, and newer areas. The city centre, which was almost completely destroyed by Nazi bombing in 1940, is in the northern part. Both our research areas are in the southern part of the city.

Between the beginning of the nineteenth century and World War II, a large amount of housing was built in Rotterdam. Building activities were concentrated in a ring around the city centre. Within this category of early twentieth-century neighbourhoods, we find notorious areas such as Delfshaven, Spangen and Tarwewijk (one of our research areas). These areas are known for their concentrations of (legal and illegal) immigrants, persistent drug problems, and poor neighbourhood quality (see for example Blokland-Potters, 1998; Botman and Van Kempen, 2001; Burgers, 1998; Burgers and Kloosterman, 1996). Moreover, there are many inexpensive dwellings of poor quality in the social and private rented sectors. A relatively low-income population is concentrated in these areas, including large numbers of first and second-generation immigrants (Turks, Moroccans, Surinamese, Antilleans, Cape-Verdians, and so forth).

After World War II, the Netherlands had to cope with an enormous housing shortage as a consequence of war damage and a baby boom. New neighbourhoods emerged in all cities, including Rotterdam. Hoogvliet-Noord (our second research area) was largely built in the 1950s and early 1960s. In areas of this kind, housing was generally of much better quality than in the prewar neighbourhoods. Early post-WWII areas were initially intended to accommodate a lower middle-class population. These areas are still very popular among the native family households. However, recent research has indicated that immigrants and their descendants can increasingly be found in these early postwar areas (Bolt and Van Kempen, 2000). This finding indicates that dwellings are becoming vacant here, either as a consequence of movements to other areas, or because the older inhabitants of these areas are gradually dying out.

The 1960s are generally considered as the decade of the high-rise boom. In Rotterdam, new areas with high-rise complexes emerged. Again, the housing quality in these areas was better than in the areas dating from the previous period. From the 1960s, central heating was standard. Because of the higher rents, it was not always possible for low-income households to find a dwelling in these areas, despite the availability of individual rent rebates. Gradually, however, low-income households began to move into the less expensive parts of these areas. This was particularly true for the area of Hoogvliet-Noord, which was also partly built in this period.

Our research has been carried out in two neighbourhoods, both of which can be characterized as poor areas: pre-WWII built Tarwewijk and post-WWII built Hoogvliet-Noord. The location of the selected neighbourhoods within the city can be seen in Figure 7.1. While Tarwewijk is located close to the centre of the city, Hoogvliet-Noord has a more remote location.

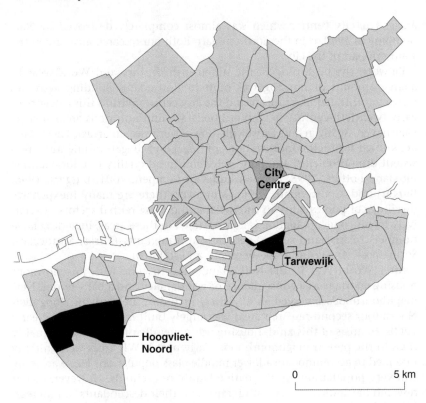

Figure 7.1   The location of Tarwewijk and Hoogvliet-Noord in the Rotterdam area

The interviews

The material in this chapter only presents a very general picture of life in the two neighbourhoods because the empirical research in both Rotterdam areas is based on a quite small number of interviews. This means that all interpretations should be made with great care. On the basis of this small number of interviews, no generalizations can be made.

In both areas respondents belonged to one of the following three groups: single mothers, long-term unemployed nationals, or ethnic minorities. Most of them were unemployed. In Hoogvliet-Noord, eight single mothers were interviewed. Five were born on Curaçao, an island in the Carribean belonging to the Dutch Antilles. Four long-term unemployed nationals were interviewed in this area. Finding representatives of this group and then obtaining their cooperation was difficult. Three men and one woman were interviewed. All four respondents once had a job. They are currently dependent on various social programmes – most of them received disability benefits. Physical problems or certain forms of mental illness give the right to an income from this source. The people interviewed had been unemployed for between four and 14 years.

In Hoogvliet-Noord, we interviewed five households belonging to ethnic minority groups. The respondents did not have a paid job. They were found through different social workers, a job agency for volunteers, and through a language course. One of the respondents came from Curaçao and so had Dutch nationality. Two were asylum seekers from former Yugoslavia and Turkey respectively. They were still awaiting a decision with respect to a residence permit. The remaining two were refugees from Iraq who had already received permission to stay. All the respondents had two or more children in the Netherlands. One Iraqi respondent still had a family in Iraq. With the exception of the household from Curaçao, all the households interviewed are young families with young children.

In Tarwewijk five single mothers were interviewed. While in Hoogvliet the majority of the single mothers interviewed came from Curaçao, this was not the case for the single mothers interviewed in Tarwewijk. Although Antilleans are less prominent in Tarwewijk, their lower representation in the study should be seen as a coincidence, because of the small number of people interviewed. Two of the mothers interviewed were Dutch, one came originally from Morocco, one from Curaçao and one from Surinam. The mothers from Curaçao and Surinam have never been married, while the other three single mothers have become single as a consequence of divorce or separation.

We have interviewed six people belonging to the unemployed category in Tarwewijk. Three of the six respondents belonged to the category of long-term unemployed nationals, while the others three belonged to the unemployed ethnic minorities (they were all Turks). The long-term unemployed Dutch were on average 20 years older than the interviewed Turks. And while the nationals were all men, the Turks were all female. Despite these differences, the two groups are taken together in the analysis, because of the low number.

Life in a peripheral neighbourhood: Hoogvliet-Noord in Rotterdam

Opportunities in the area

Hoogvliet-Noord is in most respects a typical post-WWII area. Built in the 1950s and 1960s, it follows the principle of separation of such functions as living, working, traffic, and leisure. It was planned as a satellite town of Rotterdam, so that it had to have all the facilities that belong to a small town, but at the same time good public transport connections with the main city. The town of Hoogvliet was to have a main shopping centre in the middle of the area (including such public facilities as a health centre and a police office), while each of the town's small neighbourhoods would have its own smaller shopping centres concentrating on goods purchased on a daily basis. Abundant green areas between the blocks of flats and green corridors between the neighbourhoods were planned. This means that for a lot of activities, the inhabitants do not have to leave the area.

Initially, Hoogvliet was built for the ever-expanding harbour and related industry which were in need of many workers in the 1950s and early 1960s. Workers were happy to find a home for their families in the vicinity of their workplaces. However, the population structure of the area started to change as soon as new alternatives outside Hoogvliet became available. Those who could afford to do so moved out of the area, while some apartment blocks in Hoogvliet started to suffer from vacancies. Because the rents of the Hoogvliet dwellings were not very high, lower income households moved in. Some parts of Hoogvliet regressed to dumping places for junkies and all kinds of criminal activities, making the atmosphere in the area increasingly negative, especially for those who could not afford to move out.

The distance to the centre of Rotterdam is an influential factor in the lives of the inhabitants of the area as will be shown later. The journey from Rotterdam Central Station to Hoogvliet takes more than 30 minutes by metro. Although trains run frequently (every 10 minutes on average), many people consider the city of Rotterdam to be far away.

Hoogvliet is basically a residential area and has few job opportunities. Of course, there are jobs in shops and other parts of the service sector. Moreover, in the vicinity of Hoogvliet employment can be found in the harbour and related activities. Because of computerization however, many jobs have become redundant. Growth in jobs can no longer be observed in and around Hoogvliet. Moreover, the educational levels and work experience of the residents of Hoogvliet, especially the unemployed, is often insufficient for them to have any chance of a new job.

One of the strong points of Hoogvliet is its village character. Social life in the area is important. Hoogvliet has been an important place for social contacts not only for immigrants, but also for the Dutch residents. Many Dutch people have lived in the area for decades and so have many contacts with their neighbours and other people in the neighbourhood. An extensive number of associations helps facilitate contacts between people. Nevertheless, it cannot be said that mutual affection is universal. The impression is of many separate communities in the area. Hoogvliet is seen as home for many different kinds of people. For the Surinamese and the Antilleans just arriving in the Netherlands, Hoogvliet has been an important catchment area, because a relatively large amount of people from these countries already lived there. People arriving from Surinam and the Dutch Antilles came to Hoogvliet, because relatives or friends from the home village were already living there and were able and willing to provide the new arrivals with support and a place to live, at least for a certain period of time.

Next to these opportunities, there are also some threats. The influx of new households is not seen as a positive development by many of the sitting inhabitants. They see the neighbourhood developing in a wrong direction, from a pleasant area into one with social conflicts and tensions between different groups. Many of the new inhabitants are immigrants. The present residents of Hoogvliet complain, for example, about the noise the newcomers make and their aggressive behaviour on the streets. These immigrants are sometimes blamed for the increasing criminality and vandalism. It is evident that many people who have been living in the area for a long time now have a less optimistic view of the future of the area.

Single mothers in Hoogvliet-Noord: Market exchange

None of the single mothers interviewed had a paid job; they were dependent on money from other sources. All the women found that their children hindered access to the labour market. The reasons for not finding a job had at least something to do with the kind of job they were looking for. The mothers wanted part-time jobs (in order to be at home for the children at appropriate times) or a job in the vicinity of their homes (also in order to be able to return home quickly for their children). The problem is that not many jobs are available in Hoogvliet-Noord. And because of its relatively isolated location it is also not easy to find a job in the vicinity of the area.

Because of their low incomes, the single mothers interviewed appeared to live a large part of their daily lives in the neighbourhood itself. None of the single mothers had a car. Not possessing a car is related to their low incomes, not with any voluntary choice made for environmental reasons. Within Hoogvliet, they walk or cycle to get around. If they want to get to other places in Rotterdam, they have to use public transport, but they rarely do this, as it is considered to be too expensive: 'Public transport is fairly expensive. There goes a meal I think when I buy my ticket, but you have to do it sometimes, otherwise you don't ever get out of here.' The role of the neighbourhood for these single mothers is clearly present.

Single mothers in Hoogvliet-Noord: Redistribution

Dependence on *redistribution* is obvious for single mothers, because they rely on social benefit for their income. Seven of the eight women interviewed depended on social welfare for single parents, which is around 800 Euro per month. One woman received a pension for orphans and widows, which is about the same amount.

Three of these four women had found another way of enhancing their income through redistribution. They had voluntary jobs in the area with a project known as the Non-utilized qualities bank (*OK bank*). This is a voluntary job centre for the long-term unemployed. Individuals who work through this project for ten hours a week receive a bonus of 45 Euro on top of their social benefit. The importance of the area where the inhabitants live is not so big in the redistribution sphere. However, the opportunity to have a voluntary job is clearly linked to the area.

Single mothers in Hoogvliet-Noord: Reciprocity

With respect to the dimension of *reciprocity*, a rather positive picture emerges. The neighbourhood clearly has to offer something in this respect. Seven of the eight single mothers reported good and frequent contacts with neighbours, family or friends. Many of these family members and friends lived in Hoogvliet. Family members seemed to be more important than friends. Visits were paid at least once a day to some family members in the neighbourhood. They drank coffee, or had lunch or dinner together. These family members helped them occasionally with their financial problems. In most cases this help took the form of lending between 10 and 30 Euro at the end of the month, or by paying a large bill that the single mothers could repay at regular intervals. The mothers of the Antillean mothers also lived in the neighbourhood and took care of their grandchildren for a few hours a week.

A way of obtaining social contacts is through having a voluntary job, or by participating in activities in the community centre. For four of the respondents this was an important way of getting to know people, feel useful and gain emotional support. Six mothers received emotional and financial support from family members in the neighbourhood, although not abundantly. Usually, a mother or a sister they felt close to helped them financially now and again. This support is a positive aspect of family relations, but from the information of the respondents it is also clear that family histories are often complex and fraught with frustrations and arguments.

All single mothers with contacts in the areas considered these contacts very important. They also said, however, that the opportunities of making these contacts were declining, largely because of people moving to other areas. In their opinion, it was often difficult to make contacts with new neighbours. Some respondents extended this view to the whole neighbourhood: 'The mentality of the neighbourhood is getting less social.' The overall picture that emerges with respect to the role of the Hoogvliet area for single mothers is that the area is of great importance with respect to social contacts. Contacts are mainly with people 'of their own kind', such as families and other single parents. For the people involved, these contacts are very important. It even serves as a motivation to stay in the area. The loss of these contacts makes living in the area less attractive.

Long-term unemployed in Hoogvliet-Noord: Market exchange

With one exception, the respondents felt that they would never find a job again. Most of them quit searching for a job years ago. Moving for job reasons would make no sense, in their eyes: it is not that jobs are not available, it is just that employers are not interested in these people anymore, for example because they have been out of work for a long time already and because they are considered disabled. Clearly, the neighbourhood does not play a role here.

Long-term unemployed in Hoogvliet-Noord: Redistribution

Incomes ranged from 534 Euro to 886 Euro per month. These amounts are not very high – even when compared to the incomes of the single mothers. Some of them looked for a job in the voluntary sector. Voluntary work is used as a strategy to stay in contact with people. Voluntary work also gives them something to do. Voluntary work was a strategy to stay in contact with the regular labour market for only one of the respondents. The availability of jobs in the neighbourhood was mentioned as important for taking up such a job.

Long-term unemployed in Hoogvliet-Noord: Reciprocity

All respondents stated that the number of their friends was small. All in all, the respondents claimed having from one to four friends who supported them emotionally. The neighbourhood was clearly important for social contacts for these respondents: most of these friends lived in the neighbourhood. They obtained their friends through voluntary jobs, through former jobs in the area, or through family. Friendships had been maintained ever since. For all of them, joining some sort of club was a strategy to stay in contact with people. A kiting club and a social club for ex-psychiatric patients in the social centre are examples.

Contacts with neighbours were said to be reasonable to good, but they did not seem to be very important. Neighbours greeted each other, sometimes they had a brief chat about trivialities, but that was all. Little actual support was obtained from immediate neighbours. Other people in the neighbourhood were considered more important.

Also for the long-term unemployed nationals, the area they live in is of great importance with respect to social contacts.

Immigrants in Hoogvliet-Noord: Market exchange

The interviewed asylum-seeking families waiting for permission to stay in the country did not have the right to work, or to apply for social benefit. While awaiting a (hopefully positive) decision they were taking Dutch courses, the only courses they were allowed to take while they had no residence permit.

The two refugees who did have residence permits had been allowed to work since 1997, but had not found a job yet. At the time of interview they had been looking for a job for more than three years. They were still taking Dutch classes, because they consider language an important factor in finding a job. Only one member (the mother) of the household from Curaçao had a labour market history.

Immigrants in Hoogvliet-Noord: Redistribution

Redistribution can take many forms. While the most important role of this mode of integration seems to be the redistribution of money in the form of unemployment benefit or social benefit, earlier sections in this chapter have shown that redistribution has more to offer, such as training and education, and the opportunity to talk with social workers and psychologists. It is in this respect that the unemployed ethnic minorities clearly differ from the single mothers and the long-term unemployed nationals. Compared with these two groups, the ethnic minorities only use the redistribution dimension in a passive way. They receive the money to which they have a right, but they make no further use of the other opportunities. Redistribution is a source of money and a way to survive, but that is about it. Most families simply did not seem to know about these further opportunities. They were still too busy trying to survive in a strange country to be fully aware of their rights and of the opportunities the neighbourhood might offer.

Immigrants in Hoogvliet-Noord: Reciprocity

Since, with the exception of one household from Curaçao, these families are refugees, they did not have any relatives in the Netherlands (one male from Iraq had a cousin living in another city). These families had to leave their home country and leave their families behind – in some cases even their wives and children. They had to flee for various reasons, from Yugoslavia because of the war, from Turkey because they were Christians under an Islamic regime, and from Iraq because they were politically active Kurds. To have to leave family and friends behind is a significant cause of loneliness for these households and meeting new people is important to them. For these families the neighbourhood, or joining a club like Amnesty International, provided particularly important opportunities for meeting people. The Dutch language classes were another welcome opportunity to meet people.

None of the interviewed immigrants has any social contacts, other than with family, outside the area of Hoogvliet. For this group of respondents, the neighbourhood is a very important dimension in their lives.

Life in a central neighbourhood: Tarwewijk in Rotterdam

Opportunities in the area

Tarwewijk is a typical urban pre-WWII neighbourhood. In contrast with Hoogvliet, no clearly planned separation of the functions of living, working, traffic and leisure can be discerned in Tarwewijk. Built originally in the beginning of the twentieth century, Tarwewijk can be characterized by a mix of functions. Housing is mixed with shops and small premises for all kinds of businesses. Some streets show concentrations of shops, but shops, bars and small cafes are also located in other streets. South of the Tarwewijk area, no more than a kilometre away, lies the large shopping centre of Zuidplein, which offers a greater variety of shops including some of the big chains that offer all kinds of goods relatively cheaply. The shops in Tarwewijk itself have a clearly local function: they are used by people living in the neighbourhood rather than by people living elsewhere.

Unlike post-WWII Hoogvliet, there are few green areas in Tarwewijk. Tarwewijk is a relatively densely built area, with many dwellings per square kilometre. Planning green areas for recreational purposes was not considered important at the end of the nineteenth and beginning of the twentieth centuries.

The housing stock of Tarwewijk can be characterized as relatively inexpensive. Many dwellings are small and have only three or four rooms. This description applies not only to the social rented sector, but also to the private rented and owner-occupied dwellings. The small and inexpensive dwellings have always been occupied by relatively low-income households. Before World War II and in the two decades after 1945, most families living in Tarwewijk had at least one household member working in the harbour or some associated activity.

Most of our respondents came to Tarwewijk because an inexpensive dwelling was available here. They would probably have moved to another, similar neighbourhood had an affordable home there been allocated to them. In general, households looking for a home do not move into Tarwewijk because the area has advantages to offer.

Tarwewijk is located in the south of Rotterdam. The distance to the centre of the city, on the other side of the river Maas, takes only about 10 minutes by Metro. It is however well known that people living on the south side of the river are not very interested in going to the northern part of Rotterdam. Despite the relatively short distance, people are oriented more towards their own neighbourhood and other places in the southern part of the city.

Despite the functional mix, Tarwewijk does not offer many job opportunities. Enterprises are generally small. Developments affecting Rotterdam as a whole also affect Tarwewijk (and Hoogvliet-Noord): the declining number of jobs in the harbour and related activities has had severe implications for the inhabitants of Tarwewijk. Only in the past few years have unemployment figures declined in this area. The fall has resulted in part from a booming economy, but also to some extent because people have moved away to escape from the (threat of) demolition activities.

Earlier in this chapter, Hoogvliet has been praised for its social life. The same may be said about Tarwewijk. The older inhabitants in particular mention the fact that in previous times everybody knew each other, talked to each other, and took part in the many social activities that were organized in the neighbourhood. This strong social structure was clearly one of the neighbourhood's assets.

But some things have changed, however. Like most deprived urban neighbourhoods, present-day Tarwewijk cannot be considered an area with a stable population structure. While it previously used to be quite normal to remain in the neighbourhood for decades (or even a whole lifetime), many households have decided to move. Those who could afford to do so have moved away to better housing in more attractive areas. In addition, many older inhabitants have died. The direct results of these demographic processes were vacancies in the housing stock and disturbed social networks. New households, often belonging to immigrant groups, occupied the empty dwellings. This change affected the contacts between people.

Single mothers in Tarwewijk: Market exchange

With respect to aspects that relate to *market exchange*, the first aspect to be noted is that all the single mothers interviewed have had jobs in the past. The second aspect is that two mothers had a small (in terms of working hours) cleaning job, while the other three had no paid job. One of these three was about to start a job very soon. It seems clear that the single mothers cannot be seen as totally detached from the labour market. It looks as if the children of these mothers were less central than in the case of the single mothers in Hoogvliet. In Hoogvliet many mothers were not interested in a paid job, because they wanted to be available for their children as much as possible. It is not clear if the jobs are located in the neighbourhood.

Single mothers in Tarwewijk: Redistribution

As in Hoogvliet, dependence on *redistribution* is obvious for all single mothers. They all received a social benefit of about 800 Euro. Those with a job received a smaller benefit, but in the end they had more money to spend than those without a job. Part-time work is clearly worthwhile, although the net gain was not more than about 100 Euro per month.

Single mothers in Tarwewijk: Reciprocity

All the single mothers interviewed in Tarwewijk had numerous social contacts within *and* outside the neighbourhood. As in Hoogvliet, there were good and frequent contacts with neighbours, family and friends. But in contrast with Hoogvliet, family members did not usually live in the respondent's neighbourhood. The field of reciprocity is important for the single mothers in various respects. The advantages are mainly in terms of emotional support and talking about everyday life. Financial support was only obtained from certain family members.

All in all, for the single mothers in Tarwewijk, the neighbourhood does not seem to be very important in terms of reciprocity. Most of the single mothers had several people they relied on (in several respects), but the most important people – often family members – did not usually live in the neighbourhood. There were contacts with neighbours and other people in the neighbourhood, but they were either superficial or of minor importance.

Unemployed nationals and immigrants in Tarwewijk: Market exchange

The long-term unemployed nationals interviewed had all had working experience earlier in their lives. One of the Turkish women never had a job, while the other two women had only worked for a few months in the past ten years. The limited work experience, the fact that most of the respondents had not worked for many years, and their low educational level would not make it easy to find a job in the near future, either in the neighbourhood, or somewhere else.

Unemployed nationals and immigrants in Tarwewijk: Redistribution

Two of the three Dutch unemployed respondents had a disability benefit of about 820 Euro. One of them received a small salary (136 Euro) from delivering leaflets. So these two people did not really belong to the lowest income categories. The third person received social assistance at the social minimum (635 Euro).[2]

The three Turkish women all received social assistance, but two of them had additional money from their husbands, who also had a right to some social assistance. The husband in the household of the third Turkish respondent had the right to full social assistance. Altogether, the Turkish households also cannot be seen as representatives of the lowest income brackets: they received about 907 Euro per month (but in contrast with the Dutch unemployed, they had to divide this amount among more household members).

Can they survive on this amount of money? Usually, they make it last until the end of the month. In some cases, by the end of the month some things, like cigarettes and coffee, cannot be bought anymore. One Turkish woman had the problem that she could not buy the things she would really like, such as new furniture, a car, or toys for her children. One other Turkish woman said that while the total household income was sufficient, the problem was that she received too small a share of money from her husband to run the household. The characteristics of the neighbourhood itself do not seem to play a role here.

Unemployed nationals and immigrants in Tarwewijk: Reciprocity

Relations with neighbours were, in general, rather superficial among the respondents interviewed. Most of them stated that they had no problems with their neighbours. Most also stated that they greeted their neighbours when they saw them. But in most cases they did not visit each other; neighbours did not belong to their intimate circle of friends.

Sometimes opinions about neighbours were slightly more negative. One of the long-term unemployed Dutch stated: 'We live with six families here, using the same stairs. But I don't know any of them. I know their faces, but that is all. They are all immigrants. I greet them, but I do not speak Turkish. Especially the women, they run away when they see me.' The respondents did not take part very frequently in other social activities in the neighbourhood. None of them had important contacts in the area. Although most of them knew that a variety of social activities were organized, they did not seem very interested in participating (with the exception of the Turkish women who visited a women's group once a week).

Living in Tarwewijk did not seem very important for these respondents. Most just lived there because they had managed to find a dwelling in this neighbourhood. In terms of reciprocity, there were not many indications of relationships within the neighbourhood. This is a clear difference with the situation in the more peripheral area of Hoogvliet.

Conclusions

The presence of a fairly large number of family members in Hoogvliet and their importance for the respondents can be seen as one of the most surprising results of this part of the research. There was considerable interaction between the respondents and their relatives in Hoogvliet, although it does not automatically follow that there was a large supportive network in terms of emotional and financial support. Often only one person (a sister, a mother) fulfilled this function. The others were more important for drinking coffee, having lunch or dinner together, and talking about all kinds of things. It has become clear that loneliness or a lack of social contacts was not a feature of life for our respondents in Hoogvliet.

There was a considerable fear among the respondents that social contacts might decline in the near future. There has always been some migration from the area, but it has increased in the past few years, at least in the eyes of some respondents. The deterioration of the area in terms of social and physical decline seems to be the most important reason for this. The demolition plans (see also later in this section) can be seen as a second threat to the social structure of the neighbourhood. Respondents thought that they would lose their important and enjoyable contacts, because others would have to move. They did not seem to place much faith in the newcomers.

Although formally part of Rotterdam, Hoogvliet-Noord is located at some distance from the city. Not many activities are possible in the immediate vicinity of Hoogvliet, because meadows, the river, industrial complexes, and the suburban municipality of Spijkenisse surround it. Earlier in this chapter it was suggested that the distance from Rotterdam might hinder the inhabitants of Hoogvliet in several ways. First, looking for a job outside Hoogvliet does not seem a very common activity. Second, undertaking activities outside the area also occurs quite rarely. People spend a large part of their lives in Hoogvliet and do not seem interested in doing anything outside the area. They also do not seem to feel that the activities they undertake take place predominantly in Hoogvliet is in itself problematic. More often than not, Hoogvliet is praised for its village character, including the many opportunities for social contact.

Tarwewijk is physically part of the city itself. Located on the right bank of the river Maas, it is easy to go from the neighbourhood to other neighbourhoods in the vicinity by bicycle or even on foot. The metro takes the inhabitants to the centre of Rotterdam in a few minutes. Compared with people living in Hoogvliet, respondents in Tarwewijk have more contacts outside their own neighbourhood.

Much of the literature on neighbourhood effects focuses on the detrimental influence of spatial concentrations of poverty (see also earlier in this chapter). The critical issue is that a high degree of spatial separation could inhibit contacts between different groups. Indeed, there are no indications that our respondents have important social contacts with people who are totally different from themselves. Single mothers talk to other single mothers and with their families, immigrants seem to prefer contacts with their own group, the long-term unemployed nationals seem to have most contact with people in their vicinity and with people they meet through their voluntary jobs. No respondents mentioned any important people in their lives that were completely different from themselves. Role models are found among people with the same lifestyle and among those who are in the same economic or social situation. In some cases, the respondents have learned to take only themselves as a standard. These people do not have a strong supportive network, nor do they care very much what others think of them. Again, bonding capital seems to prevail, while bridging capital seems to be almost totally absent.

Mutual contacts seem to be a survival strategy. For many respondents, the importance of their social contacts is enormous. Both neighbourhoods clearly provided opportunities for these contacts, if only because they are areas with a concentration of low-income households.

The social structure of the research neighbourhoods is not stable. On the contrary, in terms of population structure many changes have taken place in the past two decades. Hoogvliet has changed from a quiet, suburban neighbourhood with an almost totally Dutch population into an area that is attractive for all kinds of low-income people, including immigrants from Turkey, Morocco, Surinam and the Dutch Antilles. The area is becoming even more multicultural through the influx of asylum seekers and refugees. The Dutch inhabitants who have lived there for so many years are in general not very positive about this population change. This attitude may to some extent be derived from prejudice and stereotyping. But real disturbance also plays a part: loud music and criminal activities hardly improve the attractiveness of living in the area, especially for those used to the peace and quiet of the past.

In the beginning of this chapter it was hypothesized that low-income households in the more central area have more possibilities than those living in the more peripheral area, because more central areas would offer more opportunities than the peripheral area, not only in the neighbourhood itself, but also in the immediate vicinity. This hypothesis cannot be confirmed. Especially with respect to social contacts, peripheral Hoogvliet seems to offer more for the respondents than central Tarwewijk, while in terms of market exchange and redistribution massive differences between the two neighbourhoods cannot be detected. For example: those looking for a job in central Tarwewijk do not seem to be in a more advantaged position than those living in Hoogvliet. It cannot be concluded that, in terms of market exchange and redistribution, it would be better for a low-income household to live in an urban setting (Tarwewijk) than in a more distant suburban setting (Hoogvliet). In terms of reciprocity, Hoogvliet might be a better place to live, but especially for those who do have their relatives in that area.

A brief look into the future

We will end this chapter by paying some attention to the policies that are aimed to differentiate the housing stock in both Hoogvliet-Noord and Tarwewijk. In Hoogvliet-Noord 5,000 of the 13,000 dwellings – almost all in the social rented sector – are to be demolished within the next ten years; in Tarwewijk demolition has already started. In both cases the intention is that the new construction would not take the form of inexpensive social rented dwellings. To attract more middle and higher-income households, new dwellings would be constructed for the more expensive rented sector and the owner-occupied sector of the housing market.

Where these plans are the result of the idea that part of the present housing stock was deteriorating and that action was needed to safeguard the quality of the dwellings (and the environment) in both areas, there is nothing to be said against demolition and restructuring. The aim of creating a more mixed population does however raise some questions. To make life more bearable in the neighbourhood, it would be better to get rid of people such as drug dealers. But using restructuring as a method will only move the problem on to other neighbourhoods. Tarwewijk may become free from the drugs scene, but other parts of the southern part of Rotterdam might experience an inflow of drug-related activities. Some inhabitants and key persons have already noticed this 'waterbed effect': push on one side and the effects are felt on the other side. Restructuring other parts of the neighbourhoods will only bring about a new move of problem activities to other neighbourhoods. The main point here is that social problems cannot be solved by housing and spatial policy alone.

The decreasing number of low-income households in the country and even at city level might be a reason justifying a reduction in the number of social rented dwellings. The problem is that at the neighbourhood level social structures might be affected negatively. This research has revealed that, especially in Hoogvliet but also in Tarwewijk, local social contacts are very important for many inhabitants. Also, many people do not want to move from the area where they now live (particularly in Hoogvliet), mainly because of these social contacts. If they are obliged to move out, their social contacts might be seriously affected, damaging one of the big assets they have at the moment. Policy makers should be fully aware of this.

Notes

1. This chapter is based on the URBEX-report written by Botman and Van Kempen (2001).
2. None of the six respondents in this section earned additional money in an informal or illegal way.

8

Paris: Neighbourhood Identity as a Resource for the Urban Poor

Elise Palomares and Patrick Simon

The spatial dimension of social exclusion

The decline in the Fordist model of production initiated the industrial restructuring of the French economy at the turn of the 1970s – rapid and costly in terms of job losses – and transformed the customary forms of waged labour (Castel, 1995). As a result, France experienced massive rising unemployment, affecting growing numbers of low-skilled workers, women and young people who are denied access to the labour market. Where once exploitation in the workplace was the main issue, social and economic exclusion seems to have replaced it. The 'struggle against exclusion' became a key objective for public policies at the beginning of the 1990s and this new leitmotiv has been largely debated over in the media and between the social scientists. The welfare state alleviates poverty in the weakest sections of the population by extending its social safety nets. Never before has France known such a proliferation of schemes to assist people excluded from the labour market – from financial support (minimum welfare support, incentives to encourage integration and solidarity) to courses in professional training and social integration.

In this context, the concentration of ethnic minorities and deprived population in urban clusters is seen as a symptom of the breakdown of the welfare state's social safety system, and as embodying the ongoing process of ethnic and social segregation. As they emerge, the so-called 'ethnic enclaves' or deprived neighbourhoods are perceived as the sign of the failure of – and simultaneously, a threat to – the French model of integration, that is, the universalist republican model. The outbreak of urban riots, with gangs of youths fighting the police, burning cars, looted supermarkets and vandalized facilities, has shown to all that urban 'marginality' breeds in a specific type of environment. Along the lines of the 'social breakdown' (*fracture sociale)* theme, whereby people with low social status are 'abandoned' and kept apart from the more successful groups – through processes of 'disaffiliation' (Castel, 1995) or 'disqualification' (Paugam, 1991) – segregation is seen as the geographical illustration of the disintegration of social ties. In this context, the word 'ghetto' became widely popular in reference to areas where segregation processes have produced high levels of concentration of ethnic minorities or/and deprived population. Critics have often denounced the exaggerated use of this word, pointing out that it lacked precise definition and was often improperly used to describe situations far from what, historically, came to be called 'ghettos' (Wacquant, 1992). The stigmatization of the neighbourhoods, described as 'ghettos', is one of the main burdens that urban and social policies have to tackle. Nevertheless, this vague concept now plays a central role in the symbolic management of social conflicts and underscores two strategic issues: 1) the recognition of ethnic diversity and of its impact both on social organization and national symbolic representations; and 2) the management of the territorialization of social inequality, in other words the attempt to control a segregative system, whereby populations are confined to specific areas according to their socioeconomic status or, which is worse even from a French perspective, to their position in the hierarchy of ethnic origins.

The perception of social disorders as linked to specific areas has gained consistency ever since the elaboration, in the early 1980s, of local social development policies under the cover-all label of 'Urban Policy' (*Politique de la ville*). Spatial concentration and social disadvantage thus became increasingly amalgamated, in such a way that causality is inverted: the segregation of 'disqualified' populations is no longer considered as a consequence of social deprivation, but the cause of it (Simon, 1995). Observing the social and urbanistic disintegration of postwar social housing estates – and the deepening social and ethnic segregation leading to concentrations of increasingly impoverished groups in run-down housing projects lacking in basic urban services and amenities and located in depressed labour market areas – the government launched a programme of positive discrimination toward so-called 'sensitive areas' or 'deprived neighbourhoods'. The programme strives to restore balance to the resources of these deprived areas by boosting the necessary funding and other means. The *Politique de la ville* is a truly multidimensional programme, tackling housing (measures to combat residential segregation, urban regeneration) and integration – both social (community support, access to urban rights) and economic (tax assistance for companies, local training and integration schemes, education support). Its application is designed to take place at the local level and, despite the fact that the policy has been devised and is being financed by central government, municipalities – and even neighbourhoods – are putting their own schemes in place. The *Politique de la ville* has set itself some pretty ambitious targets and focuses the bulk of public action on combating 'exclusion'.

The development of these 'territorial social policies' relies on the strong assumption that neighbourhoods matter, or to use a more scientific concept, that there is a neighbourhood effect on social exclusion (Ostendorf *et al.*, 2001). In a certain way, the whole URBEX project is concerned with the debate on neighbourhood effects, initiated by the totemic Wilson's book *The Truly Disadvantaged* (1987). The question whether inequalities are due essentially to individual's characteristics or can be in part explained by the additional effect of the concentration of deprived population in particular areas, is a crucial one (Jencks and Mayer, 1990). It has been addressed by sophisticated mathematical models, which have reached ambiguous answers (Buck, 2001; Ellen and Turner, 1997). The objective of the URBEX project to analyse the spatial dimension of social exclusion takes place in this debate, and this chapter aims to bring some insights from the Parisian case.

Fieldwork in the poor neighbourhoods of the Paris metropolitan area

In 1999, the Paris area was made up of 396 municipalities containing 9.6 million inhabitants. This massive entity has extremely strong spatial and social differences and, just like the other major metropolises in the world, it is highly polarized. It is therefore easy to find neighbourhoods where disadvantaged populations are concentrated and whose socio-urban characteristics match the criteria defined in the URBEX project. However, the rationale behind the distribution of functions (political, administrative, economic, residential and leisure functions) and of social and ethnic groups, is based on a centre–periphery pattern (Paris-suburbs) crossed with a western–eastern opposition (roughly speaking, the bourgeois South and West versus the proletarian North and East).

For the purpose of this study, we have chosen neighbourhoods in two emblematic *communes* of Seine St Denis, a departement located at the east-north periphery of the city of Paris: La Courneuve and Montreuil. These two towns differ by their urban structure and social dynamics. Whereas Montreuil is an old industrial neighbourhood that is undergoing a process of gentrification, La Courneuve is one of the poorest cities of the Parisian outskirt and received on its territory a huge social project built in the sixties, *les 4000*.

The *department* (city district) of Seine St Denis lies against the eastern and northern borders of the city of Paris (see Figure 8.1). It is considered as one of the districts confronted with the greatest difficulties, to such an extent that it is now widely seen as epitomizing urban and social crisis, as shown by its major socio-economic indicators (in 1999):

1. More than 32 per cent of social housing as opposed to 21 per cent in the whole Ile-de-France region;
2. A 14 per cent unemployment rate (versus 9.3 per cent in Ile-de-France), 53 per cent of which is long-term unemployment;

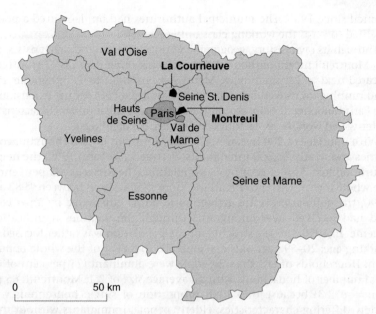

Figure 8.1 Ile-de-France, with the two neighbourhoods of Montreuil and La Courneuve

3. A proportion of industrial workers and employees which remains high: 66 per cent of the working population as opposed to 52 per cent in the whole Ile-de-France region;
4. A rate of people on minimum income benefit (RMI) and of isolated people facing hardship twice as high as the regional average;
5. A remarkable presence of immigrants, both in terms of demographic figures (immigrants counted for 29 per cent of households in 1999, the highest rate in France before the city of Paris), of their visibility in public spaces and of their contribution to the social organization of many neighbourhoods.

Gentrification in the Bas-Montreuil: Protection and risks

Located in the eastern periphery of Paris, Montreuil, with 90,735 inhabitants, is the main town in the department of Seine St Denis and the third in the Ile de France region in terms of population. Next to the residential bourgeois enclave around Vincennes, Montreuil is part of the 'red belt' or *'banlieue rouge'* as, until very recently, it featured as some its stronger characteristics: big industrial business activity within its own territory, an overrepresentation of industrial workers in the working population, large areas of social housing, and a communist majority in charge of the municipal council since 1935. The municipal authorities had implemented a policy oriented towards the working class until recently.

Through its own history, geographic settings, and social characteristics, the Bas-Montreuil neighbourhood differs from the other districts of Montreuil. Located next to Paris, enjoying Métro stations and the 'Périphérique' ring road running on its western side, the Bas-Montreuil is a former extension of the Paris Faubourg de Saint-Antoine and features similar urban characteristics (intertwined workshops, factories and residential buildings).

With a surface of 200 hectares, the Bas-Montreuil hosts a thousand companies and nearly 20,000 inhabitants. Between 1990 and 1999, the neighbourhood lost 3.5 per cent of its population (the loss was 4.3 per cent in the whole town). This move is all the more significant as between 1982 and 1990, the population in the neighbourhood had increased by 5 per cent, and had received new immigrants through the 'families reunification' scheme. In 1990, the age structure of the population was rather focused on working age: 20–59 year olds made up 60.1 per cent of the whole population. Households of less than 2 people were dominant (71 per cent of the total number of households with an average size of 2.1; Montreuil: 65 per cent and 2.3) because of a high proportion of single households with widely differing characteristics: elderly people, immigrants without their families and young working people. Lone parent families who made up 13 per cent of the population were over-represented compared to the other districts of town.

Although it is undergoing renovations, the total available accommodation of the Bas-Montreuil remains very old (71 per cent of housing was built before 1949), dilapidated, and basically made up of small apartments (57 per cent of flats have just one or two rooms). In 1990, the available accommodation was by and large made up of buildings that included few social housing apartments (13 per cent of accommodation; Montreuil: 28 per cent). The supply of furnished accommodation is still relatively high (4.3 per cent; Montreuil: 1.3 per cent), showing the persistence of a traditional form, in the housing of isolated immigrants. In a vast majority of cases, households rent their accommodation, but social housing is relatively scarce.

By and large, the socio-economic characteristics of Bas-Montreuil residents paint much the same picture as those of the city as a whole, albeit with a more marked representation of manual workers (33 per cent of the total labour force, versus 30 per cent for Montreuil) to the detriment of clerical staff (25 per cent to 29 per cent for Montreuil) and middle-ranking professionals (18.5 per cent to 20 per cent for Montreuil). The fact that the balance is tipped more in favour of the lower-skilled occupations explains the higher rate of unemployment than in the rest of the city – 13.3 per cent versus 11.4 per cent. Having said that, from the standpoint of trades and professions, Bas-Montreuil features a certain degree of genuine social mixing, tying in with the area's industrial calling. Rare indeed are the Bas-Montreuil housing blocks where one will not find mixed communities combining all groups of the population. The mobility of the population has remained rather high over the past 20 years: 56 per cent of the inhabitants in 1990 did not live previously in Montreuil in 1982 and similarly, between 1990 and 1999, the population has been renewed by 54 per cent.

The rental market in Paris and in the near suburbs is experiencing outstanding pressure. In this context, Montreuil becomes an 'attractive place' as the average rent in private housing is lower than in Paris and it provides nice places for rehabilitation. The pressure is, therefore, all the more strong as the rehabilitation of older buildings or the transformation of factories into loft apartments offers new opportunities. The general re-appreciation of the neighbourhood considerably improved its attractiveness for middle and upper class householders.

With the gradual reduction of dilapidated private accommodation, households living in this type of housing (insalubrious buildings, furnished hotels, homes) and facing the most precarious conditions are gradually rehoused in social housing. The access to social housing for the deprived population and ethnic minorities relies on emergency housing procedures. Household of these groups are offered a place in the less attractive sections of social housing where one can find a high vacancy rate (Menard *et al.*, 1999). The trends in private and public housing alike are characterized by a gradual eviction of the least well-off households and their replacement by middle- and upper-class households coming from the Paris area or from other neighbourhoods of the city: a typical gentrification process.

A restricted local job market

Local opportunities are relatively marginal as the relevant geographic level for both job seekers and employers is the region. This is confirmed by looking at the occupational trajectories of the people we met: only two of them got access to the local job market through contacts in the neighbourhood. Most of the others work or have worked through opportunities located in other areas. Those with a part-time job spent more than two hours a day commuting.

The neighbourhood sometimes offers some opportunities for work. This is true of many ethnic bars, hotel-restaurants and shops. Numerous informal activities (either partly or totally unregistered, undocumented employees and/or with no residence permit) started thriving in the neighbourhood: 'illegal' hairdressers, garages or cigarette and alcohol sales with equally illegal opening hours and various cases of trafficking stolen goods in connection with the flea market. The relative tolerance, which allowed these economic niches to expand, has decreased with the gentrification of the neighbourhood. The common idea is that commercial areas should be 'normalized' and 'gentrified' (quality, opening hours) by means of a renovation policy and by reducing the allocation of commercial leases. In the same way, a municipal decree has declared illegal the market inside the Malian migrant hostel.

Following Hatzfeld who studied ethnic shops in the Faubourg St-Denis (Hatzfeld *et al.*, 1997), one may hypothesize that recruitment through community networks reaches far beyond the neighbourhood. The 'labour pool' of Kabyle bars, which also includes the twentieth arrondissement of Paris, seems to operate pretty much in this way. In the past, these bars used to be informal 'job centres' for the unemployed industrial workers who attended them. Today, however, they no longer offer an alternative for long-term unemployed industrial workers to find a job; neither do they provide relevant information on the job market. In the case of the only person we met who managed to get temporary access to the job market through ethnic networks, both the job and the employer were located in central Paris and contacted through business networks with no connection with the neighbourhood.

The people most actively looking for a job, who have also the highest academic degrees and/or the most extensive professional experience, were considering working in Paris or in the residential part of the western Paris region. They had not thought of the possibility of mobilizing ethnic networks. People relying on redistribution for their income and for assistance in finding a job seemed quite unlikely to take advantage of these opportunities, which do not seem to represent any real alternative to the 'mainstream market'. The informal market does not seem to offer a real alternative for the most precarious individuals of the ethnic minorities.

The neighbourhood's artists and the managers of small enterprises in the graphic, cyber and audio technology industries are an exception to this. They combine their professional life, housing and sociability in a small perimeter that can be described as a local community (Hatzfeld *et al.*, 1997). Their networks include people in work with various qualification levels, and provide a favourable context for the emergence of job opportunities for unemployed people with any kinds of skills in the related fields. Their idealization of the neighbourhood, of the work/housing proximity as an alternative way of life, of local professional relationships based on mutual help, and the joint achievement of common projects with interchangeable positions, participation in local associations, the series of emblematic rallying places and the active support from the municipality, all in the end make up a dense network over the whole Bas-Montreuil, even if such networks reach far beyond to the neighbourhoods of eastern Paris. Still, one should not overestimate the potential of integration brought by these networks to the most precarious individuals: older long-term unemployed people, especially, have no access to them.

Public policies and the dynamics of the local job market

Most employment policies encompass wider territories than the one of Montreuil, like the national young people's job scheme (*emploi-jeunes*): 50 per cent of the young people hired in Montreuil are not living in the city. The local employment agency for young people (*mission locale*) is shared between several municipalities. This agency and the job centre (*ANPE*) do not consider that the home/job proximity is a priority criterion.

With the emergence of new service businesses in the context of the gentrification, territory-based urban development policies are attempting to establish Bas-Montreuil as a working area designed for the least qualified workers. Through a partnership with recent businesses and collaboration with local associations for economic insertion, the municipal services try to increase the attractiveness of the neighbourhood. The urban social development programme mentions two types of measures to attract 'citizen businesses' who care for their environment: creating businesses offering services for companies and their employees (restaurants, day-care centres, sports activities) and organizing local recruitment procedures (recruitment clauses, direct placement, training schemes matching existing needs, and so on). The purpose of this is to avoid a gap between the deprived section of the population and a flourishing economy.

Redistribution, reciprocity and the local identity

The local identity is built by the multiple social and cultural events coming up regularly in the neighbourhood's collective life and the municipality's active communication policy. Despite a high residential mobility, the sense of belonging to the city and to the neighbourhood is shared by the different social and ethnic groups. This identity feeling, which partially transcends ethnic and social cleavages, does not in any way lead to a generalized exchange of goods and services. While only exceptionally offering direct opportunities to the most precarious households, it is nevertheless favourable to the development of formal and informal types of associative or militant life. Numerous activities of this kind are carried out by various figures on the local scene: some of them come from the long tradition of communist and trade union militant action, others belong to middle class circles who have recently moved to the neighbourhood while others are members of former or recent immigration groups. Relative mutual acquaintances between these voluntary groupings of people produce collaborations of either a short or long-term kind. Authier (1999) stressed that:

> contrary to a common representation, the categories with the strongest feeling of identity relative to their place of residence are young graduate students (in a phase of residential mobility), and white collar workers or intermediate professions (well established) – who are also the people with the strongest connections to their neighbourhood, who have most deliberately chosen to live in it, and who most accurately identify it – and certainly not elderly people, women or any members of the 'captive' groups.

The presence of many such better off households in the Bas-Montreuil makes it a lively neighbourhood but only produces low opportunities for precarious groups.

National social policies are made more efficient by being echoed by many local parameters: a very dynamic associative and militant set of activities improves and diversifies access to redistribution. Apart from this process, when groups with better social and cultural assets get involved in the neighbourhood's life, the benefits for deprived groups are mostly of a symbolic nature. However, the resources of the neighbourhood are not systematically used: several women surveyed had a very negative relationship to the neighbourhood and chose to focus their strategies (in terms of job, residence, social networks) on the 'city centre' or on more well-off cities in the area. Rejection of the neighbourhood is based on a strongly racialized perception of it: a Senegalese respondent thinks that the concentration of 'Africans and poor people' in the neighbourhood strengthens her stigmatization, and two others living in social housing were trying to escape from the neighbourhood as they refused to live next to ethnic minorities, regarding it as degrading and even dangerous:

> 'I don't like living in Montreuil, it's a ... dark neighbourhood. I can't stand all these people in the rue de Paris staring at me. When I went to Annecy [a city in the French Alps], I don't mean to say that everybody is rich there, but, well, things look ... brighter. Here in Montreuil I am feeling ... stuck'.

Such a negative perception of the neighbourhood is based on the feeling of being outcast in comparison to their initial social position.

Scarce reciprocity from family and friends

Reciprocity between individuals, beyond public and semi-public initiatives in the neighbourhood itself, is very unusual. Diverse socialization places are of course constitutive of common or distinctive symbolical reference spaces, but they are actually tools for the construction of an identity ('Montreuil' or 'neighbourhood' or 'Kabyle' places) rather than a real base for exchange of commodities and services. Moreover, most marginalized people, hardly if at all (or no longer) take part in the numerous daily exchanges or in the short-term excitement over local events.

Direct exchanges of commodities and services (financial help, furniture, clothes, food) are more generally limited to the family, and the local dimension is, therefore, no longer very relevant. On the contrary, spatial proximity actually reinforces the daily reciprocity of those very few people who have family links inside the neighbourhood. Household solidarity between precarious neighbours, on the other hand, is usually inexistent or very unusual.

Finally, family and friends' networks are often of little extent and what's more, they provide virtually no information on the official job market as in many cases, the people in the socialization network have few opportunities available. Apart from offering temporary housing at the time when immig-

rants arrive in France, the pragmatic help, especially financial, is often provided by one single family member or friend and their spatial localization
is then fairly unimportant to the process.

The '4,000': Can the neighbourhood be an obstacle to getting jobs?

La Courneuve, population 34,139 is a traditional working-class residential
area mainly inhabited by manual labourers. It used to be an important
industrial site but is now having to contend with the difficulties of redevelopment. With the highest unemployment rate in Seine St Denis (25 per
cent of the labour force), and the largest number of RMI claimants in 1993,
La Courneuve and most of the surrounding *communes*, barring Le Bourget,
stand at the heart of what the *Caisse d'Allocations Familiales* (CAF: Office for
Family Benefits) refers to as a 'poverty zone'.

The A1 motorway in the north and the A86 in the south section off the
neighbourhood. Its housing stock divides into two distinct areas separated
by the 'Six-Road' crossroads: the more outlying Northern District, skirted
by the A1 and the La Courneuve landscaped gardens, contains the '4,000'
housing project plus a few local shops; the Southern District, situated in
the far west of La Courneuve and bordering on the *commune* of St Denis, is
closer to the town centre and equipped with a shopping precinct and cultural amenities. The commercial infrastructure of the neighbourhood has
undergone a severe collapse since its construction. All the shops in the
commercial centre of la Tour – whose ambition in the 1960s was to attract
customers from the whole department – have now gone out of business.

The combination of long, 15-storey blocks set perpendicular to one another, small 4-storey blocks, and a 26-storey tower block, make the neighbourhood something of an enclosed space. This may be seen most clearly
in the south where the large north–south blocks loom like 16-level barriers
between the housing project, the old town and the rest of the urban fabric.
Aubervilliers train station is a five-minute walk away, and from there it
takes about 12 minutes to get in to the centre of Paris by the RER suburban
railway.

The neighbourhood owes its name – '4,000' – to the 3,700 homes built
there by the City of Paris public housing department from 1956 on. It
houses 12,300 people (36 per cent of the *commune* population), yet 44 per
cent of foreigners aged 15 to 41. The neighbourhood is central to the life of
La Courneuve, not only because of its demographic contribution, but
rather as it became a symbol of the 'high rise projects' (to such an extent
that the whole town has been identified with it), with a dereliction of
social life, an atmosphere of insecurity which is fed off by a partly real and
partly fantasmatic delinquency. Finally, a strong immigrant population of
various origins and highly visible in public places gave the neighbourhood

the reputation of being an 'immigrants' neighbourhood', a perception which is further strengthened by the fairly recent emergence of associative or business structures facilitated by some immigrants' groups. Large households – one in five households living in the '4,000' project is a couple with three or more children, that is three times more than in the region as a whole – and an overrepresentation of young people (the 15 to 24 year olds accounted for half of the total population) characterized the population in the neighbourhood.

More than a third of the neighbourhood labour force and half of the 15 to 24 year olds claim to be out of work. Long-term unemployment is also a marked feature here, with two in three of the unemployed belonging to that category. Three in five single parents are unemployed. Neighbourhood households can largely be described as deprived: half the monthly incomes per unit of consumption coming to less than 580 Euro. Earned income counts as the chief source for 60 per cent of households – yet only half in the case of single-parent families, another quarter of whom remain reliant on social benefits.

The estate of the '4,000' was a pioneering neighbourhood for the enforcement of '*Politique de la ville*' urban policy programmes since its early phase in 1977. Since then, the 4,000, and therefore the town of La Courneuve, have gained a terrible disrepute and are considered as 'the' typical deprived neighbourhood (Bachmann and Basier, 1989). The estate of the '4,000' has gone through every territory-based public policy scheme since and was considered as a laboratory for evaluating their effects. The town's three secondary schools were included in the territorial positive action scheme called *ZEP* (*Zone d'Education Prioritaire*: priority education zones). A regeneration project for one of the high-rise building was initiated in 1984, involving the state, the municipality and the inhabitants.

In spite of these heavy intervention programmes, the neighbourhood seems to continue a seemingly unstoppable decline. As social issues remained unsolved, the authorities decided to move to another dimension in handling the tower block. Demolitions have become a strategic mode of intervention on the neighbourhood: in the initial projects of urban re-development, the total or partial destruction of five buildings had been planned. Actually, the 'Debussy' housing block (370 apartments) was demolished, in February 1986, as a prelude to the construction of the urban development zones (ZAC) of l'Orme Seul. A second 360 apartment housing block (Renoir) was torn down by dynamite in June 2000. 'Presov' and 'Ravel' housing blocks were pulled down in 2003. The last operation has been highly publicized, which has contributed to the emergence of a memory of the estate of the '4,000'. On this occasion, the history of the building has been re-appropriated and stimulated the formation of a collective identity.

An inexistent local job market and an inaccessible regional market

As in the case of the Bas-Montreuil, the relevant scale in analysing the dynamics of the job market is the whole Paris region. The town of La Courneuve alone has 1,400 shops and commercial companies, 4 per cent of which represent 50 per cent of the jobs. The economic fields of small local businesses are widely diversified (biotechnologies, textile industry, food processing industry, precision engineering, and so on). From this perspective, the location and the excellent transport connections of the '4,000' estate are certainly not an obstacle for reaching the labour pools. The main causes behind the high local unemployment rate and under-employment are not of a territorial nature, but rather the region's massive de-industrialization, the increasing precariousness of the type of jobs available and the mismatch between the skills wanted by employers and those offered by long-term unemployed people. The neighbourhood's very high stigmatization (living at the wrong address), certainly increases the ethnic and racial discrimination of a large section of ethnic minorities on the job market. In fact, Champion and Marpsat (1996), in their work on targeted neighbourhoods in the *Politique de la ville*, have shown that more than the place, the ethnic origin of young jobseekers is a discriminating factor in access to the job market, even if the residential indicators are controlled. The relatively weak influence of the areas on social trajectories has also been pointed out by Fieldhouse and Tye (1996) for the UK.

The discrepancy of a local job market is a twofold reality, both in terms of job supply and demand, and if nothing is done to reverse the social 'disqualification' of the inhabitants, any installation of businesses may fail to create jobs for the local unemployed. The employees of the local branch of a bank and of La Poste (the national postal service also involved in banking activities) in the neighbourhood live outside the neighbourhood. A nearby fast-food restaurant has no inhabitant of the estate of the '4,000' among its employees. Still, a majority of the employees in question have very limited qualifications, which confirms the above hypothesis of discrimination against the inhabitants. In the same way, the nearby supermarket, the shopping place for many inhabitants of the estate of the '4,000', has only one employee from the neighbourhood. The 'hard-discount' store in the neighbourhood closed down alleging a *'lack of personnel'* but it seems that security matters was the real reason behind this failure.

In addition to the scarcity of the job offers in the neighbourhood or in its vicinity, the very strategies of the unemployed is based on other towns of the Paris region, or on the 'focus town' itself. Irrespective of the duration of the unemployment period, the value of work is internalized, even though short- or middle-term opportunities seem limited or nonexistent. In this respect, getting a job outside the neighbourhood is an ideal 'first stage' for escaping the neighbourhood and its twofold stigmatization in terms of residence and status. But this stigmatization is precisely one of the obstacles to entering the job market.

Existing 'community' networks in the neighbourhood are not job providers for unemployed people from ethnic minorities: solidarity is more effective in terms of providing accommodation to immigrants at the time that they arrive in France, of socialization and monitoring for administrative procedures.

The size of any illegal activity is, by its very nature, difficult to evaluate. Still, these were mentioned over and over again by the inhabitants and the interviewed. This illegal business seems to consist mostly of receiving stolen goods, such as clothes or cars, and drug trafficking – recently, drug trafficking is said to have shifted from hard drugs to soft drugs. The economic fallout of trafficking is equally impossible to assess. Social workers often mention the discrepancies between the value of domestic appliances or common consumer goods in some families and their official earnings. A parallel economy actually exists in the neighbourhood, but it can only be approached through a complex and long-lasting research strategy.

Redistribution: The use of local amenities

There is a striking concentration of social services in the neighbourhood, which are also used by the inhabitants from the other parts of the town (especially the municipal health centre, the cultural centre and the social security centre). There is no clear strategy for the local authorities to implement territorial development in the neighbourhood. The idea is that any improvements in the amenities in the city centre also benefit the inhabitants of the estate of the '4,000'.

Access to the national public assistance schemes is locally taken care of by many public institutions, whose offices are located in one single building of the southern neighbourhood. Except for family allowances and the minimum income, however, access to the numerous existing schemes (concerning excessive debt, transportation, telephone and electricity bills, credits, food tickets) is fairly unequal because the schemes are extremely fragmented and opaque. The social care of precarious households is mostly done by the social service of the Familly allowance centre (*Caisse d'Allocations Familiales*) and, to a lesser extent, by the social service of the social housing landlord. In conjunction with a very well established local semi-public association, both institutions are making up for the obvious deficiencies of the social assistance service.

Most of the surveyed have developed alternative strategies to get information on their rights, mostly by turning to local associations and, to a lesser extent to the communist party. But these organizations may not actually totally compensate existing schemes because they cannot make any direct financial contribution. Integration through redistribution thus complements integration through the community sphere, but the latter is more male-oriented. And one should bear in mind that priority targets of social policies are families, leaving childless households with very little social assistance and highly dependent on the job market.

Lone mothers, all of whom belong to ethnic minorities, more often apply for – and obtain – selective assistance for themselves and their children. The work of the social centre is mostly dedicated to them, focusing on literacy (39 per cent of those older than 18), sewing, cooking, silk painting, pottery work and knitting. The social centre also runs activities addressed to children. The deliberate focus of integration schemes on immigrant women was confirmed by the social service's assessment: out of 456 members using the social centre, 252 are younger than 18 (55 per cent of the public) and 92 per cent of the adults are women.

Living in the Hood: Sharing territory on an unequal basis

Because of the stigmatization of the neighbourhood's inhabitants, most of the people we met had a very negative view of it. Very often, people just try to avoid the neighbourhood by either shutting themselves up in their apartment or by making connections outside the neighbourhood or town. The opposite move, that is, receiving outsiders at home, is not an easy one.

In the '4,000', meeting places like bars and restaurants or public places are scarce resources. Exchanges and socialization take place in inappropriate places, like halls, alleys, squares for children, and so on. Appropriation of public places (staircases and parking places) by the 6 to 15 year olds is very much resented by the interviewed and other inhabitants. Benches and bus stops are home to some of the 'older ones', from North Africa and sub-Saharan Africa, and a few Comoros nationals. By default, the market in the *Place du 8 Mai 45* and the commercial centre – two important gathering places, are also meeting places to various groups at different times of day and night. The coexistence between them – usually an uneasy process – is based on this implicit sharing of the territory along gender, generation and ethnic group lines. The absence of police forces, as repeatedly mentioned in the interviews, reinforces the 'let go' feeling among the inhabitants, who see the estate of the '4,000' as a different, dangerous and rejected territory. The supposed homogeneity of the collective identity of the estate of the '4,000' is mostly at work outside the neighbourhood, whose internal fundamental features are a social and ethnic segmentation (or even fragmentation) and a divide between the northern and southern part of the neighbourhood.

The neighbours' committees created by the local authorities are little popular with the inhabitants who see them as control bodies. One of the most important initiatives of the municipal team for creating more cohesion and identity in the neighbourhood has been to work on the memory of the 'Grand ensemble'. The idea has been implemented in 1997, at the time of the demolition of the Renoir housing block, with the purpose of magnifying 'local history' through its earliest inhabitants. The creation of 'resource inhabitants', picked among people who already fulfilled informal mediation tasks, was part of this scheme. The strengthening of the scheme is now being considered through a system of 'resource adults' who would be municipal employees and whose task would be a mix of cultural and social mediation between the inhabitants and public institutions. In this perspective, from a stopgap, the status of 'resource inhabitants' could be a real strategy for professional retraining.

Inside the neighbourhood, daily socialization is mostly articulated around women's associations and community and/or religious associations. Muslim prayer centres are socialization places for adults and increasingly for young people, partly because of the imam's credibility with them, and partly because of the identity 'revival' based on religious symbols, especially at the time of the Ramadan.

With a little help from friends and family

The length of residence, for precarious households, brings no advantages in terms of local integration, just like the density of the family network (a fairly usual case) does not imply the availability of any substantial assistance. Two common features to the experiences are a major dependency on redistribution and a relative isolation from family or 'community' networks. Among various reasons, many women say that they are trying to escape from forms of social control that they find too intrusive.

The type of exchange at work in community networks is mostly based on non-financial help (minding children, small services, shopping and delivery, information). Financial help does exist but is not very common, because all in all, households are faced with the same kind of socio-economic difficulties. In the same way, there are isolated instances of solidarity between neighbours, but, according to the interviewed, it is a limited process and most of the time, the relations with next-door neighbours will not go beyond saying hello to each other.

Attempts at evaluating the strength of the links between neighbours, and their capacity to bring about some solidarity are very contradictory. One may even hypothesize that the contradictions in the evaluation of relationships with neighbours – sometimes considered to be strong and at other times weak – reflect a deliberate attempt to keep the stigmatization away by looking at any kind of links with neighbours from a distance. The social attitudes are dominated by isolation, a fear of 'retaliation' in the event of 'problems' and distancing oneself from the whole situation in order to get rid of the stigmatization by passing it on to others. In the estate of the '4,000', the strategy of seclusion in the domestic sphere is especially true of lone women, but the picture is not so clear-cut: some people have family members in their own building, and everyday life solidarities between neighbours may occur.

Local identity matters

Both neighbourhoods under survey offer resources in all three spheres of integration. These, however, are not accessible in the same conditions to any inhabitants. If target groups do not use local resources on an equal basis, the differences are even greater between precarious households as a whole and the middle and upper classes living in the neighbourhoods. In the end, the initial hypothesis should be changed to include the fact that social exclusion *also* has a negative impact on the use of local resources. However, the local configuration (Elias and Scotson, 1965), which under-pins and produces local identities, has a definite impact on the individual integration trajectories.

The local job market as a deceptive alternative

The lower employment rates in the department of Seine-St-Denis have trig-gered massive unemployment among the least qualified of its inhabitants. Moreover, a socio-spatial segregation has strengthened as people who had lost their job were 'forced' into the most depreciated zones. The develop-ment of local job markets in order to act against this negative spiral is not a real alternative. The reason for this is because we are faced not so much with a spatial mismatch between the jobs and residence locations, but rather with a discrepancy between available jobs and the low level of skills offered, of the 'assets in terms of representation', and of the social networks of the unemployed in order to afford these jobs.

A sharing of wealth?

Contrary to initial hypotheses, reciprocity between households is fairly similar in mixed social urban contexts and areas with concentrations of urban poor. In the socially mixed area of the Bas-Montreuil, reciprocity may potentially transfer wealth at the benefit of the poorer population, but in practice networks are highly segmented. The potential benefits for deprived households are limited because functional relations are scarce, except for the connections made in the school context on the initiative of a pupils' parents association and the more or less direct advantages derived from the action of numerous socio-cultural associations. Poverty levels are more significant in La Courneuve, and the objective social and economic conditions are more homogeneous. However, such a concentration of pre-carious households does not in any way encourage the emergence of more effective collective solidarities: the territory-based ethnic differentiation is even more clear-cut than in the Bas-Montreuil.

The ubiquitous presence of the welfare state

The one typical aspect about the French case is the sphere of redistribution, which, in both neighbourhoods, has comparable levels, with differences in the organization of the benefits. In both cases, needs are relatively well met, in spite of a deficit in public facilities which is particularly sharp in the estate of the '4,000'. In the peripheral neighbourhood, municipal structures are more systematically present than in the older neighbourhood, because in the latter case, the structures come as a complementation of existing local initiatives. The history of local social policies in the estate of the '4,000' has developed along other lines. In a first stage, public intervention was a compensation for the gradual decline of militant and associative structures which were a real catalyst for the organization of social life. In a second stage, these structures became 'thoroughly dominant': the neighbourhood became an experimental field for public intervention. At this stage, the public authorities act as a substitute to stimulate the local networks in order to reinforce social cohesion. Following a process of concentration of precarious ethnic minorities, other 'community' structures emerged to make up for the failures of standard social policies. But, as the contents and the modes of operation of such gatherings of people are not well perceived by the institutions, complementarity between the two turned out to be limited.

In the end, the historical, urban and social differences between the neighbourhoods have little impact 'in themselves' in the three spheres of integration (job market, redistribution and reciprocity), even though interrelations specific to each local context are visibly at work between the three spheres of integration. Moreover, strategies, among the unemployed, aiming at using the neighbourhood's resources are very unusual in both cases.

The choice of our observation protocol, based on the hypothesis of opposing peripheral neighbourhoods and older neighbourhoods, presupposed the existence of different forms of urban operation as a result of different social contexts. We insisted on the importance of challenging the hypothesis on many aspects, but still, it remains quite valid in terms of *the experience of poverty*. The designers of the tower blocks tried to provide quality housing but widely disregarded the environment. The lack of public facilities in peripheral neighbourhoods is in sharp contrast with the integrity of the urban space and its social functions in older neighbourhoods, whose typical feature is the poor quality of housing. On an urban level, the experience of poverty in the estate of the '4,000' is having a decent home in a deficient environment, while for the poorer inhabitants of the Bas-Montreuil, it consists in having a timeworn and small home in a relatively better environment. But the differentiation of the experiences of poverty between these contrasted urban contexts is not limited to the above as the neighbourhood's renown is an additional determining factor.

Could the neighbourhood's renown be counted as a fourth sphere of integration?

Concerning the various potential local resources, the Bas-Montreuil differs from the estate of the '4,000' on one fundamental aspect: the renown of the neighbourhood. Although the location of the Bas-Montreuil in the department of Seine-St-Denis – often simply mentioned by its number (the '9-3') – is in itself a potential reason for stigmatization, the town's differentiation and its specific, deeply rooted representation (the media are now calling it the '21st arrondissement of Paris') gives it a special status inside this 'indiscriminate' and depreciated territory of the Paris urban area. The social mix inside the neighbourhood does not provide any special opportunities for the poorer sections of the population of the Bas-Montreuil, and the benefits derived are mostly symbolic: especially, the interclass and inter-ethnic socialization during festive events, as well as the representation of the neighbourhood stimulate the construction of a positive collective identity. On the contrary, the renown of the '4,000' is in total opposition with the case of the Bas-Montreuil: the estate of the '4,000' has become a symbol of poverty, degradation and violence, all typical features of the '9-3' in collective representations, and the inhabitants have internalized the stigmatization closely associated with their place of residence in all aspects of their daily life.

Now, the survey has demonstrated that the representations of the place of residence are a strategic resource at various levels of social integration. First, the disrepute suffered by the inhabitants of the estate of the '4,000' by the simple fact that they live 'there' has real effects on their access to professional integration. An obvious effect is their discrimination on the job market, and this also applies to the perception by the unemployed of their chances of getting a stable job. This, again, has an impact on the institutional management of 'social exclusion': unlike the Bas-Montreuil, social services in the estate of the '4,000' are much more developed than professional integration services. Besides, subsidized jobs are very marginally staffed by local people, and especially by young people, whose bad collective renown is too overwhelming.

Second, integration into society does not boil down to simply having an apartment, a job, and social connections with peers: participation in the local collective life is also a fundamental resource. In this respect, the positive collective identity of a neighbourhood has a comforting effect over the social identities of the most destitute. In summary, inclusion in a positive local identity is a resource *inside* one's own socio-spatial borders and *outside* them, and concerns all aspects of daily life.

This is why we may consider the renown of one's place of residence as a genuine fourth sphere of integration. Of course, this additional sphere does not provide any direct access to the job market, nor any significant improvement in government help or any increase in the volume or quality of the practically exchanged goods and services between households, but by simply providing the most precarious households with a status, it is an essential basis, improving access to all other spheres. If the neighbourhood offers an identity potential that individuals can use to build up a positive social identity in contrast with their real social and economic situation, the urban poor will enjoy a better initial position as a result. The opposite relationship has even more systematic effects: negative renown is vastly harmful in terms of accessing the job market, participating in exchanges and benefiting from certain aspects of public policies (subsidized jobs, professional integration, improving the school system, and so on). The poverty experience is even more difficult in the '4,000' because of the poor quality environment and of the negative representation of the neighbourhood.

In the end, the initial hypothesis opposing peripheral neighbourhoods and older neighbourhoods is little relevant in terms of objective differences in access (or denied access) to the three spheres of integration defined according to Polanyi's model. But the expected difference regarding renown has more significant effects than we had initially considered. For this reason, we would like to complete this analysis model with a fourth sphere of integration inside which the neighbourhood remains as an equally relevant entity: the local identity.

9
London: Deprivation, Social Isolation and Regeneration

Justin Beaumont[1]

Introduction

Research undertaken for the London case study of the URBEX project forms
the basis for this chapter. Evidence is presented from a number of in-depth,
semi-structured interviews with residents felt to be the victims of social
exclusion in two council estates (one core, the other peripheral), as well as
from interviews with other local key-informants connected with the
estates. The findings reveal that the processes and experiences of exclusion,
and strategic responses, vary considerably with respect to Polanyi's spheres
of economic integration among the three groups, and that certain contextual factors distinguish the neighbourhoods. No evidence for a distinctive
core–periphery 'neighbourhood effect' is found. Political tensions concerning the wider local regeneration efforts reflect similar conflicts elsewhere in
London and the UK at large. Problems of low-income, poor housing and
social isolation are common to all target groups in both estates. All groups,
moreover, value and utilize their neighbourhood as an important resource
as part of their struggle to make ends meet. Attachment to place, however,
is paradoxical, reflecting socio-spatial immobility among deprived people,
and the necessity of having to make do with spatially fixed assets such as
housing. Residualization of council housing in London concentrates many
marginalized people in areas where unemployment, deteriorating council
housing, petty crime, drugs and prostitution are mounting problems,
although historical and institutional specificities prevent deprived neighbourhoods assuming more extreme 'ghetto' features.

The first section situates the London case within processes of deindustrialization, social exclusion and socio-spatial segregation, and in the context
of the welfare regime debate. The second section links these issues to the
process of residualization of council housing in the city, followed in
the third with a brief outline of the characteristics of the London Borough
of Lambeth. The next two sections present findings from the interviews,
the first with respondents from the Ethelred Estate located in the vicinity of

London's core in the north of the borough, the second with respondents from Clapham Park, another council estate located between Clapham and Brixton towards the periphery to the south. The concluding section discusses implications for alternative approaches for combating social exclusion in London and elsewhere.

Deindustrialization and socio-spatial segregation

Since the 1960s, economic restructuring in various countries in the West has led to the decline of full employment in large-scale manufacturing industries, alongside service employment growth and the rise of mass unemployment (Mollenkopf and Castells, 1991; Rodwin and Sazanami, 1989; Savitch, 1988). New expressions of poverty and inequality in social and spatial terms wrought by deindustrialization are increasingly apparent. A number of scholars point to these new expressions, relating to the notion of an 'underclass' in the US and to the concept of 'social exclusion' in Europe (Mingione, 1996; Wacquant, 1996; Wilson, 1987), so there is no need to revise the arguments in detail here. These commentators show that internationalization (the extension of economic relations across national boundaries) and globalization (the functional integration of economic process across national borders) combine to expand the population of low-skill, low-wage workers and high-skill and high-wage staff in the same urban system. Cities display sharp socio-spatial disparities between rich and poor and excluded areas. These disparities reflect deindustrialization, the rise of mass structural unemployment, the rise in levels of poverty and social exclusion and the consolidation of a more or less permanent pool of people marginalized from the formal labour market and largely resident in certain deprived neighbourhoods.

For some observers the shift to postindustrialism in world cities (like London) entails the increasing polarization between those on the lowest incomes and an expanding high-income stratum (Friedmann and Wolff, 1982; Sassen, 1991, 1994). Critics contend that rather than exhibiting polarization tendencies, economic restructuring in London leads to professionalization. For example, analysis of occupational change in the London and Randstad regions indicates employment growth among professional occupations but in the absence of a parallel growth in low-income jobs, at least in the formal labour market (Hamnett, 1994; Hamnett and Cross, 1998). More recently, debates have focused on the ever growing number of people in cities, including asylum-seekers, minority ethnic groups, lone parents and long-term unemployed, who are often marginalized from work and dependent on benefits, isolated from the social and economic mainstream and increasingly concentrated on deteriorating housing estates in certain parts of the city (Buck, 1996; Gans, 1993; Philo, 1995). One of the more intriguing aspects of the geography of deprivation in London is that as a result of large-scale gentrification, pockets of deprivation in many inner London boroughs are adjacent to pockets of affluence and wealth. The social geography of inner London today reflects an intricate, small-scale mosaic of alternating wealth and poverty, affluence and deprivation, partly explained by the changing occupational structure and housing market and the associated social differentiation by tenure (Beaumont and Hamnett, 2001; Hamnett, 2003).

The downward effects of deindustrialization are particularly marked in inner city locations, like Barking and Dagenham in East London (but also south of the Thames), where manufacturing activity has declined and moved away and where little diversification into new sectors has taken place (Beaumont, 2004). To illustrate, the Ford Motor Company first acquired land on its riverside site in 1924, and the famous Dagenham plant was built between 1929 and 1931. Ford simultaneously pioneered new forms of shop-floor production, based on mass-production principles in large production complexes, and established new relationships with workers through high wages and unionized labour. The crisis of Fordism and the transition to post-Fordist forms of production from the early 1970s onwards means that this plant and others like it have dramatically reduced the size of their work-force. In 2000, Ford at Dagenham announced that it would end production in 2002 with profound consequences for the economy of East London.

Embedded in path-dependent characteristics, there are at least two ways to highlight London's specificity. The first refers to contextualization within a wider welfare regime framework. Recalling the typology of welfare regimes (Esping-Andersen, 1990; 1996; see also Gallie and Paugam, 2000), some countries stay broadly within a regime-type over time, for example Sweden (social democratic) and Italy (corporatist), while others show sharp shifts between regimes, such as the UK which was broadly social democratic until the 1960s and (neo)-liberal since 1979 under the influence of Thatcher and subsequently Blair. The second indicates variation across space as cities within any national regime may show different institutional characteristics, such as the private housing market. Evidence suggests that London and Birmingham in the UK are more segregated than cities in other European countries as a consequence of a more liberalized welfare regime at the national level. There again, patterns and processes of segregation, closely linked to the incidence of poverty households in the private rental sector, are closer in Birmingham to those in, say, Brussels or Amsterdam, than in London. The trend towards concentration of low-income households in the public sector is more pronounced in London.

Residualization of council housing

The residualization of council housing refers to the increasing concentration of deprived people within the council stock, in terms of the proportion of council tenants receiving state benefits and other measures (Forrest and Murie, 1988; 1991). While the social structure of council estates has altered through the Right to Buy, and low income households are not only limited to the council sector, the special nature of the housing market in London means that processes of exclusion are more concentrated on council estates.[2] People from minority ethnic groups often find themselves housed in the council sector in certain parts of the city. It is important, however, not to make a simple conflation of ethnic diversity with deprivation and exclusion. Residualization of council housing is accompanied by residualization in other dimensions of welfare provision as an increasing onus is placed on the private and voluntary sectors for service delivery. Transfer of council stock and the deregulation of public transport are significant in this respect, as are creeping privatization within pensions and health services. While indicative of changes across the country, the resulting differential access to welfare services, from those that can afford private schemes and those that can not, is an important factor in determining processes of exclusion in London.

London Borough of Lambeth

The London Borough of Lambeth ranks as one of the more deprived areas of London with a long history of policy initiatives against deprivation. The two areas chosen for detailed study were the Ethelred Estate built in the late 1960s and early 1970s, and the Clapham Park Estate, partly constructed in the 1930s and completed as part of postwar reconstruction in the 1950s. Both areas are local authority redevelopments. The Ethelred Estate is located in the northern part of the borough near Vauxhall, while the Clapham Park Estate is situated in between Brixton and Clapham town centres in the southern part of the borough.

Lambeth is one of a ring of 13 local authorities constituting inner London (see Figure 9.1). The River Thames bounds the north of the borough, opposite the Houses of Parliament, and Lambeth's proximity to central London and the location of the Channel Tunnel International Rail Terminal at Waterloo situates the northern part in reach of London's core. The central part of Lambeth extends from the Oval in the north to Clapham Common and Brockwell Park in the south. Mainly a residential area where many of the council's housing estates are located, some pockets of commerce and industry can be found in the area including the borough's largest shopping area in Brixton, traditionally the cultural centre for the capital's Afro-Caribbean community (Western, 1993) and a major gentrification zone south of the Thames. Many council offices are located in the area contributing to the high proportion of employment in administration and public services. From the north of the borough through the densely built-up areas of

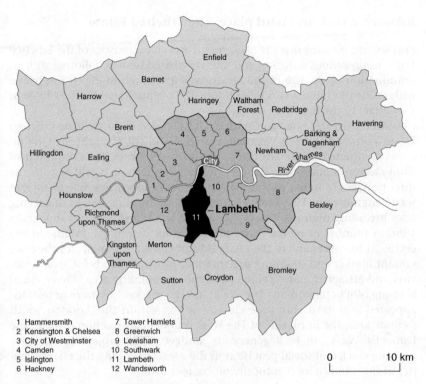

1 Hammersmith
2 Kensington & Chelsea
3 City of Westminster
4 Camden
5 Islington
6 Hackney
7 Tower Hamlets
8 Greenwich
9 Lewisham
10 Southwark
11 Lambeth
12 Wandsworth

0   10 km

Figure 9.1   London and its constituent boroughs

Vauxhall, Oval and Brixton one reaches the inner-suburbs of Streatham and Norwood. The south of the borough is predominantly private-rented and owner-occupied residential in character, but does contain smaller pockets of deprivation.

Despite certain exceptions – like the Central Hill estate in the Gypsy Hill area on the southern tip of the borough – the more deprived areas are located in the central and northern parts of the borough. Brixton town centre and the South Circular Road to the south are often regarded as dividing the north and the south of the borough. Areas typically cited as deprived are the various north Brixton estates in the Vassall ward, such as the Myatts Field, Moorlands and Loughborough estates. Stockwell Park is another highly deprived estate in the Stockwell area bordering on Wandsworth. Due to the recent desirability of living in the vicinity of central London, land values have boomed in the north of Lambeth, leading to various regeneration and 'stock transfer' proposals in the Vauxhall and Waterloo areas.

Between a rock and hard place: The Ethelred Estate

This section presents first the background and characteristics of the Ethelred Estate using various statistical and interview-based sources, followed with an examination of the use of the area revealed through in-depth interviews with residents (Table 9.1). Similar information is presented for the Clapham Park estate in the following section.

A former Greater London Council (GLC) 'concrete jungle', the Ethelred Estate – situated between Vauxhall, Waterloo and The Oval Cricket Ground – was completed in the late 1960s and early 1970s. Built as the result of slum clearance and bomb damage in the aftermath of World War II, the intention was to house people away from heavy industries, like metal and waste engineering. The estate comprises many housing blocks of varying sizes including high-rise blocks. The estate was transferred to Lambeth in 1986. A number of medium rise blocks are located in the middle of the estate. At the other end of the estate is Lambeth Walk, famous for the once vibrant market and shopping precinct that provided goods for local residents and attracted many people from the surrounding area. Two council housing blocks remain on 'The Walk' but the market has more or less disappeared and most shops are closed. Falling within the 'London South Central' area, the north side of The Walk is under construction through the Lambeth Walk Single Regeneration Budget (SRB) project to improve housing stock and social provision in the area. Describing the characteristics of the estate, a local authority officer revealed:

> '[The Ethelred] was the heart of a thriving heterogeneous community based around Lambeth Walk. The various factories that existed down there have gone, [as have] those at Nine Elms ... [and as a result] the social structure that supported the shops and social amenities that went with it have also been lost. The Ethelred is seen as the cause of the decline of Lambeth Walk shops ... You've got the changes that are happening along the Embankment, those offices traditionally provide a large number of relatively low skilled clerical jobs for particularly young women and part-time jobs for married women. They've gone ... So the division by the railway line is distinct. [There's] 200 metres sanitized by the railway, its an unpleasant place to walk any time of the day but particularly in the evening, and that isolates people.'

By 1991 the Ethelred was typical of many similar estates in terms of social and economic composition. A total of 88 per cent of households rented from a social landlord: over three quarters (77 per cent) rented from the local council and 11 per cent from a housing association. Of the 2,424 residents aged 16 and over 61 per cent were economically active, of whom 33 per cent worked full time and 8 per cent part-time, 4 per cent were self-employed and 14 per cent were unemployed. Employment opportunities are limited in the area. Male unemployment was 20 per cent compared to female

Table 9.1 Profiles of interview respondents on the Ethelred Estate, 2000–1

Interview number Category	Nationality/ Ethnicity	Age (years)	Housing	Marital status	Children	Duration unemployed	Sources of income	Strategies
1 Lone mother	British/White European	35	Council tenant	S	1 Son (9) 1 Daughter (7)	10 yrs	Income Support Child Benefit	Calculation
2 Unemployed male	British/White European	42	Council tenant	S	None	3 yrs	Incapacity Benefit Informal Work	Retreatist Alternative
3 Ethnic minority female	Ugandan/ Black African	33	Sharing with tenant	S	Pregnant at interview	6 wks	Maternity Leave (90%)	Conformist
4 Lone mother	British/White European	47	Council tenant	S	2 Sons (26, 16) 3 Daughters (27, 13, 11)	15 yrs	Income Support Child Benefit	Calculation
5 Ethnic minority male	Ugandan/ Black African	30	Council tenant	S	None	6 mths	Job Seekers Allowance	Conformist
6 Other	British/Spanish/ White	38	Council tenant	S	None	1 yr	Incapacity Benefit	Retreatist Alternative
7 Unemployed male	British/Italian/ White	54	Council tenant	S	2 Sons (27, 22)	6 yrs	Job Seekers Allowance	Resignation
8 Unemployed male	British/ Jamaican/Black	38	Council tenant	S	2 Sons (10, 7) 1 Daughter (4)	5 yrs	Job Seekers Allowance Informal Work	Autonomy Rebellion
9 Lone mother	British/White European	44	Council tenant	S	1 Son (22) 2 Daughters (16, 1)	25 yrs	Income Support Child Benefit	Calculation

Table 9.1 Profiles of interview respondents on the Ethelred Estate, 2000–1 *continued*

Interview number	Category	Nationality/ Ethnicity	Age (years)	Housing	Marital status	Children	Duration unemployed	Sources of income	Strategies
10	Other	British/Black Caribbean	50	Sharing with tenant	S	3 Sons (30, ?, 3) 3 Daughters (16, 14, 12)	PT work	Official Labour	Conformist Retreatist
11	Lone mother	British/Jamaican/ Black	36	Council tenant	S	5 Sons (15, 12, 7, 6, 3)	Never worked	Income Support Child Benefit	Calculation
12	Lone mother	British/White European	40	Leaseholder	S (div)	1 Son (1) Pregnant at interview	1 yr	Maternity Leave Savings	Conformism Calculation
13	Ethnic minority male	Vietnamese/ British	89	Council tenant	Wid	1 Son (64)	21 yrs	Income Support	Dependence
14	Unemployed male	British/White European	49	Council tenant	S	1 Daughter (4)	2 yrs	Job Seekers Allowance	Conformist Alternative
15	Unemployed male	British/Jamaican/ Black	40	Council tenant	S	2 Sons (20, 4) 1 Daughter (17)	9 mths	Job Seekers Allowance	Conformist Enterprising

Notes: div=divorced; Wid=widowed

unemployment of just under 10 per cent. In addition, a further 39 per cent of the population aged 16 and over were economically inactive. There are some predictable differences in economic activity status by ethnic group and gender, with the numerically dominant indigenous white group (67 per cent of all residents) and persons born in Ireland having a higher proportion of economically inactive males (a product of the age distribution of residents), but a lower proportion of male unemployment (16 per cent) than black groups (26 per cent) or Indian and Pakistani males (37 per cent). Where females are concerned, Indians and Pakistanis had the highest levels of economic inactivity (72 per cent) compared to 52 per cent among the Irish and the white group and just 36 per cent among Black groups. A local primary school head-teacher spoke of ethnic diversity in the area:

> 'This area is a kind of exemplar of things about this city. You have got yards away such wealth and such deprivation, they are side by side, but there is a lot of energy, trouble and strife and apathy, but a lot going on. They stick to their parallel universe. The kids go down the river, the iron works, on their bikes along the embankment. We don't see any of them, we see a few middle class people that send their kids here and that's really good, so you do get different perspectives.'

Many residents on the Ethelred are housed on short-term agreements rather than 'assured tenancies'. Many immigrants are allocated housing on the estate because they could not be accommodated elsewhere. As a result there is quite a high tenant mobility rate, some with limited historical connection to the neighbourhood and presenting cultures that sometimes conflict with those of longer-term (often white) inhabitants. A relatively settled community, the Ethelred is also elderly and many of the problems associated with deprivation concern age. Little crime is reported on the Ethelred, certainly relative to notorious estates in the Brixton vicinity where drugs and prostitution are rife, partly explained by the age profile of the estate. Employment opportunities are limited in the area, although ironically the estate is effectively the closest, single large body of council property ripe for re-development within five miles of Big Ben and the Houses of Parliament. The largest single employer in the wider Vauxhall area is the Fire Service, which despite some attempts at local recruitment does not tend to employ residents from the Ethelred.

Utility of the area

The neighbourhood undoubtedly acts as an important resource for residents of the Ethelred in terms of housing. If a feeling of attachment to place exists for the people living on the estate it is a tenuous one. A problem of design was cited as a possible explanation. As one resident, a single mother and leaseholder, stated:

'No, I don't like the Ethelred – it's a dump ... [O]verall the Ethelred has some serious problems ... in terms of the structure. I can't help but feel the social side is but a reflection of the structural side – the design and outlook and density of it all ... Before Kerrin Point, [one of the Towers], was demolished I found it difficult to tolerate the tower blocks – it looked ominous and overcrowded. Now I can put up with the remaining ones on the estate. And I think that's probably the pitfall of the area – it's too dense ... The roads don't look like roads, they look like alleyways ... They've got these concrete slabs all over the show – and I think that just makes it look like rabbit warrens ... [The design] affects the attitudes of the residents.'

The Project Vauxhall initiative, a proposed 440 million pound re-development of the estate through public–private partnership, was thwarted at resident ballot stage.[3] The tension between the poor quality of local housing stock and the desire to hold on to neighbourhood identity, harking back to romanticized notions of community solidarity along the Lambeth Walk, is a revealing one. Historical identities associated with The Walk go a long way in explaining the importance of the neighbourhood. While increasingly redundant among younger residents and newcomers (especially from other countries), memories of the days when everybody knew each other and people could trust one another are still relevant for the older residents. As memories associated with 'The Walk' continue to fade, notions of community solidarity based on these memories are mobilized by local community and political activists. As a local leaseholder and activist illustrated it:

The traditional community from the 1860s onwards on Lambeth Walk was very much like the East End communities. It was self-supporting and particularly dependent on migrant communities with their own internal social, family and community links. After the war when something like 40 per cent of the area was bombed out and deemed to be uninhabitable, massive amounts of slum clearance went on and a great deal of social housing was built ... That process broke up the community networks but did not disperse the community. The community remained here, retaining its particular attitudes and historical links with the community.

Proximity to central London is a strong plus factor for the people living on the Ethelred. All respondents spoke of the ease of access to the rest of the city – for special shopping trips or visits to cultural institutions and parks, as well as outings to family and friends. While many people are dependent on public transport, the cost of fares restricts the number of trips to the city. More frequent trips are possible on foot or by bicycle, which is less feasible for people living in more southern parts of the borough. Some residents do not consider themselves as part of the Ethelred but with the more affluent Kennington that borders the estate and where many higher income people own properties. These residents, often lease-holders, tend to be more aspirational and pro-development, holding on to more conformist attitudes and viewing the area in terms of market value. The majority opinion among respondents was ambiguous about re-development. Many were interested in substantial physical, social and economic investment, while sceptical as to the benefits for ordinary people, particularly in light of the hotly contested 'guaranteed right to return'.

Another respondent of Scottish and Irish origin, mother of five and living on The Walk, expressed her opinion about proposed re-developments:

> 'Yeah, there's a problem of stigma here, there's a big percentage of black people here. My new man's black. When you apply for a job I think they really want to ask you what culture you are, but it's racist and they can't do it. They just think this is a bad area. But people down here are all right, there's a lot of black people here that hold good jobs. Lambeth [council] has a bad reputation – I think they should leave [the estate] alone and let it pick up and get on, the people living in it, not the people they want to bring in. There is a bit of stigma here ... The council robbed people ... that doesn't look good on the residents here and it has nothing to do with them. Instead of building private accommodation they should build stuff for us. They've got developments here but not for us – for the yuppies and tourists instead. They should make recreation areas for the kids. Those should have been in at day one.'

For some of the respondents the neighbourhood acts as an important resource in terms of reciprocity, particularly among lone mothers and ethnic minorities. Active support networks – either familial, extended family or social – are sometimes explicitly local for people, especially familial networks as family members often huddle for mutual support. As one lone mother revealed:

> '...all my family [offer support] – there's four of us and between three of us there's only a year between us [in age]. We're very close. Those difficult times – like my mum's death which was really difficult, we were really close – we had each other then, but it's made me tougher, that and other things. I'm pretty independent now. After splitting up with my partner, he doesn't help at all. I don't rely on other people. Not me.'

For the long-term unemployed males reciprocal relations between family, friends and neighbours were less significant, but not totally unimportant. The unemployed men interviewed appeared the most isolated. Those interviewed were usually living alone, without partners, and increasingly marginalized from the labour market. A degree of retreatism following marital break-up, personal trauma and independent bachelor lifestyle goes some way towards explaining these findings. One man in his fifties spoke of his labour market marginalization following a divorce from his wife of 34 years:

> 'I worked in a carpet sales centre, doing the carpets, for three years, and after that I went into the painting – I learnt off an old man. I did that 'til Maggie Thatcher come along. All this self-employed ... is nonsense. The old man I worked for

really suffered; she ruined their lives. Since that happened every one got greedy – they'll pay you what they want to. In those days you could get a job in and out, in and out. I was working with different contractors [so] you didn't know when the next one was coming. Six years ago I was laid off [and] the job came to an end. I couldn't get any other work. I was too old.'

The strategies adopted by the respondents from all three groups vary between and across groups, change over time in some cases and sometimes relate strongly to the neighbourhood. Strategic diversity was apparent across and between groups; the only exception was the 'lone mothers' category. The long-term unemployed males all adopted different strategies to deal with their situation: from retreatism (accepting means but abandoning hope) to alternative lifestyle and rebellion. All the lone mothers were resigned to their situation and were making the best out of benefits in order to be at home to look after their children. With meagre benefits spending has to be restricted to essential items:

'You juggle from one week to the next and hope that nothing comes up that week. Food is what I spend most money on. You hope that you have enough to last the week, otherwise you borrow to get by. I'd have to cut back on the food, the luxury items or a bill – you hold it over to the next month. I have direct debits that just come out, but anything else I just keep back ... I cut down on luxuries, like cake and crisps, but I want my children to have these things, you know, go to the cupboard and get what they want. It makes you feel bad if they ask for food or to go to the café and I have to say No.'

For these women to be classified as 'calculators' should not be confused with fraudulence as they all attributed their exclusion from official labour in relation to their full commitment to motherhood. The people from ethnic minorities were conformist in accepting the main cultural goals and means of society, while one of them was more sceptical due to his weak position in the labour market. The respondents from the Other category, falling outside the main three, were more complex strategically displaying tendencies towards ritual, calculation, retreat and rebellion.

On first appearance the strategies adopted by the lone mothers and the people from ethnic minorities are relatively stable over time. The strategies followed by the long-term unemployed males and people from the other category appear dynamic, altering according to new circumstances. An element of active engagement followed by resignation and withdrawal is an important part of this change, particularly as these people get older. An element of ingenuity in the face of adversity is also apparent. There are two areas where the strategic role of the neighbourhood is important. The first of these refers to the 'calculating' strategies of lone mothers, where local familial, extended family and social networks are important as part of their survival strategies in the absence of other forms of childcare and fathers.

The second refers to those adopting elements of retreatist and oppositional strategies, where the neighbourhood – in terms of local history, identity, and intra-community tensions – often becomes a resource for the mobilization of individual political interests in the name of community solidarity.

Managing decline: The Clapham Park Estate

Following interviews with residents (Table 9.2) and other key informants, this section presents the background and characteristics of the Clapham Park Estate. The utility of the area is indicated. The Clapham Park Estate is the largest estate in Lambeth with over 2,400 households. The estate is divided into two parts. Clapham Park East comprises pre-WWII blocks that are mostly without lifts, with four or five floors, pitched roofs and solid brick construction. These units were built in the 1930s after slum clearance with the desire to construct better quality homes. Clapham Park West is located on the other side of Kings Avenue; for the most part brick built, slightly lower rise (three or four floors) with flat roofs. The western part of the estate was built in the immediate postwar period around 1952–3 in the aftermath of the war, bomb damage and slum clearance. Most of the council stock in both locations was originally built and owned by the London County Council (LCC), passed on to the GLC and finally assigned to the management of Lambeth. The neighbourhood as a whole has not received major social, economic or physical infrastructure investments of any kind; whatever limited intervention has been undertaken was characterized by one former resident and activist as 'managed decline' rather than fostering improvements for residents. The housing stock has deteriorated dramatically over time. As a resident and activist elaborated:

> 'I've been here [Clapham Park] 15 years, the character of the estate, is one of the quintessential Lambeth estates where there's a good mix – there always has been. Different ethnic groups, different genders, different lifestyles. It was quite a fun place to be on until about five or six years ago ... But things like leaking roofs you could actually live with, until the level of deprivation reached a critical point. From my personal point of view, you just arrive at a particular point and you get very angry and then you look around and say "My God" it's happened everywhere on the estate, it's not a personal thing and you start to question things. That's how I got involved working in the community ... lots of things going on, you had your gangsters, you had guns, you had people who would go to the local newsagent and put a gun on the counter and I say I need cigarettes and I have no money. Common place? No. But it does happen ... The drug dealing, oh, the drug dealing.'

All the Enumeration Districts within the neighbourhood rank in the 25 per cent most deprived in Lambeth (CPP, 2000). The report identifies crime – namely nuisance, robbery and drug use – as a major local concern. The

Table 9.2 Profiles of interview respondents on the Clapham Park Estate, 2000–1

Interview number	Category	Nationality/ Ethnicity	Age (years)	Housing	Marital status	Children	Duration unemployed	Sources of income	Strategies
1	Ethnic minority female	Ecuadorian/Latin	37	Council tenant	M (sep)	2 Daughters (13, 11)	3 yrs	Income Support Child Benefit	Conformist Dependence
2	Ethnic minority female	Black African/ Ghanaian	38	Council tenant	M (2nd)	2 Sons (15, 9) 3 Daughters (17, 7, 0.5)	FT Work	Official Labour Maternity Leave Child Benefit	Conformist Resignation
3	Lone mother	British/Jamaican/ Black	42	Council tenant	S	1 Son (11)	12 yrs	Income Support Child Benefit	Calculation Dependence
4	Other	British/White European	48	Council tenant	S	None	7 yrs	Incapacity Benefit	Alternative Dependence Resignation
5	Unemployed	British/Jamaican/ maleBlack	39	Council tenant	S	3 Sons (20, 16, 9) 3 Daughters (22, 13, 8)	10 yrs	Job Seekers Allowance Informal Work	Calculation Dependence
6	Unemployed	British/White maleEuropean	33	Council tenant	S	1 Daughter (14)	1 yr	Job Seekers Allowance	Dependence Resignation
7	Lone mother	British/Indonesian	32	Council tenant	S (clw)	2 Daughters (2, 5)	5 yrs	Partner's Incapacity Benefit	Conformist Dependence
8	Ethnic minority	Portuguese-Angolan/Mixed	29	Council tenant	M	2 Sons (8, 10 mnths) 1 Daughter (10)	PT Work	Official Labour Child Benefit	Conformist
9	Lone mother	Black Caribbean/ St. Kitts	46	Council tenant	M (sep)	1 Son (10) 1 Daughter (27)	FT Work	Official Labour	Conformist

153

Table 9.2 Profiles of interview respondents on the Clapham Park Estate, 2000–1   *continued*

Interview number Category	Nationality/ Ethnicity	Age (years)	Housing	Marital status	Children	Duration unemployed	Sources of income	Strategies
10 Lone mother	British/White European	29	Council tenant	*S	1 Son (4) 1 Daughter (10)	2 PT Jobs	Official Labour Child Benefit	Alternative Conformist
11 Lone mother	British/White European	37	Council tenant	S	2 Sons (19, 14) 1 Daughter (2)	14 yrs	Income Support Child Benefit	Dependence Calculation
12 Unemployed male	British/White European	53	Council tenant	*M	2 Sons (32, 29)	10 yrs	Incapacity Benefit	Dependence Resignation
13 Ethnic minority female	Black African/ Ghanaian	37	Council tenant	M (sep)	2 Sons (8, 6) 1 Daughter (4)	3 yrs	Income Support Child Benefit	Calculation Dependence
14 Ethnic minority female	Black Caribbean/ Bahamas	31	Council tenant	S	3 Sons (6, 4, 2)	7 yrs	Income Support Child Disability Child Benefit	Conformist Calculation
15 Ethnic minority female	Portuguese/ White European	29	Council tenant	M	1 Son (9) 1 Daughter (12)	5 yrs	Official Labour Child Benefit	Conformist Dependence
16 Lone mother	British/Jamaican/ Black	47	Leaseholder	S	2 Sons (30, 21)	Temp. Work	Official Labour	Conformist Resignation
17 Ethnic minority female	British/ Nigerian/Black	35	Council tenant	M	1 Daughter (4)	FT Work	Official Labour	Conformist
18 Ethnic minority male	Irish/ White European	47	Council tenant	M (sep)	1 Son (18) 3 Daughters (25, 23, 20)	7 yrs	Income Support	Dependence Resignation

Table 9.2 Profiles of interview respondents on the Clapham Park Estate, 2000–1 *continued*

Interview number Category	Nationality/ Ethnicity	Age (years)	Housing	Marital status	Children	Duration unemployed	Sources of income	Strategies
19 Lone mother	British/ Jamaican/Black	44	Council tenant	S	1 Daughter (3)	3 yrs	Income Support Child Benefit	Calculation Enterprising Dependence
20 Ethnic minority male	Irish/ White European	42	Leaseholder	S	None	FT Work	Official Labour	Conformist Autonomy Alternative
21 Ethnic minority female	Irish/ White European	34	Council tenant	M	2 Daughters (8, 10)	5 yrs	Income Support Child Benefit Carer Allowance Disability Living Allowance	Dependence Resignation
22 Ethnic minority female	Black African/ Ghanaia	44	Council tenant	*S	3 Sons (11, 6, 4)	Temp. Work	Official Labour	Conformist
23 Lone mother	British/ White European	57	Council tenant	S	2 Sons (35, 21) 1 Daughter (19)	3yrs	Incapacity Benefit	Conformist Dependence
24 Unemployed male	British/ White European	45	Council tenant	S	None	7 yrs	Job Seekers Allowance Informal Work	Dependence Resignation
25 Lone mother	British/ Jamaican/Black	40	Council tenant	S	3 Sons (23, 18, 2) 1 Daughter (12)	5 yrs	Income Support	Conformist Enterprising

Notes: sep=separated; *S= cohabiting with boyfriend; clw=common law wife; *M=second marriage; M (2nd)=widowed and remarried; div=divorced estate lacks an institutional focus for community activities and community facilities are thin on the ground. The recent closure of the local library removes one of the last remaining community facilities from the area. Local schools suffer problems of deprivation, with high proportions of pupils eligible for free school meals and special educational needs. At any moment in time 20 per cent of Clapham Park tenants are seeking transfer to another part of Lambeth, while over half (57 per cent) of tenancies are relatively new. A majority of tenants on the estate (54 per cent) receive Housing Benefit. The absence of adequate security in the housing blocks encourages petty theft and anti-social behaviour, according to one local activist, partly the result of social instability in the area: 'There's an awful lot of 'dumping': housing application dumping. They [Lambeth] decide to put in a lot of people that don't have many skills, don't know how to look after themselves very well, would be able to if they were given a little help, but they are just pushed into this particular area.' The same respondent elaborated on problems of crime:

'Six years ago you suddenly had an increase and influx of crime, almost over-night. There was the "cleaning up" of Streatham. Pimps, prostitutes, their dealers, the whole lot moved "lock stock and barrel". Streatham was cleared out [and] they displaced it to here [Clapham Park]. Even early in the morning you began to see "working women" trying to stop cars on the main road. They had serious drug problems – every so often you'd see them crying and shaking ... a sense of fear began to develop. The crack dealers had moved in. Mugging began to increase ... Crime was moving in, lack of money; but nothing happened ... Active neglect, I think it's active neglect ... it wasn't in a sense planned, but it becomes habitual – habits become active habits.'

Utility of the area

The most vulnerable and marginalized members of society, including asylum seekers, tend to find themselves housed on the estate, sometimes compounding the problems. As one resident explained:

'There are probably more asylum seekers on Clapham Park than others. The problems that will not just be dealt with by dialogue are those that Social Services put that are vulnerable (mental health, drug addition and so on). Social Services don't provide back-up support. The [drug] dealers take over. People are people. There will be crooks and undesirables too. The undesirables will ruin it for the rest. The Portuguese are the group here that get the most flak. Some heavy drug dealers come in amongst them, more so than other groups ... It's creeping up to Clapham Park from Brixton and the other [Town] Centres. They will be a bigger problem to deal with because they are more organized.'

The estate is classically residualized and an area of last resort. None of the people I spoke with said that they chose to live on Clapham Park and all expressed the desire to move away. For the most part they were transferred from less desirable properties elsewhere or simply allocated housing there by the local authority. All the respondents were vocal about the poor and rapidly deteriorating condition of their housing, particularly on the west side.

Expressed housing grievances are exacerbated by the perceived negligence on the part of the neighbourhood housing office. None of the respondents had anything positive to say about the housing office or about Lambeth council in general. As one woman commented:

> 'Lambeth ...are a load of w*****s. Shamefully and criminally neglecting Clapham Park. They want to make it into a ghetto and that's what they've been doing. I felt that. I think it's conscious on their part: the people they put on here (to contain us), we're not important, we've never had any respect from anybody until New Deal and then we're still fighting for that respect. I think we've just cracked the ice. "We're not important, we don't count, so why bother?" Most people think that way. Anti-Lambeth. I've never met anybody yet say a good word about any member of staff. I wouldn't of thought that Clapham Park is worse than any other estate.'

Most agree that the housing on the east side is structurally sound but in desperate need of major investment for maintenance and repair. There seems to be a stronger attachment to place expressed by residents on that side. These properties are older and many of the more elderly and long-standing tenants reside there. The feeling is that if offered the chance, a lot of people on the west would quite happily move away and support some form of demolition and rebuild.

There is a distinct lack of social, community and economic facilities on the estate. Local shops are few and far between. The majority of residents interviewed bemoaned the lack of community spirit in the area, explaining that no one cares or looks out for each other any more in an increasingly selfish world. People tend to keep to themselves, and in the absence of suitable public areas and meeting places tend not to interact for mutual benefit beyond a nod of the head or a quick Hello. As one respondent elaborated:

> 'I hate living here. It's a notorious neighbourhood – the drugs, the prostitutes ... With the repairs it's ridiculous. Last year, July, there was a shooting incident outside my house ... I don't feel part of this neighbourhood, there's no community here, no togetherness, no one trusts each other. I do feel isolated, but there's nothing I can do. I feel excluded from lots of things – there's nothing to do here, no social things. If you had money you can go to all sorts of places, have a better lifestyle. Poor people don't consider themselves poor. [But] the poor gets poorer ... Clapham Park don't offer anything for their tenants. I don't speak to my nearest neighbours because of the drugs, they're still there, you can't report them because the police won't protect you.'

Not all lone mothers were resigned to a life dependent on benefits, although the ones now working were claiming beforehand. All the long-term unemployed men were resigned to a life of benefit dependency, increasingly sceptical about their chances of ever finding work with the passing of time. As with the Ethelred, all the respondents from minority ethnic groups expressed conformist attitudes through acceptance of the main cultural goals and means of society. As one lady originally from the Bahamas and resident in the UK since 1988 revealed:

> 'I went to school in the Bahamas, and then in London I did a degree in political science at Richmond College (I wanted to go into politics). I have no professional qualifications and for the last seven years I haven't worked since I got pregnant with my first boy ... [Before] I was always working ... always wanted to be a diplomat – that's why I chose a politics degree. Because of my children, my career then became to look after them ... With a regular job you can plan ahead, you can have insurance and things ... this way you only have enough to make ends meet. You have less privileges; just on the edge.'

Certain trends are apparent regarding strategic change over time and the strategic role of the neighbourhood. The strategies adopted by the people from minority ethnic groups were relatively stable, as they tended to express the same conformist attitudes about work and welfare when they entered the country as today. The slight modifications that have occurred are arguably less to do with a rejection of their conformism but rather creeping dependence and resignation when faced with certain problems finding work and fully integrating into British society. The underlying desire to work and enjoy financial independence from the state remains. The strategies followed by the long-term unemployed men are also relatively stable over time; all are dependent on benefits and rather resigned to their predicament. Incapacity Benefit received by some of these men takes on long-term strategic significance, mobilized as a way-of-life where formal job opportunities are few and far between. While all the lone mothers adopted a calculating strategy at some point during their motherhood, evidence suggests that individuals are re-entering the labour market and undertaking paid work. Where re-entry was possible these women were benefiting from active support structures, either through new co-habiting or visiting partners or through local support networks. Those women still excluded from work were increasingly resigned to a life dependent on benefits and sceptical about entrusting other people to care for their children. As a 37 year old divorcee and mother of three children stated:

> '[Now] I'm not looking for employment. The thing is I've been out of work for so long that nobody's going to pay me a fortune ... all the bills ... who's going to employ me and pay enough to pay all that? Even if you get a full-time job you don't get Housing Benefit and Council Tax relief. Only if you work part-time. I think it's defeating the object. I would love to be at work ... the positive thing [about being out of work] is that I get more time to be with the children. I don't fully trust people to look after the 'litt'lun'.'

While noting that the neighbourhood does not provide many positive resources, there are perhaps two areas where the neighbourhood assumes strategic importance. The immediate locality is vital for those lone mothers who have withdrawn from the labour market in order to raise their children. They are reliant on social support for their survival, especially in the absence of fathers. Second, for certain residents, problems of deprivation, exclusion and neglect serve as a spur for active involvement in community politics, as with the recent New Deal for Community initiative. Other people utilize the neighbourhood for activities like drugs and prostitution.

Conclusion

Findings from a number of in-depth, semi-structured interviews with residents from the Ethelred and Clapham Park estates in the London Borough of Lambeth were presented in this chapter. Evidence from practitioners and activists involved in the improvement of those estates was also presented. The research in London did not find evidence for a pronounced core–periphery 'neighbourhood effect'. As residualized council estates at the interface between redistribution and reciprocity spheres, with the redistribution sphere dominant, this observation is hardly surprising. While problems of low-income, deteriorating housing and social isolation afflict all three groups of respondents on both estates, experiences of and strategies towards exclusion vary among those groups. On both estates, long-term unemployed men were the most difficult to access and most likely resigned to their exclusion from work and to a life dependent on benefits. Women were more easily accessed and willing to talk candidly about their lives and experiences. Respondents from minority ethnic groups were more likely to display more conformist attitudes regarding education, work and welfare. In general, very few respondents spoke of positive, stable and enduring marital and emotional bonds with partners. Almost all lone mothers interviewed felt that the vocation of child-rearing was a justifiable reason to quit the world of work and focus on building familial bonds, sometimes within wider social webs in the reciprocity sphere. Interviews with residents on both estates revealed a paradoxical attachment to the immediate locality because of a relative lack of choice in determining housing mobility. While resources, facilities and activities are severely lacking in both neighbourhoods, people tend to make the best of a difficult situation in the absence of viable alternatives. Experiences of deprivation, problems of loneliness and deteriorating housing combine to produce areas that are increasingly marginalized, offering breeding grounds for vice, drugs and other informal survival strategies. The estates also provide socio-spatial conditions that nourish a degree of political contestation among residents to avert further deterioration and address possibilities for change.

Despite clear similarities based largely on the dominance of the redistribution sphere and elements of strategies rooted in the reciprocity sphere, certain specificities distinguish the two estates. Proximity to central London, in view of the Houses of Parliament on the opposite side of The Thames, provides a more integrated feel on the Ethelred estate, at least in terms of access to central city facilities. The estate represents an enclave of deprivation in rapidly gentrifying surroundings. Within the context of Lambeth, Clapham Park is more peripheral, located at a greater distance from the city centre between Brixton, Clapham, Balham and Streatham town centres, a kind of 'non-place' (Augé, 1995). People tend not to venture to the city centre for goods, services and activities, preferring to draw upon more local resources, adding to the socio-spatial isolation. While certain residents from both estates engage eagerly in political activism, in the context of the demised Project Vauxhall initiative on the Ethelred and the New Deal for Communities on Clapham Park, different perspectives on the neighbourhood underlie their activities. Whereas romantic notions of working-class solidarity, historically associated with memories of Lambeth Walk, form an important strategic element within Ethelred's antagonistic neighbourhood politics, similar historical imagery is not mobilized on Clapham Park. Rather, the problems and difficulties increasingly evident on the estate are utilized by activists to raise awareness and support claims for substantial investment, upgrading and improvement of the neighbourhood for its inhabitants.

Due to greater pressures on the economy and housing market, the more distinctive role for council housing, the inaccessibility of more of the housing market to people on low-incomes and the pressure of demand for council housing and other rented housing mean that, in practice, it is more difficult to negotiate movement between properties in London than in Birmingham. As a consequence, poorer London households have less choice on the housing market, are more likely to leave if their circumstances improve and are more inclined to feel trapped. It would be misleading to suggest that only poor people live in London's council sector. Housing quality and levels of over-crowding and sharing are lower in the council sector than in the private rented sector. Council sector waiting lists tend to be very long in London and have generally not declined significantly over time. Taken in the context of more concerted council sector residualization, on the one hand, and the wider political economy of fiscal scarcity, 'stock transfer' and gentrification on the other, the distinctiveness of the London case comes to the fore.

With regards to implications for policy, I recognize the problems associated with 'best-practice' and transferability through international comparison. Contextual variation, among case studies at neighbourhood, city and national levels, in organizational, institutional and political terms, severely limits the extent to which so-called 'success-stories' in certain places can be feasibly replicated elsewhere. It is, therefore, important to draw attention to general themes for policy that cut across all case studies. One remarkable finding from the London research is the widespread breakdown in stable marital bonds among the residents of both estates, presenting a sharp indication of the stress placed on relations of reciprocity in poverty neighbourhoods (contrast with the Naples case). Support for people with this predicament through targeted activities at local associations is a priority in London.

Overall processes should be conceived in the context of path-dependent neoliberalization, where pressures for state withdrawal and market integration are playing out differently in diverse welfare regime contexts. Despite the contextual variation, neoliberalization is directing cities and their neighbourhoods concertedly towards the market-exchange mode of integration, threatening the viability of redistribution and placing stress on relations of reciprocity. Policy-makers require sensitivity to the changing balance between market, redistribution and reciprocity spheres at various scales in order to enhance the likelihood of successful policy interventions, whether spatially targeted or socially generic. An appreciation of the wider urban political economy, moreover, would augment the capacity of intervention for effective and lasting change, particularly when combined with strategic alliances with all relevant stakeholders including residents (Beaumont *et al.*, 2005).

In conclusion, I claim that despite growing socio-economic disparities between those people integrated into mainstream society, and those excluded, historical and institutional specificities prevent deprived neighbourhoods in London, like the Ethelred and Clapham Park estates, assuming more extreme 'ghetto' characteristics (Darden, 1995; Rex, 1988; Wilson, 1987). Institutional legacies of the postwar welfare state in the UK alongside deindustrialization and gentrification in London explain a large part of the distinction. Additional conceptual, theoretical and empirical analyses of relations between welfare systems and institutional specificities, on the one hand, and in-depth sociologies and politics of poverty on the other, would help clarification. On a final note, our findings suggest that if neoliberalization continues unchallenged, a degree of convergence with US poverty neighbourhoods might result. New neighbourhood politics based on progressive strategic alliance among all relevant stakeholders, including residents and, at the very least, alternative policies for social inclusion where residents are central to decision making, are a matter of some urgency.

Notes

1. Interview and statistical data were acquired through the URBEX project between 1999 and 2001 with Chris Hamnett at Kings College London. The author would like to thank Ronald van Kempen, Alan Murie, Maarten Loopmans, Katleen Peleman and Pete Somerville who commented on earlier drafts. Responsibility for the final version naturally rests with the author.
2. While recognizing this trend, it is not the intention to create a 'tenure fallacy'. The greater concentration of deprived people in the council sector does not mean that all council tenants are poor.
3. For some critical observers, especially within the council, the outcome was the direct result of the 'Save Ethelred Homes' (SEH) campaign that mobilized sufficient local support on an anti-commercial development ticket. For those sympathetic to SEH's arguments the housing stock on the Ethelred was structurally sound but in desperate need of investment for proper maintenance and repair. If properly maintained, local housing would be more than adequate for those residents wishing to stay.

10
Birmingham: Narratives of Neighbourhood Transition

Peter Lee, Alan Murie and Riette Oosthuizen

Introduction

Economic and social changes and the policies adopted by a succession of governments have left British cities more unequal than their counterparts in other European countries (Musterd *et al.*, 1998). The postwar welfare settlement in Britain had been significantly eroded before 1979 and was further weakened by neo-liberal policies after 1979. Consequently the differences between key features of the British welfare state and the more generous welfare states elsewhere in Europe increased. The UK is left not with the liberal welfare system suggested by Esping-Andersen (1990) but with a very unevenly developed, hybrid, welfare system with elements both of universal redistributive and liberal approaches (see, e.g., Murie, 1997).

Birmingham is a major regional industrial city with strong international links. It has gone through a major period of adjustment but the finance and services sectors remain relatively underdeveloped and international migration has a much smaller impact than in London. Previous studies have described some of the distinctive features of spatial and social polarization in Birmingham and links with housing (see for example Lee *et al.*, 1995; Lee and Murie, 1997). Lower income and especially lower income ethnic minority groups in Birmingham are not concentrated in the rented sector in the way that they are in London. The low-cost homeownership sector plays a significant role in housing deprived households and older inner city housing as well as slum clearance and peripheral council estates house the poorest sections of the community.

Birmingham

Birmingham is the second city in the United Kingdom with a population of just over 1 million. It is an industrial city, an industrial revolution city and a city of immigration – initially migration from rural parts of England and subsequently, from Ireland, Scotland and Wales and then the British Commonwealth.

The city has been associated with strong municipal government and is the home of the modern party system and big city politics in Britain (see Briggs, 1952; Sutcliffe and Smith, 1974). The enthusiasm with which the city tackled urban housing problems generated a very large stock of council housing which remained of a higher standard than most of the private sector through to the 1970s. The high quality of this stock was crucial to the characterization of urban conflicts within the city – most notably, Rex and Moore (1967) in their classic portrayal of conflict and competition to enter the council housing stock. In the 1970s older, inner city neighbourhoods of mixed tenure and private rented housing played a key role in housing newer residents to the City and ethnic minority groups who were excluded from council housing. New migrants accessed the most dilapidated, privately owned housing. The established white population who left for higher quality housing elsewhere no longer valued much of this. The housing they left behind was low priced and owner occupation among minority ethnic groups was associated with easy access, preferences and discrimination over council housing. Subsequently the concentration in particular areas was enhanced by a preference for living in the same neighbourhood as other households with family links, similar cultural traditions and faiths.

New patterns of deprivation

As in other British cities, the 1970s and 1980s was a period of major economic, welfare and urban restructuring. In Birmingham the process of deindustrialization, the decline of manufacturing, rising unemployment and increasing social polarization has been fully described elsewhere (Spencer *et al.*, 1986). The advantage associated with council housing was also eroded as the most attractive council housing was sold to sitting tenants (Forrest and Murie, 1990; Murie, 1975). Previously privileged labour market and housing market situations were no longer the focus of competition. Ironically the owner occupied housing that was bought by ethnic minority households excluded from council housing was now generally a sector of advantage.

The map of deprivation for Birmingham at the turn of the century shows new patterns of segregation in peripheral and inner city council estates, as well as the mixed tenure, inner city neighbourhoods previously associated with deprivation. As council estates became less the subject for competition, they developed different dynamics. While the earlier movers to these estates stayed in houses that met their aspirations, later cohorts saw them as staging posts and places to move on from. The rented housing stock became marked by high rates of turnover and voids. Mixed tenure estates, areas of obsolete private sector housing, and increasingly residualized council housing were unlikely to form these privileged neighbourhoods of choice and were affected by lack of demand rather than competition.

The council housing estates associated with deprivation were of different vintages, with different types of dwellings, different histories and different locations. Many high-rise estates had a high proportion of one and two bedroom properties, whereas most council housing consisted of three bedroom family houses with gardens. Council estates had different levels of home ownership but high-rise and non-traditional housing estates developed less tenure mix (Jones and Murie, 1999). Some council estates had substantial populations from ethnic minority groups but these were more likely to be Afro-Caribbean households and the ethnic mix in council estates differed. Peripheral estates were more associated with unemployed, and elderly white households, while inner city estates showed a greater diversity, in terms of ethnicity.

The deprived inner city areas were not generally council estates and were the same areas that were deprived before the economic shocks of the 1970s and 1980s. They had dilapidated, substandard housing stocks, with overcrowding and lack of amenities, lack of security of tenure, low investment by private landlords, and populations with low employability and low wages (see for example, Groves and Niner, 1998; Karn *et al.*, 1985; Rex and Moore, 1967). Much of the housing in these neighbourhoods was over a hundred years old and properties were in poor condition and overcrowded. Residents were often home owners, but often with low incomes, family problems, unable to move elsewhere and increasingly affected by poor health (Lee, 2001).

Researching neighbourhoods

The URBEX research was designed to get below this surface appreciation of differences between 'deprivation' neighbourhoods. The central question addressed in Birmingham was whether neighbourhood makes a difference in the experience of social exclusion. Does it make a difference whether you live in a purpose-built council house on a relatively isolated, peripheral but once-privileged council estate that has been affected by a loss in status; or whether you live in older, more dilapidated and patched up housing in a neighbourhood which has long been regarded as a zone of transition? Do these different neighbourhoods, associated with different forms of exclusion and differences in the level of social cohesion, have different resources which benefit some or all of those living there? Can the neighbourhood itself enhance or mitigate exclusion? Or are labour market position and income all important?

The research carried out followed the URBEX programme in two neighbourhoods (Figure 10.1):

- *Sparkbrook*: an inner city neighbourhood of mixed tenure and population with a large, established ethnic minority community. The study area in Sparkbrook was adjacent to the opportunities and services of the city centre.

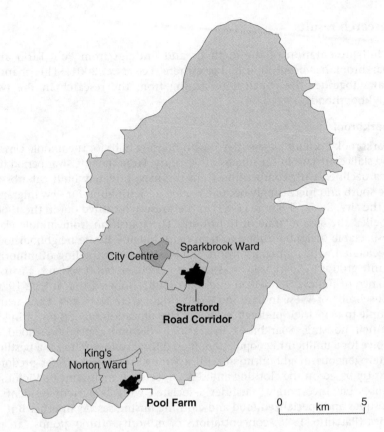

Figure 10.1 Location of study areas in Birmingham

- *Pool Farm*: part of a larger council estate approximately 9km south of Birmingham City centre and adjacent to the Green Belt and expensive private housing. The estate consists of a mix of non-traditional and traditional dwelling types built at a lower density than Sparkbrook and influenced by the planning and architectural fashions of the 1960s.

These two deprived neighbourhoods have different legacies in terms of housing tenure, design and class and ethnic composition, local facilities and resources and political activity. The research enables us to move beyond this perspective in two ways. We carried out in-depth interviews with long-term unemployed persons in both neighbourhoods and can refer to how the neighbourhood made a difference to households experiencing long-term unemployment. The narratives provided by these and other interviews in the two neighbourhoods highlight the different attributes of neighbourhoods identified by local residents.

Research results

A full presentation of the methods and findings from Pool Farm and Sparkbrook has been published elsewhere (Lee *et al.*, 2001). This chapter draws together the conclusions arising from the research in the two neighbourhoods.

Sparkbrook

Sparkbrook's origins are associated with housing built for the middle classes and skilled artisans in the nineteenth century. From the inter-war period the area declined with competition from the new, privately built suburbs to the south and increasingly became a popular destination for new migrants to the city. Rex and Moore (1967) in their research carried out in the 1960s labelled the area a 'zone of transition'. The transition from middle class 'respectable' neighbourhood to temporary lodging house neighbourhood accelerated with immigration into the area. The channelling of minority ethnic groups to Sparkbrook was seen as a problem but it was also a consequence of policy. Henderson and Karn (1987) showed that in the 1970s households of West Indian and Asian origin were less likely than white people to have their preferences met in the allocation process operating in council housing. Sparkbrook increasingly became a neighbourhood of choice for a multiethnic population. It established a new status as a bustling heterogeneous neighbourhood with a strong cultural character predominantly based on the clothing and service sector. It maintains its Victorian houses but incorporates facilities associated with its current residents – mosques and specialized food and clothing businesses. As in other British cities (Ratcliffe, 1996) concentrations of minority ethnic groups can no longer be adequately explained by the discriminatory practices associated with bureaucratic housing allocation but these are still a contributory element, explaining residential patterns.

The households interviewed in Sparkbrook reflect the design of the study in terms of employment, ethnicity and household structure. At the same time they reflect the role of this neighbourhood. Sparkbrook has a high proportion of ethnic minority households and the interviews reflect this. Lone parents are not a major group within the population, partly because of the nature of the neighbourhood and the community, but different ethnic minority groups and households in different positions in relation to the market are well represented.

The in-depth interviews carried out in Sparkbrook show significant differences in the way that households experience exclusion and integration. However, the overwhelming impression is that the categories themselves (lone parenthood, membership of ethnic minority groups, long-term unemployment) are not homogeneous with common origins or experience of exclusion. At the same time, with the exception of refugees, most households in each of these categories had a similar experience of the welfare state and redistribution associated with the benefit system. Those long-term dependent on benefits did not regard the benefits as particularly constraining and did not refer to any great complications in relation to benefit. Those in low paid employment faced a more complex set of regulations, but still did not see these as central. Refugees faced a much harsher regime with very limited cash payment and received vouchers which both limited and stigmatized their situation.[1]

People in Sparkbrook had a different experience of welfare state services other than benefits. This particularly related to schools. Families with children made use of the educational system, and some of their aspirations for the future related to the quality of the education provided. Critical comments related to schools were made but were not common. Those working in schools in the area, however, felt that it is difficult to move beyond the bad image of inner city schools created by the press. This had a knock on effect on teacher recruitment in the area. According to a head teacher in the area some parents preferred to send their children to schools outside the area as they expect better quality education in schools without a dominant ethnic minority population. This reflects an expectation that standards are lowered where language barriers play a large role. The other major area of redistribution relates to housing provision, but in Sparkbrook there is a great variety of housing circumstances with some households owning their property, others renting from family and others renting from different social landlords.

Households were excluded from participation in the market, by a variety of factors. Women in particular were excluded because the brunt of childcare responsibilities fell on them – especially if they were lone parents. Others were excluded because of low skills and employability or illness and disability. There were further exclusions which relate to gender roles within the family and language difficulties. Finally, there are exclusions related to age. Refugees were totally excluded and not able to work without breaching their status. There were also people temporarily excluded from the labour market or in low-paid employment. For these groups exclusion related more to job insecurity and quality, the potential for promotion and getting a better job. These aspects related to skills, employability and employers' practices.

Sparkbrook residents had different experiences of reciprocity, particularly related to length of residence in the UK and to family status. At one extreme there were households that benefited enormously from family support and active exchange systems. This was most apparent among British-born ethnic minority households whose families were well established locally and who had strong family and friendship links.

At the other extreme, refugees were the most isolated section within the community. They had no right to work and were also excluded from the normal operation of the welfare state in that they had a separate voucher system which segregated them from other people receiving state benefits. The refugees interviewed had a short history in the area and were unfamiliar with the neighbourhood. They did not have family and kinship links in the area and were unfamiliar with services and facilities. Nevertheless, because they were in an area with a high proportion of ethnic minority households and because of the diversity of cultural and religious facilities, they felt relatively comfortable in the area. They were eager to adapt to their environment, although they have a fatalistic view reflecting their experience.

Lone parents were relatively isolated without strong family and friendship links and little contact and support where kinship links existed. Lone parents were generally excluded from the market because of childcare responsibilities and lack of (suitable) job qualifications. They were wholly dependent upon welfare benefits and made considerable use of other state services especially for their children. The neighbourhood tended to be familiar: most had a significant history in the area and regarded shops, buses and access to the city centre as presenting a resourceful environment. Although they were more isolated than other groups, there was no comparison with the situation of refugees. Some, however, had a sense of hopelessness, a fear of crime and a sense of being trapped. Some strongly desired to move away and escape from the area and some were forced into various illegal coping strategies (such as shoplifting).

The non-British-born ethnic minority households who are unemployed or in low paid employment had less robust family and kinship networks but made substantial use of voluntary organizations and the faith community. These particularly included households with larger families. Those in employment were more likely to have been long-term residents with more support and were more familiar with the environment. There was generally a distinction between this group and British-born households from ethnic minority communities. The non-British-born group had more problems over language and less supportive family and kinship systems. Consequently they made more use of voluntary organizations rather than the family. They used local services, especially those available in their first language. The area was attractive because these services existed. The cultural affinity, the big Asian community, the accessibility of shops and places of worship were all extremely important and provided robust support systems, albeit of a slightly different nature than for the British-born ethnic minority community. Particular issues within this population related to gender: the language skills and roles played and expected of women. In this sense the non-British-born group had a distinctive set of factors contributing to exclusion and the coping strategies adopted. They had lower expectations than the British-born group with their ambitions related to the next generation and their own strategies to adapt to their circumstances. As with the British group there was no great urgency to leave the area, but for different reasons: cultural affinity and local facilities were important rather than family and familiarity with the area.

Pool Farm

Pool Farm, like many other estates in Britain, was built in the 'fifties rush' typifying 'modern monument(s) of municipalism' (Campbell, 1984: 33, 47). It was built as good quality public sector housing but the area quickly declined and vandalism, violence and disorderly conduct have been associated with the estate for many years. The design of the estate is typically modernist, based on the concept of separation of vehicles and pedestrians, high rise buildings and vast open spaces that remains un(der)claimed by residents. The estate is designed around a series of cul-de-sacs not intersected by any main through routes with the effect that circulation of people through the area is minimal. People enter the estate only if they live in it or have specific reasons for visiting. Supportive facilities and services on the estate are minimal. These physical characteristics are overwhelming and it is difficult to escape the feeling that the estate is cut off from the rest of Birmingham.

The estate was originally one of three adjacent estates built by and managed by the council. New residents were largely white working class families – mostly moving from private rented accommodation in inner city areas. Pool Farm had been in general decline over a number of years and has suffered from under investment while regeneration money went to the city centre and inner city (NDC, 2001).

In Pool Farm we completed interviews in the categories identified in the URBEX programme but also to reflect the neighbourhood. We did not seek out household types that were highly unusual within the neighbourhood. Consequently, we completed very few interviews with ethnic minority households – Pool Farm has a low ethnic minority population and was regarded as unsafe by many ethnic minority households. The experience of social exclusion in this neighbourhood is reflected through households from the white community, especially lone female parents and people in different employment situations.

The lone female parents have some strong elements in common. Very few had a long educational history, the majority were currently unemployed because of child care responsibilities and disabilities. For these reasons finding employment was either impossible for the time being or very difficult. Very few of the lone parents had a history of family relationships that were stable and supportive and most had little or no contact with parents. Very few had continuing contact with partners and few men seemed to play a significant role in child care. Most of these young women were housed in social rented housing.

Beyond these factors the lone female parents category breaks down in two significant ways:

- Five of the lone female parents received additional benefits related to some form of disability and this disability status has a significant impact on current ability to work and long-term coping strategies.
- Some of the single mothers came to the area by choice because they knew the area or had family or friends in the area, while others arrived as a consequence of being allocated emergency housing because they were homeless because of family or relationship breakdown.

While all of the lone parents interviewed had been in the area for a considerable period of time, the different circumstances determining their original move to the area are important.

Lone female parents in Pool Farm were more dependent upon the state and services provided directly by the state than in Sparkbrook. Their dependency on state benefits was just as great but, in many cases, there were more complicated arrangements because of either disability or complicated family and living arrangements. There was also a greater dependency on state housing and the references to family and kinship support or to wider voluntary organizations and services were fewer. The quality and extent of local services from shops to buses was much more limited and problematic. This is not to argue that support networks did not exist, but they were more based upon friendship and neighbouring rather than family and more related to a small number of formal support arrangements provided by the state and the voluntary sector. Lone female parents, however, adapted to their circumstances. While some did not expect them to change many were keen to change their circumstances by accepting training opportunities.

In many ways the long-term unemployed had a similar set of circumstances to the lone parents. Although they had different ages and household compositions, they had similarly low skill levels and low employability. Their dependence on the state in terms both of income and housing was similar to lone parents. Differences in circumstances related to age, gender and household composition. There were more references to support from family members than among lone parents, but otherwise the overall impression is of a similar set of circumstances, reflected in residents' own views that 'most people in the area are in the same boat.'

In Pool Farm a much more uniform pattern of exclusion and integration emerges than in Sparkbrook. It is associated with a peripheral estate with a limited range of services, relatively isolated with poor facilities of shops and transport, with a greater dependency on a less dense and diverse layering of services: predominantly provided by the state and, to a lesser extent, voluntary organizations.

None of the residents were particularly attached to Pool Farm. People were acutely aware that they lived in an area with a poor reputation and were stereotyped by it. Again, this was more apparent than in Sparkbrook. While Sparkbrook was recognized as having an ethnic minority population, it was not stigmatized in the same way as Pool Farm and crime and drugs were not so commonly referred to. At the same time there was a more uniform view in Pool Farm about exclusion relating to employment. In Sparkbrook low paid employment and welfare dependency was not always seen as fundamentally unacceptable and aspirations related to the next generation. In Pool Farm similar circumstances were seen as highly unsatisfactory – the strategies adopted included resigned submission and active adaptation but there was a greater emphasis upon escaping from the situation.

This broad picture is also applicable to younger, unemployed people in Pool Farm. This group struggled with low employability and most of them were limited by child care responsibilities and disordered family lives. Some had significant illness. In a more positive sense, the exclusion of this group from the labour market seemed temporary. There was more support (including financial support) from family and friends than among others in Pool Farm.

Comparing and contrasting Sparkbrook and Pool Farm

The research carried out in these two neighbourhoods highlights differences between neighbourhoods and the people living in them. We did not interview perfectly matched samples of households because such perfectly matched samples did not exist. The neighbourhoods have different roles and house different people. Because they house different people the services and facilities that have developed in the neighbourhoods have distinctive patterns. There is a mutual reinforcement involved. The nature of the population contributes to the types of services and facilities which develop locally and the presence of these services and facilities makes the neighbourhoods attractive or accessible to different people: consequently the population that lives there has developed in a different way.

The two neighbourhoods have developed along divergent trajectories with an increasing specialization in who they house and what they offer. Although some of this distinctiveness can be connected to the location of these areas within the city and their degree of connectedness to the rest of the city and the city centre, the distinctiveness between the two neighbourhoods is not simply a product of geography but is rather a product of the evolution of population and services over a longer period of time. Nevertheless, in describing the differences between these two neighbourhoods and accounting for them, it is appropriate to start with the geographical and historical background to the two neighbourhoods.

Sparkbrook is part of the older, inner city of Birmingham. It is has gone through a number of transitions but people living there have good access to different facilities within the city centre as well as locally. They have the capacity to take advantage of choices in relation to schools, transport and housing. In terms of housing there are a mixture of tenures and a mixture of property types. Sparkbrook is a neighbourhood marked by diversity as well as by poverty. The cultural distinctiveness of the area has become a major feature of it. Services such as restaurants, which were developed for the local resident population, have come to be valued by other residents within the city and there is a thriving restaurant quarter that provides employment and income. It reduces the isolation and separateness of the area. While the area has a strong identity with low income households and the Asian community, it is used by other people and is much more integrated within the economy and society of the city. Sparkbrook is an older residential area than Pool Farm but in recent years has benefited from a more sustained pattern of public policy intervention. Urban renewal programmes have targeted the area and provided a steady flow of resources for housing improvement and other investment. This has generated visible improvements in the physical condition of the area and individual properties.

All of this contrasts very starkly with the peripherality and isolation of Pool Farm. Pool Farm is located on the edge of the city and is poorly connected with the city centre. A journey by bus takes up to one hour to connect to the central city zones that Sparkbrook is connected to within ten minutes. Bus services are poor. Pool Farm is not well integrated into the economy and the society of the city. Except for people living there, very few people would visit Pool Farm. There is no equivalent of Sparkbrook's restaurant services and local shops and services are of very poor quality. There is very little employment within the neighbourhood and essentially the only people going there to work are those managing the estate and providing social services for local people.

The geographical and economic isolation of the neighbourhood was not so important when the Pool Farm estate was originally built. At that stage it was seen as providing state-of-the-art, good quality accommodation, vastly superior to the ageing and dilapidated properties in the inner city neighbourhoods such as Sparkbrook. It was attractive to a range of households including affluent, employed, working class households. However, the deterioration of housing quality and changing expectations and aspirations have reversed the attractiveness of these two neighbourhoods. The housing stock in Pool Farm has been neglected and includes unpopular dwelling types. What was once attractive has become very unattractive. There has been no sustained public policy intervention to improve or sustain the attractiveness of the area. Capital programmes have been spasmodic with major estate programmes in 1985 and 1993 and a New Deal for Communities programme currently in place. In between the approach is best described as neglect or managed decline. Lack of investment has been accompanied by deterioration in the levels of income and employment of local people.

As incomes and employment have declined so has the size of the population, with smaller families and more lone parent and single person households. This adds to declining purchasing power which reduces the viability of local services. Local shops are of poor quality because of the low spending power of the population. People with a capacity to travel to local supermarkets do so rather than shop locally. At the same time the local shopping area has developed a reputation in relation to drugs, alcohol abuse and crime. It is regarded as unsafe as well as unattractive, especially in the evenings. All of this contributes to a beleaguered atmosphere. The estate is cut off from the city and some individual households are cut off from an unwelcoming estate.

It is wrong to exaggerate the differences between Sparkbrook and Pool Farm. The interviews with residents and others in these two areas highlight continuities between them. There is fear of crime and there is entrapment in both areas. Poverty and social exclusion are major features in the experience of all households. It would be wrong to suggest that these two neighbourhoods are at opposite ends of a continuum in relation to measures of poverty and market integration. These two areas have more in common with each other than they do with the more affluent parts of the city. However, in respect of other services and connectedness to the city there is a significant difference. Pool Farm emerges as a relatively one-dimensional neighbourhood. It has a strong identity with the public sector, having been built and maintained by the local authority and remaining largely owned by the local authority. Residents rent their property from the local authority and the public sector provides the majority of services within the area. It is, in the final analysis, responsible for the shopping area, the bus services and the majority of the social infrastructure within the area. There is a poverty of private and voluntary sector provision in the area, a lack of diversity and choice and an underdeveloped network of services and cultural facilities.

In stark contrast, Sparkbrook is marked by diversity and is less dominated by the public sector. Although the public sector has provided the essential underpinning to the private and voluntary sector in the area its role is less dominant and there is a richer, more mixed variety of social provision. Public sector housing is the minority rather than the majority and there is a range of choice within the housing market. There is a significant level of owner-occupation and households interviewed as part of the study included those who were owner-occupiers or who rented, often at below market rates, from relatives. There is a diversity of property types, sizes and conditions as well as rent levels and housing costs. Some of this enables people to cope with low incomes through different mechanisms than apply in Pool Farm.

In Pool Farm rent levels are relatively uniform and the state housing benefit system is the principal mechanism for assistance with housing costs. There are problems associated with this system as well as clear advantages. In Sparkbrook some households are exposed to this same system, but others have different assistance with housing costs or have lower housing costs because of differences in ownership and control. The greater cultural and social mix in Sparkbrook has been associated with the development of a much greater diversity of social provision. There is a greater range of organizations providing services for the community. This ranges from a greater mix of shops and restaurants and the location on a major arterial route means that people who do not live in the area make use of these facilities. There is greater spending power supporting these businesses and services than is associated with the local resident population. At the same time the shops and restaurants reflect the cultural diversity within the area and people interviewed referred to the availability of doctors and dentists and other services where language differences were easily overcome. There was provision made by different faith communities and the overall impression is one of mix and diversity, a layering of social provision and a much richer environment than in Pool Farm.

Again, the position should not be overstated. Simply because there is a richer infrastructure of social provision does not mean that everybody's circumstances are easier to cope with in Sparkbrook. Nevertheless for many households, the diversity of provision is a key element. Even for the most isolated of groups – refugees – the cultural affinities within the neighbourhood are a source of security and safety. For people isolated by language differences, the presence of local services that can respond to different language needs is a great asset. For some households, however, it makes no difference and fear of crime and concerns about safety and isolation are just as striking as in Pool Farm. The answer to the question: 'does the neighbourhood make a difference to these households?' is nevertheless clear. It does not make a difference for everyone but the diversity of provision in Sparkbrook ameliorates the problems experienced by households more than do the services provided in Pool Farm. The neighbourhood ameliorates problems but does not remove them. In Pool Farm the services available locally do less to ameliorate problems.

Following on from this overview, it is important to ask some more specific questions about the particular groups included in the interviews. Do neighbourhood differences, as described above, ameliorate the circumstances for each of the groups of households included in the study to the same extent? The evidence presented suggests that this is not the case. Each of the groups are themselves diverse, and as we have emphasized, we are not always comparing like-with-like. The very fact that people live in different neighbourhoods reflects different histories and trajectories and households falling into the same category in terms of employment or ethnicity or household structure are often only comparable on this one dimension. The differences between them in relation to other factors are often profound. We need to be very careful about assuming that households in the same category are, therefore, similar rather than being more marked by differences.

Leaving this aside, however, it would appear that lone parents are less affected by where they live than the other groups. Lone parents appear to be among the most dependent upon state benefits and the most excluded from the labour market because of child care responsibilities as well as low employability. At the same time they seem to have the weakest family and kinship links. Both in Pool Farm and Sparkbrook the overwhelming impression is of isolated households with weak networks and dependency upon state provision. Although lone parents in Sparkbrook comment on the resources available within the area the fundamental similarity of experience is striking.

Where then does the difference in neighbourhood impact most? The conclusion here is complex. There are some groups present in Sparkbrook but not in Pool Farm. Refugees and non-British-born ethnic minority groups – especially those for whom English is not their first language – are not evident within Pool Farm. Arguably this is because such households find it more difficult to survive in Pool Farm. Again, the argument becomes a circular one. Because of the difference of facilities different types of households can cope. This increases and maintains the demand for diversity of provision and encourages the continuation of the very things that enable people to survive: so there is a self-reinforcing process, which impacts upon the character and nature of the neighbourhood and impacts upon the households living there.

The discussion then leaves us with a middle group of households: ethnic minority households that are British-born, the long-term unemployed and young people. Although we can emphasize the different attractions associated with the two neighbourhoods with the greater sense of security and safety for ethnic minority groups in an area which has greater cultural diversity, there are other factors which are associated with these middle groups. Two things are particularly important. First, differences in housing practices and approaches and second, differences in family and kinship networks. To some extent this discussion is around the reasons for people moving to and living in different neighbourhoods. In Sparkbrook this is associated with the greater mix of tenure, the extent to which family and friends provide housing and stronger family and extended family links. Fewer people referred to homelessness and to housing without choice. In Pool Farm there was a greater likelihood that people were housed as homeless and housing practices are more dependent on the public sector. What we are identifying is different responses to housing need and different ways of seeking to obtain housing. For this middle group neighbourhood makes a difference and affects coping strategies. The sorting of people between the two neighbourhoods reflects different practices in housing and housing choice including the propensity to stay because local neighbourhood services are valued.

Conclusion

The research carried out as part of the URBEX project in Birmingham has focused on two deprivation neighbourhoods. The underlying objective of the research that was carried out was to assess how far neighbourhood made any difference to the experience of households in specific deprived categories. From the research it is apparent that people who appear to be in the same economic or income position are living in very different environments and have different experiences of social exclusion. Some differences derive from proximity to a city centre but are more than a geographical issue; neighbourhoods have different resources and the research demonstrates the significance of a range of resources provided by public, private and voluntary sectors. Where deprived people live affects their experience of low income or unemployment. Although this appears to have less significance in relation to lone parenthood it initially establishes that the processes and dynamics of social exclusion have an important neighbourhood dimension.

Deprived households living in different parts of the city can access a different range of resources: but ultimately, does this matter? Does it assist in the coping strategies of households or does it make the experience of deprivation any different? The evidence presented here suggests that it does. The variety of different facilities and services available enables households, who feel that certain providers are unwelcoming, to find an alternative. Where there is a richer, more diverse, variety of services it is more likely that people will find coping strategies that are effective. Where there is a more limited range of resources a more limited range of households are likely to be at ease with the services available. Others are more likely to seek to leave or to become disillusioned or disgruntled.

However, at this point, it is important to acknowledge that the argument becomes somewhat circular. The reason why there is a greater diversity of services is both cause and effect of the characteristics of population. People move to and choose to stay in areas where they can cope. They are more likely to not move to or to move away from areas where their coping strategies cannot be effective. Consequently, the differences in population and the differences in facilities are interlinked. The characteristics of the neighbourhood are a product of who lives there and the people who live there are a product of the neighbourhood. This is an important conclusion in relation to debates about the significance of neighbourhood. It supports a view that neighbourhood differences do matter and where people live will make a difference in the experience of social exclusion, but it also suggests that neighbourhoods are path-dependent, that their services and facilities develop over time and will develop partly as a response to the needs of communities themselves. This perspective also begins to explain the different patterns identified in this research between Berlin and Birmingham. In these two cities the peripheral public housing estates studied have very different characteristics and in Berlin these overcome the disadvantages associated with location to a greater extent than in Birmingham.

In cities where there is significant segregation or polarization deprived households live in different kinds of deprived neighbourhoods. There are neighbourhoods which serve a largely transient function catering for households on their first arrival in the city – often for a short period until they move on. Neither Sparkbrook nor Pool Farm fall exclusively into this category. Other neighbourhoods are much more stable but serve different functions for different groups within the population of the city. What emerges is that the resources associated with neighbourhood, affect the experience of social exclusion. The processes of exclusion that impact upon households differ in different parts of the city and an important dimension of exclusion relates to neighbourhood resources. Some of this is a code for the nature and quality of facilities provided by the welfare state and relates to the sphere of redistribution. It also relates, however, to the sphere of affiliation or reciprocity where the strength of family and kinship networks and the nature of those networks are associated with neighbourhoods. Finally, neighbourhoods themselves provide different access to the market both in terms of employment and consumption behaviour. The access to city centre opportunities is different between neighbourhoods. In that sense the location and the characteristics of the neighbourhood are an important component part of social exclusion. Rather than being seen as a separate agenda that impacts on social exclusion it is important to see neighbourhood and the resources associated with neighbourhood as an integral component of processes of exclusion within a dynamic concept of social exclusion.

The conclusions that we have drawn from this study are that, in Birmingham, where you live is important. There are different resources available and differences in the policy approaches adopted. The residents of Sparkbrook and Pool Farm fall under the rather leaky umbrella of a rather ungenerous welfare system. The significance of neighbourhood and of distinctive locally provided welfare services, whether these are provided through the mainstream welfare state, the voluntary sector or special initiatives, is partly because the umbrella leaks. If the state welfare system was more redistributive and more universal the differences identified might be less important. There would not be the same need for a diverse and dense pattern of differentiated services. At the same time those households most directly affected by the provision of services by the state, especially those in public sector housing, are victims rather than beneficiaries. The poor quality of services reflects the lack of consistent spending over a long period.

This perspective on the British case is important. A stronger welfare state and a less damaged public housing sector would almost certainly mean that the experience of people living in different parts of the city would be less important. The need for neighbourhood-based policies would be reduced because needs would be met through general provisions. In our view, however a stronger welfare state and public housing sector would not remove the need for neighbourhood-based policies altogether. For those households most dependent upon welfare benefits, including lone parents, a more generous welfare regime would probably reduce the significance of where you live. However, for other households, and especially households not so wholly dependent on welfare provision, neighbourhood would continue to be important. Households most at risk from racial discrimination would continue to have a greater sense of security and safety in an area which has cultural diversity; differences in housing preferences and practices and differences related to family and kinship would still mean that some neighbourhoods would provide better support than others and that coping strategies would differ.

The housing dimension of this is crucial. The low social esteem in which council housing is now held and the disadvantages associated with the tenure contribute to attitudes in Pool Farm. The task of modernizing and raising the status of council housing is extremely difficult in Britain. The delegitimation of the sector is the consequence of a sustained process of economic, social and policy change and it may be impossible to reverse it. If this is so, there are elements of neighbourhood difference that are difficult to remedy through general welfare state measures. This argument is about the relevance of strengthening general welfare state provision rather than about neighbourhood-specific interventions. However, if the view is taken that the history of British cities leaves a legacy that would not be easily addressed through general welfare measures, then some neighbourhood differences would only be addressed through targeted neighbourhood policies – in the Pool Farm case through policies that would channel resources to change the standing of the neighbourhood.

This kind of discussion could imply that problems are greater in Pool Farm than in Sparkbrook but we should be cautious about such a conclusion. We have established that there is a different experience of social exclusion in these two neighbourhoods, but we have not established that one is better than the other or indeed that it is better irrespective of the other circumstances of households. The implications are that there is a need, however generous general welfare state measures are, for policies that respond to the strengths and weaknesses of particular neighbourhoods. While the weaknesses in Pool Farm appear greater, there are issues specific to Sparkbrook – housing conditions and quality, segregation and lack of choice, low expectations and access to educational opportunities and jobs. There are also particular issues in relation to refugees and households with different backgrounds and resources.

Finally, the research demonstrates that the opportunities and policy options related to particular neighbourhoods are path-dependent. Any policy responses in the short-term have to take into account the legacy resulting from previous policies. The legacy in British cities is highly differentiated. Households most exposed to social exclusion live in very different environments. Where this is the case policies designed to benefit those exposed to social exclusion but taking no account of the different environments in which people live will be deficient. If they assume that the Pool Farm case is the norm they will embark upon policy action that will be less relevant in Sparkbrook and vice versa. Although the extent of difference in Birmingham is a product of wider welfare state systems and economic and social histories, the conclusion about the need to be sensitive to the particular environments and resources of different sections of the community is likely to hold for other cities in Britain and elsewhere.

Note

1. This refers to arrangements at the time of interview rather than those that have emerged subsequently.

11
Naples: Unemployment and Spatial Exclusion

Enrica Morlicchio and Enrico Pugliese

Introduction

The processes of deindustrialization that have produced an increase in unemployment and poverty in many western cities, have also affected Naples, the third industrial city of Italy. As a result, the number of workers in the manufacturing sector has practically halved in only 25 years, declining from 70,000 in 1970 to just over 32,000 in 1996. However, it would be inadequate to refer exclusively, or even primarily, to recent phenomena of industrial decline to explain the tendencies toward social exclusion; they have, indeed, a much longer history.

Phenomena such as welfare dependency, ethnic segregation and disruption of family and community ties, that are often at the basis of sociological models for the study of social exclusion in many European cities and metropolitan areas (see Mingione, 1996), are also less relevant. The historical lack of economic activities, with their implications in terms of unemployment, underemployment and informal employment, are much more important. Families are poor not because they are isolated from their relatives and social networks, but because they suffer from an imbalance between income and number of consumers. This imbalance is not related to high fertility rates, but both to the high youth long-term unemployment rates and to the exclusion from the labour market of the less-educated married women. The latter is not related to the absence of social networks of support, but precisely to the fact that they are so strictly embedded in family networks and obligations. The lack of care services also plays a role (Saraceno, 2002).

Another peculiarity of the Neapolitan case has to do with the chronic housing shortage and the recent mismanagement of the public housing stock. The present housing distress – contrary to other cities whose analysis is included in this volume – can be explained only partially in terms of economic and industrial decline. Naples has always been characterized by a difficult housing situation, made worse by housing speculation and by the lack of urban planning and discipline, which culminated in the 1950s and 1960s. The existence of an unsatisfied demand for housing, throughout the course of the 1960s and 1970s, gave rise to mobilizations for better housing, which in some cases concluded with the illegal occupations, particularly of unfinished dwellings.[1] These waves of illegal occupations provoked a 'war among the poor' between the illegal occupants and the future tenants to which the dwellings had been allocated. In some cases, the protest of the homeless has been infiltrated by the 'camorra', the Neapolitan organized crime, which was seeking both to increase social consent for some of its activity and at the same time to acquire some of the buildings. Nevertheless recent intervention of local political and legal authorities has been able to bring these buildings back into public properties.

The existence in Naples of a situation of endemic and often acute material poverty – at the level of both labour and housing market – implies a re-contextualization of the commonly used categories of analysis. Therefore, it would be inappropriate to rely on the models developed by sociologists to study the 'new urban poverty', such as the spatial mismatch, racial prejudice or individual trajectories. At the same time we need to be very cautious in considering poverty and precariousness as an expression of a 'Neapolitan model of survival' to use Ada Becchi's words (Becchi, 1989, 2001) based on a precarious equilibrium guaranteed by a combination of activities of a purely redistributive nature, such as the recycling of second hand or stolen goods, or alternatively, transfer of resources resulting from the welfare system. As we will try to illustrate in the next section, which deals with the socio-spatial structure of Naples, such a representation is indeed often a misleading description of events containing many anachronistic elements. And biased representations do not help to understand how social exclusion develops, how much it is an individual or, conversely, an area-based problem and, finally, how important are large-scale changes in the labour market and in the economic and physical structure of the city.

The socio-spatial structure of Naples and the selected neighbourhoods

In comparison with other European cities, Naples has a rather mixed socio-spatial structure, mainly because vertical segregation is still very common. With the exception of the few relatively homogeneous bourgeois and middle class residential areas in the western city (Arenella, Vomero, Posillipo), we can identify three significant areas of popular settlement that we define by their socio-economic characteristics, respectively, the 'City of Allum', the 'City of Ford' and the 'City of Wilson' (Figure 11.1). The name of the first of these comes from an old and important study by the British sociologist Percy Allum (1975) in which he analyses the structure of political power and of clientel relationships in the city at that time. Allum underlined the character of precariousness and backwardness of the economic structure, particularly in the historical centre of Naples. Since then, the informal economy has changed character, rising from the almost exclusive production to cover the needs of the local poor, towards small scale productions mainly oriented towards the market. Nevertheless, the main elements characterizing the Naples of Allum – the neighbourhoods of the historical centre – are the prevailing informality of job relations and the precarious or casual nature of employment. The level of unemployment is relatively high, although not the highest in the city, but the type of employment is of low quality. In this regard, craft and service activities, in addition to retailing businesses, are the basic activities in the historical centre.

The 'City of Ford' is, or rather was, limited to one specific area of Naples: Bagnoli, where a steel mill was erected in the 1910s in an early attempt to industrialize the South. This was the only district with a vast scale and continuous production activity and with a corresponding stable class of workers. The steel mill is actually being dismantled and has been sold to a Chinese company. Not all the steel mill workers lived in the area. Indeed, the labour basin of the steel mill and of its suppliers and related businesses was the entire city, and thus Bagnoli was a vital part of the city's economy. Furthermore, its social and cultural life was strongly determined by the enterprise system of Bagnoli, especially its temporality. This 'City of Ford' was a 'company town' within the city. This industrial reality was unique in Naples, even if other industrial districts of a certain importance were present, as with the oil refinery of San Giovanni a Teduccio in the South East zone or the Alfa Romeo plant in Pomigliano d'Arco (a municipality in the northeast periphery of the city). Bagnoli is in many ways similar to the 'rust belt' in the USA, with evident decay of industrial buildings and the presence of an unemployed working class. Changes in this situation result from urban renewal and the residential and tourist appreciation of some places in the area, like the beach and some better housing estates. However, these changes have nearly no impact on the victims of the deindustrialization process, who are not seen as a priority within the renewal process.

The third representative case is the 'City of Wilson', presenting some characteristics of 'hyper ghettoes', of the highly distressed areas of American cities. In Naples, these areas are located in the northern periphery. They were developed in the 1980s as residential areas for the working class and have rapidly deteriorated and became impoverished neighbourhoods, with a strong concentration of disadvantaged households. They were conceived as monofunctional residential zones for workers of a Fordist industrial city, based upon the large-scale enterprise. In other words, these new housing complexes had been planned with reference to an employment structure that has never been prevailing in Naples and that in recent years has been reduced to an even more marginal role in the city. In this regard, we deal with a form of settlement that responds to the need of providing

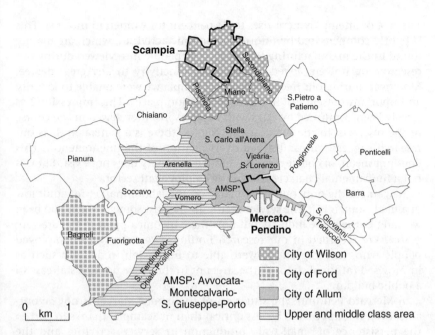

Figure 11.1 Some elements of the socio-spatial structure of Naples

housing to the low-income families, but that has never been able to guarantee them better occupational conditions. The weakness of the productive structure of the northern districts goes together with the concentration of social problems, especially the lack of occupational prospects for young people and consequently, the risk of escaping towards drug use and criminal behaviour. The social services and infrastructure that might break such a vicious cycle, in particular the schools and other supporting institutions are outmostly deficient in the 'City of Wilson'.

Following the URBEX research design, we selected two neighbourhoods to study the spatial dimension of social exclusion, namely Mercato Pendino in the historical centre and Scampia on the north fringe of the city. Mercato Pendino is an example of the 'City of Allum', while Scampia is part of the 'City of Wilson'.[2]

The labour market as main arena of poverty reproduction

The labour market is particularly relevant in the context of Naples to understand processes of social exclusion. The selected neighbourhoods display relevant differences. The situation in Scampia is the most worrying. According to the 1991 population census, the unemployment rate in Scampia reaches 60 per cent of the active population, a level much higher than the municipal level and, as we will see, even higher than that of Mercato Pendino.

The rate of unemployment rises to 73 per cent for women in the area. This is poorly compensated by informal economic activities, which are mainly found in the manufacturing sector. Indeed, people interviewed during our research are not employed in this kind of activity to any great degree. Moreover, during our frequent visit in Scampia we were unable to identify an important presence of informal production places. This impression has largely been confirmed by talks with key-persons interviewed in the course of the research. In the literature on Naples, there is a general and, as our research suggests, an unjustified overvaluation of the phenomenon. This does not mean, of course, that the hidden economy does not exist. But it is not a fundamental characteristic of the employment sector.

In Scampia the only option available on the labour market for adult low qualified women is in the service sector. In the past some of them had been working in the glove industry but now these income opportunities are very scarce. We recorded in our research findings even cases of unemployed people who, in a big effort, were able to find a job in activity such as improvised informal shops in the street or in the space under a staircase in a public building.

In Mercato Pendino, the situation of the labour market is not favourable, even if it appears to be less critical than in Scampia, thanks in part to the persistence of small-scale production or service activities and the greater extent of the informal economy. According to the census data, manufacturing employment in the historical centre dwindled from 25,000 in 1981, to 14,000 in 1991. Fifty-two per cent (over half of all people available for work) are unemployed. If we consider just the female component of the labour force, the rate of unemployment rises to 56.2 per cent. However, the marginal position of the women of Mercato Pendino is not only a matter of a high unemployment rate, but also of other authentic processes of exclusion or barriers to employment that maintain them in the role of 'housewife': the number of women who declare themselves to be housewives (7,339) is as much as six times higher than the number of employed women (1,263). This results in a prevalence of single-income families or families of irregular working poor with a high risk of impoverishment.

In Mercato Pendino, some streets have a long established tradition in craft production. In such cases, the ground floors of the buildings are at the same time sales point, workshop and home of the craftsmen. One typical example is that of the 'shepherd-makers' craftsmen who produce and often sell directly the clay figures of the traditional Christmas crib, and who live mainly in the vicinity of Via San Gregorio Armeno. Those involved in the art and craft sector (making plaster figures of San Gennaro, or plastic and paper flowers, or the above-mentioned crib figures) only amount to a few hundred people.

These activities are closely integrated into the neighbourhood because it is nearly impossible simultaneously to relocate the production, trade and housing functions, but also because these crafts have often been handed down from father to son for generations and because the clients are mainly local people. However, the area does not always provide a favourable context for these activities. For example, a survey carried out in 1992 on a sample of 809 owners of craft businesses in the city centre showed that the problems of MercatoPendino most keenly felt by the craftsmen were, in order of importance, the 'request for contribution' from organized crime, mentioned by three-quarters of the entrepreneurs, air pollution and petty crime (Società Studi Centro Storico di Napoli, 1992: 82)

Alongside the traditional craft, some manufacturing and informal economic activities also exist. In Mercato Pendino there is some evidence of leather workshops for the production of bags and shoes generally for large business groups, some of Neapolitan origin (such as Valentino). But most of these businesses are found in the Spanish Quarters (another typical neighbourhood of the 'City of Allum' located just west from the medieval city) or in suburban districts and outlying municipalities. Production and manufacturing regards mainly goldsmiths and other metal working (a whole area in the neighbourhood is known as Borgo degli Orefici, the 'goldsmith village', due to the high concentration of gold and silversmiths and the sales points for gold or silver work). These two broad production sectors of arts and crafts and small manufacturing business, not all of them regular, make up most of the neighbourhood's industrial activity. Part of the population working in these sectors is regularly registered (the official employment rate in Mercato Pendino is 28.7 per cent which means that less than one out in three people of working age is officially regularly employed). Another part comes into the category of the irregular workers or those working in the hidden economy.

Among the illegal activities of the area, the contraband and, particularly the retailing of cigarettes, is today largely in decline. An increased repression of such activity in the past few years has pushed some smugglers into higher risk criminality such as robbery and mugging, and drug dealing, which presents a worrying increase, especially in the Scampia area. More frequently, however, the alternative has been to give up illegal activity in favour of other casual work. In any case, the selling of contraband goods and the related activity, such as selling counterfeit goods or illegal reproduction of video games or music CDs, are only ways to gain some modest income in Naples. The risks related to these types of criminal activities persuaded many young men to give up their activity as soon as they assumed family responsibility to start less dangerous and less risky informal ways to gain some money, such as illegal parking control or to take the more radical decision to emigrate.

The survival strategy of lone mothers, immigrants and the long-term unemployed

Following the common URBEX research design, we have conducted 60 semi-structured interviews in Scampia and Mercato Pendino with single mothers, long-term unemployed men and immigrants. The diversity of ways to reach the poor, in particular the presence of both public and private social services and the recourse to both formal and informal channels, allowed for considerable variety in the choice of interviewees. Nevertheless some bias remains, and will be pointed out in the analysis of the interviews.

In this section we attempt to examine the rich material coming from the interviews with the aim of analysing how the subjects interviewed are able to face the situation of poverty that they find themselves in, and which of the three spheres of integration – market, reciprocity and redistribution – has a more significant role for each of the categories identified in relation to the two contexts studied by the research.

The market

The lack of productive activity at a local level, the lack of employment possibilities in the district and the scarce opportunity even abroad, are translated into the statistical data, such as the unemployment figures that we have examined at the beginning of this chapter. The interviews of long-term unemployed and lone mothers, mainly of large families, have allowed us to document the experience of unemployment as a daily experience in its main aspects. This has enabled individuating life in the forms and factors of a kind of 'emergency income' (income coming from casual work opportunities, sometimes on the margin of illegality). Indeed inevitably, both in Scampia and Mercato Pendino the majority of long-term unemployed people in reality do some kind of working activity to survive. As an unemployed interviewee describes it, 'in Naples we are all unemployed, but no-one is staying without doing anything' (long term unemployed, male, 49 years old, Scampia). Since 'everyone in some ways is doing something' the main question becomes how can we better understand the ways in which these different activities are perceived by the actors that carry them out and conversely how they are perceived by the laws that regulate the labour market. From the interviews it has repeatedly emerged that in the majority of cases they deal with informal occasional activity, often marginal and sometimes invented by the same subject, are used as simple strategies of everyday surviving. The following examples emerged in the course of our research:

> 'I did few odd jobs, such as selling T-shirts on the street but obviously I've never done a day of regular work.' (Long-term unemployed male, 25 years old, Scampia)

'I work as a pizza maker on Saturday and Sunday. In the past I have worked as barman and street vender.' (Long-term unemployed male, 33 years old, Mercato Pendino)

From other interviews a sharp 'skidding' process is clearly observable:

'In the past, before I got married, I made glasses in a glass works. After my marriage I worked as a mason and in the past I even sold notepads and pens as a street pedlar. In this moment I'm not doing anything and I would work even without contributions.' (Long-term unemployed male, 42 years old, Scampia)

'As a boy I did a bit of everything, a mason, a waiter, then in 1970 I went to work in a carpenters, in 1983 the carpenters went bankrupt and all of the workers were laid off in "Cassa Integrazione" (redundancy pay) and then on the mobility list and now I do socially useful work ... to survive (by doing lots stuff) selling contraband cigarettes or going to make removal service and dismantling furniture.' (Long-term unemployed male, 34 years old, Scampia)

Often for the same casual or precarious jobs, when performed by local unemployed immigrants, the worker receives lower payment: 'I'm used to building work; I did it in Yugoslavia. I tell you the truth; here in Naples they give you 15 Euro a day. What can you do with so little?' (Macedonian immigrant male, 26 years old, Scampia)

It is difficult and debatable to consider street sales of t-shirts, paper handkerchiefs or notepads as jobs connected to a real market demand. However, it has also emerged that jobs that meet the demands by the local labour market – wherever there are odd jobs in building, transport, catering, carpentry or cleaning work – all have an unstable nature. There is also lack of respect for norms regulating such working activity in terms of working conditions, pay and pension or other contributions. Furthermore, it is the failure itself in trying to find regular employment that pushes individuals to accept irregular activities, so that it is the occasional, casual or illegal character of such activity which excludes the possibility that with time the work can become stable and can enable both promotion and social mobility. A dynamic of this kind, however, has been found in the case of an immigrant from Senegal, resident in Mercato Pendino who started from an initial situation of casualness and low pay, who has been able to acquire a condition of greater stability both of work and of income.

From the interviews conducted with lone mothers we can argue that the degree of discomfort, but also quality of work are interrelated with their need and more general plans, regards the family in its entirety. In this specific state, the heavy weight of domestic work and the lack of any skills, even basic or traditional skills, makes the opportunity of finding work even more scarce, even among the vast typology of relationships of casual work that require low qualifications. This contributes to reduce the expectations such individuals have in relation to work. This can be seen in our research, for example, in the statement of an illiterate widow, who's last search for a job involved going to the local church asking to do the cleaning:

> 'I don't ask much of a job, I can't afford to, what I would like is to wake up in the morning and not have to worry about what to do to get by. Of the same kind is the fact that I can't read or write and I can't leave the house because of the children, what else can I do besides clean?' (Lone mother, 37 years old, Scampia)

A particularly interesting aspect that has emerged through the interviews of the lone mothers is the contradictory factors of the process of creating identity in relation to the labour market (see Dubar, 1991). Even if the working history of many lone mothers, both from Scampia and Mercato Pendino is characterized by frequent and often premature experiences of work, the casual character of the work makes them perceive their employment state with difficulties and pessimism:

> 'The work I have always done and I'm still doing is not regular, I do not know if this means that I am unemployed.' (Lone mother, 38 years old, Mercato Pendino)

> 'I never had regular work, and then I have always been unemployed. I have done just housewife work.' (Lone mother, 33 years old, Mercato Pendino)

> 'I work in a supermarket, but I'm not regular ... Then I am unemployed.' (Lone mother, 40 years old, Scampia)

Nevertheless, the desperate condition in the labour market could, in some ways, drive the condition of people getting used to a situation in which the majority of women still seem to be actively looking for a job. This represents without doubt an expression of the phenomenon of female emancipation, one related to the processes of female mass education, which happen in the South, despite the inefficiencies of the school system and the high rate of truancy among the poor. Young women who have satisfactorily completed their compulsory education are different not only from young rural housewives in the 1950s (when in the South the work for females was, on the whole, rural work) but even from their aunt and mother and the typical urban housewife of the past with a low level of education and destined – for lack of opportunities, and for prevailing values – to be the family mother and nothing else besides. The lone mothers interviewed in this research are not all with a low level of skills and qualifications. Among them are many with a high level of education. It might be argued then, that indeed the system of values and the whole of the cultural model that form the basis of the labour market are very different in respect to the one of the previous generation – even if the impact of the deindustrialized economy and labour market can frustrate these expectations and values, and lead to a closure of this more liberated perspective, which in turn can lead to a closure of horizons.

In relation, more specifically to the activity of consumption, the evidence suggests that such people are limited to the satisfaction of merely their basic needs. To the question pertaining to what they are obliged to give up by their low income, the most frequent responses in our interviews has been: 'too many things' or 'lots of things' or 'I don't know because I do not pay attention any more to the many things I've given up.' The main problem for the interviewed subjects is how to face the economic expenses with just the income that comes from *work* that is not just insufficient, but discontinuous. The patterns of consumption are shown to be based on some typical priorities. The main part of expenditure is absorbed by the expense of groceries, mainly food, and fixed expenses such as electricity, gas, petrol and public transport. Families mainly tend to make sacrifice in three key areas: in the area of transport, as is illustrated by the fact that no lone mother interviewed has a car, in the expenses for the house, and for clothing. In one case the interviewee has admitted to not always being able to ensure to provide a complete meal for her children, specifying that 'if sometimes we don't have the second course or the fruit, the children understand that they do not complain' (lone mother, 37 years old, Scampia).

In relation to clothing, the reduced capacity to go shopping has obliged the interviewee to get second hand clothes, given mainly by friends, relatives or the families where the woman does the cleaning, or else from the local market, which provide cheap but low quality clothing. The research has also shown that such families are not easily able to do work for self-consumption, because this kind of integration of the income is only possible in a rural context and not in urban areas such as Scampia and Mercato Pendino.

The compression of consumption in the case of immigrants is often tailored to the area of sending money to their country of origin, much more than in the area of meeting the needs of a family with scarce resources, as with the long-term unemployed and lone mothers of Naples.

Reciprocity

In this section we now turn to the second sphere of integration, taking into consideration the factors associated with reciprocity. The first important dimension of reciprocity that we need to address is the exchange of resources both in monetary and non-monetary terms, inside the family network. The majority of those interviewed – with the exception of the immigrant subjects which belong to the first immigrant generation and are much more isolated from kinship networks – declare to have frequent relationships, in particular, with close direct relatives such as their mother, brothers or sisters. Even the relationships with friends are described as quite frequent. They are often made more stable in Mercato Pendino by the fact of being born and brought up in the same district, and in Scampia by having shared some moment of political organization or activity.

The majority of the interviewed subjects also declare themselves as being enclosed in quite dense networks in which all the subjects know each other very well. The problem is that subjects that are a part of this network have very little to offer in terms of useful contacts, or in information relative to vacanct jobs, or material resources to exchange, because they generally share the same condition of unemployment and a scarcity of income. In the interview it is possible to find many examples of the situation of the 'impotence' of strong ties (see Granovetter, 1973).

> 'As far as money is concerned I can't ask my family for anything, my mother brings me shopping once a week ... that's already a great help ... they have so many problems themselves.' (Lone mother, 44 years old, Scampia)
>
> 'I often take the bus and go and see my mother ... I eat with her ... she gives me a smoke ... my mother sells contraband cigarettes ... sometimes she gives me a bit of money.' (Lone mother, 45 years old, Scampia)
>
> 'Fortunately we know how to organize ourselves even with little money, but surely in the case of need we would ask for help from relatives even if they also were not very well off.' (Long-term unemployed male, 34 years old, Scampia)

In analysing these statements in more detail, other aspects of particular interest emerge. In the first place, we have to remark upon the fact that despite the over-burdening of the kinship network, help is not denied by the families. It seems that everyone, for what they can, is doing their part. Second, it is mainly the mothers interviewed rather than the father that gives help, from small amounts of money, food, cigarettes, or even giving simple emotional support. In other cases, nevertheless, the personal difficulties that face the same lone mother are multiplied in that they often have to help the married children who also find themselves in a disadvantaged condition. This is shown in the following comments:

> 'My daughter often comes to see me; she lives quite near with her mother-in law ... I look after the children for her ... we eat together ... she doesn't have an easy time of it either; her husband is a drug addict and treats her badly. My other daughter is even worse off.' (Lone mother, 45 years old, Scampia)
>
> 'My married son lives two doors away from me, he lives with my mother, because she has got more room, my son cannot get a house of his own, he is working for a furniture shop, they give him 250 euros a month. When I can, I give a bit of money to him and to my mother too.' (Lone mother, 58 years old, Scampia)

Family, then, mainly through the figure of the mother, is a central component of the survival strategy both of the long-term unemployed and the lone mothers. Nevertheless, having very little to offer, family often functions as 'transmission belts' of poverty. Furthermore it is important to keep in mind that families do not just represent a source of help and emotional support, but even, or indeed especially, as a factor of social control. One of the interviewed women, a young widow who lives with another 11 family members, belonging to four different family groups in a house of five rooms, has expressed with a great deal of yearning the wish for greater autonomy, but this wish is frustrated by her chronic situation of poverty: 'I would like to live by myself, its since I got married that I had this wish, I can't stand it any more' (Lone mother, 35 years old, Mercato Pendino).

The protection given by the community network is very important also for the immigrants, even if it changes according to the community the immigrant belongs to (the diversity among the different immigrant groups does not allow any strong generalization to be made). Above all, the fact that is particularly interesting that has emerged though the research is the existence of relationships of mutual help among immigrants and the indigenous families in Mercato Pendino where the living structure, consisting of houses on the ground floor (the so-called 'bassi') with common public spaces, such as courtyards and alleyways, helps the neighbourhood relationships to develop. To give a concrete example, an interviewed immigrant from Sri Lanka has declared to have sometimes received help from the neighbours both in money to pay the bills or in order to pay for shopping. In another case the interviewee, a Polish immigrant who works as a domestic cleaner, has declared to have given support to people from her building without asking for any money for the service. We can say then, that the class condition and the analogous situation of precariousness, imposes and effects the social relationships – including the degree of solidarity – much more than the effect of ethnic and religious differences.

Redistribution

The unfolding of the sphere of redistribution inside the survival strategy of poor families has compensated in very few ways that are of relevance in relation to the complex weakness of the local system of welfare that reflects the low concern given in Italy to the politics of the fight against social exclusion (see Saraceno, 2002).

In that which specifically concerns the unemployed and the lone mothers, state intervention is limited to a sporadic and typically insufficient income support. The very limited nature of this support, in relation to other EU countries, while avoiding the severe situation of welfare dependency, provides few opportunities in escaping poverty. The response that we have received suggests that generally welfare does not enable any real improvement in the life of the very poor people in Naples. Indeed, if the opportunity of full time school allows the lone mothers to lighten the domestic burden and the basic income she receives allows her to give some improvement to the house and pay bills, we cannot conclude that these measures actually help to solve the problem. On the whole, it is clear to those interviewed that the benefits do not change the trajectory of life, even though they represent an important form for material and psychological support. Indeed, some of those interviewed have been very sceptical about the possibility of using these measures indefinitely (and justifiably so when such measures are characterized by great uncertainty), while others emphasize the fear of not being able to escape the condition of state assistance. It is necessary, however, to specify that the interviews had been done at a time of great transformation of the local welfare system, changes characterized by a measured effort to intervene to a greater degree in favour of the very poorest families and this transition does not allow us to fully evaluate the capacity of the sphere of redistribution to tackle impoverishment in the long run. We have to underline, however, that we found within the interviews, a clear awareness by the interviewees of their rights and entitlements:

> 'I believe that it is my right to be taken into consideration, considering my state of difficulty.' (Lone mother, 38 years old, Mercato Pendino)

> 'Services are lacking in giving you information ... many fear the social workers. For instance, my daughter is scared that they can take her child away ... in reality they haven't got much time because there are too many of us.' (Lone mother, 36 years old, Mercato Pendino).

Inside this general picture of the weakness of the local welfare system, the situation of immigrants is even more problematic as the following comment underlines: 'I have never seen any social workers; every now and then some council workers come to count us and then go away again' (Macedonian immigrant, 41 years old, Scampia).

Indeed, the specific services for these groups are still very lacking. On the other hand, services already available are scarcely used by immigrants, both because of a lack of information and because of the lack of engagement or indeed documentation necessary for having access to the service itself. By this, it is not just a problem of language or having a legal right to remain. For example, it is difficult for an immigrant, even if legal, to have the medical support because for this document you need to have residence documents, which are only available to those that have rent documents, which are not generally made available to those with informal housing contracts.

An important source of help for all the interviewed subjects is represented by the Catholic parish church or organizations such as 'Caritas'. In this case, it is mainly emergency help, such as providing medicine, pasta, occasional jobs and the payment of bills. It is important also to note that in Scampia, the parish priests have typically been very active in denouncing the condition of life in the area, often pushing the public institutions to intervene in the area.

The role of spatial location in reinforcing social exclusion dynamics

As previously stated, one of the objectives of the research was to find out the way in which individual and family strategies differ in the two contexts, which are different in terms of the forms of urban settlement and the social composition of the population. This question regarded the variable that is a key to the whole research, and which we can define in general terms as 'space'. We posed the question of how an event such as poverty, clearly of a levelling nature, could be absorbed and metabolized in the two neighbourhoods. To state that two different neighbourhoods 'explain' different trajectories and strategies would be an obvious conclusion in many ways. We have, therefore, attempted to understand how the different demographic, social and economic structures of Mercato Pendino and Scampia prevent or encourage individual and collective strategies for exiting the condition of poverty.

The interviews that we have done suggest that the experience of unemployment in Scampia, where employment opportunities represent a scarce resource and where almost everyone is poor, is more destructive and suggest less chance of a way out of poverty than that of Mercato Pendino. Indeed, the lack of work opportunities impoverishes the network of social relationships and this limits the channel of access to the possibility of finding work, even if in a reduced way the situation exists in other neighbourhoods. The generalization seems to hold that unemployment generates further unemployment, and this generalization is the case both for the local population and, at the same time, the immigrants. 'Obviously one who lives in this district has more difficulty in finding a job because the contacts and the knowledge are missing, here everyone needs but no one can help you' (Macedonian immigrant male, 41 years old, Scampia).

We need to observe, furthermore, that while the situation of Scampia is shown to us to be difficult, the social representation of it – the image of the district that prevails in Naples – is surely much worse. This problem is not exempt from further concrete and severe implications (that is, the bad image of the district and its population is reflected in the social conditions and the prospects of the inhabitants). In the interviews, many different cases of discrimination were reported, from access to work and services, to difficulties concerning school.

The presence of organized criminality further serves to feed the bad image of the district. Undoubtedly in a district like Scampia, for poor families it is easier to get into a network of illegal activity such as the one connected to the drug dealing and the illegal arms trade. It is, of course, simplistic to make recourse to the absence of prospects or to the influence and availability of such opportunities afforded by the district, to explain the large number of people involved in such activity in Scampia. The explanations are however much more complex and concern factors such as socialization and the lack of perceived opportunities in education (see Pugliese, 1999). But within the fieldwork, we found some paradigmatic cases such as a family with many difficult problems that in the end found themselves involved in drug dealing and other petty criminality in order to survive.

> 'It's easy to fall into drug dealing when you find yourself with your back against the wall. And so, in our economic situation, we have gone down the easier road so to speak, because in fact we sink more and more ... the district has influenced our choice of dealing drugs because there are many opportunities to get into the network ... there are many points of reference.' (Lone mother, 42 years old, Scampia)

Often in cases where the legal system places someone in prison, other members of the family are affected, making it even more problematic to search for a new and different equilibrium inside the same nucleus. The deep-rootedness of organized criminality, while representing an income source, more frequently also represents a big obstacle for the development of every kind of legal activity. Indeed robbery, extortion and blackmail of different kinds discourage any entrepreneurs, big or small, from investing in the area. This does not represent a problem just for Scampia, but for the entire city and metropolitan area of Naples. In Scampia, however, the problem is much worse and a concrete example of this kind of factor is illustrated by the following comment:

> 'Sometime ago I had problems with my work, in the sense that they asked me for money to keep on doing transport, the amount they asked me was so high that I would have had to give up working, it has been a very difficult period, I didn't know what to do or who to go to, in the end I understood that they were interested in giving the transport to someone else that they protect and so we found a deal, I can transport just in determined areas and leave the others to them. Anyway, since then I lost a bit of money.' (Long-term unemployed male, 49 years old, Scampia)

It is evident then that in this type of environment, those who suggested self-employment and entrepreneurship risked seeming merely rhetorical and strongly punitive in comparison with the unemployed people that would need to take the risk.

The great majority of those interviewed from Scampia are in a condition of illegality with regerd to payment of the rent, the consumption of electricity and water. This situation does not just concern the immigrants that live in shantytowns, but even families. To give some examples:

> 'I do not pay the rent.' (Lone mother, 40 year old, Scampia)
> 'I don't pay rent electricity or water bills.' (Lone mother, 42 years old, Scampia)

'We haven't paid rent for years.' (Lone mother, 40 years old, Scampia)
'Luckily we don't pay rent, electricity or water bills.' (Long-term unemployed, 34 years old, Scampia)
'I should be paying rent but I don't.' (Long-term unemployed, 43 year old, Scampia)

While in Mercato Pendino we found many of the problems present in Scampia, starting from the difficulty of finding a job, they seem less exasperated due to the higher level of social cohesion and the major functional complexity of the district.

(Do you like living in the neighbourhood?) 'It is all right' (What are the positive aspects of the neighbourhood?) 'Mutual help, we always help one another out'. (And the negative aspects?) 'None'. (Long-term unemployed, male, 39 years old, Mercato Pendino)

(What are the positive aspects of the neighbourhoods?) 'Mutual help'. (Long-term unemployed, male, 33 years old, Mercato Pendino)

Among the advantages quoted more often, there is the possibility of acquiring goods at low cost in the numerous wholesale shops within the district.

'I'm very well here in Mercato, even if its not quite a nice district … the positive aspect are that Mercato is a quite central district, with a little bit of everything for everyone, its a district in which you can live decently even with a few coins in your pocket.' (Sri Lanka immigrant, female, 36 years old, Mercato Pendino)

'Its a quiet district, it isn't very expensive and I manage to live well here … there are a lot of shops so there is a wide choice of goods to buy. There are things to suit all pockets and that's positive for people like us who don't earn much.' (Senegalese immigrant, male, 30 years old, Mercato Pendino)

If on one side the presence in the district of numerous markets, and wholesale shops and the area's centrality represents some undoubted advantages, on the other hand, the immigrants and the lone mothers interviewed underlined the danger represented by petty criminality and by the absence of space for the socialization of young people and, in particular, children, apart from the inappropriate space of the streets.

Last but not least, for Scampia we have to mention an aspect of the environment that relates specifically to the urban configuration of the district and that reflects some of the contradictions of the popular public housing at the time in which the district was built. There is the presence of large areas built without respect for urban planning criteria and without a sufficient quantity of space reserved for green. This has resulted in the existence of an enormous empty space which is unusable, and at the same time, a lack of space available for effective socialization. The possible agoraphobic reaction that this can cause leads to a negative sensation even with the simple first observation of the district. But the large-scale dimension of this abandoned space even makes it dangerous to pass through this area to

get to the underground station. From this point of view, the urban structure of the district adds to the other forms of negativity in determining a
negative effect that leads to the segregated and homogenous character of
the district itself.

Concluding remarks

In Naples, the removal of low income families from the historical centre
and their resettlement in the periphery of the city and in the hinterland –
due first to the creation of new neighbourhoods on the basis of the public
housing programmes (Law 167) and followed by the rebuilding programme
after the earthquake of 1980 with exclusive residential function – has
favoured the concentration of social groups with high risk of social exclusion in specific areas of the city, and particularly in the North East belt. The
most disadvantaged districts are in the urban periphery, unlike the model
represented by the American inner city area. Another specific characteristic
of Naples, from this point of view, is that no single ethnic quarter within
the city can be identified. The spatial distribution of immigrants in the city
is fairly homogeneous, up to now there is no evidence of concentration of
ethnic groups. Immigrants are more present in the historical centre of the
city (like in Quartieri Spagnoli) were they can find cheap accommodations
very close to their business or their work place, but also in the upper class
neighbourhood (like Posillipo, Vomero) as they often live as domestic
workers in the same house as their employer. The more casual, precarious
and segregated accommodations are found mainly in the rural area outside
the city.

Although racial and ethnic variables do not have the same prominence
in the socio-spatial configuration of Naples, our analysis seems to reinforce
Wilson's ideas on the concentration effects (which emphasizes the depar-
ture of higher-income people from impoverished ghettos). This is on the
basis of the hypothesis that attributes more importance to the characteristics, of a specific area such as the mixture of residential and business use,
in explaining socio-economic outcomes. In the case of Naples, indeed
such concentration effect is more related to the processes of forced internal mobility of the poor families towards the marginal districts than to the
mismatch between the skill of central city residents and the demand of
employers in knowledge-intensive service industries in the suburbs
described by Wilson. Even if the incidence of unemployment in Naples is
high in both Mercato Pendino and Scampia, in the latter case it is exacerbated by the social stigma of belonging to a district well known for its
deviant behaviour and by the higher weakness of the informal networks,
which produce effects of concentrations, and not to the movement of
middle classes and economic activities from these districts as in the case
described by Wilson.

Notes

1. The earthquake of 1980 brought this problem to the attention of local and national institutions, and the public in general.
2. In Bagnoli, households receive redundancy income to offset the loss of regular income. In addition, much of the public housing has been sold to the tenants and is passed on by the parents to their children. Thus income and housing stress in the Fordist city is not (yet) comparable to those in the Allum and Wilson cities.

12
Brussels: Neighbourhoods as Generators of Integration

Christian Kesteloot and Pascale Mistiaen[1]

Introduction: Deprived areas in Brussels

When the geographical and historical context is taken into account, spatial concentration of poverty in Belgium can be expected in three situations: working class areas in the nineteenth-century inner city belts, in industrial regions, and recent social housing estates. The second one is not relevant in the Brussels context.

As a result of the industrial revolution, the working class neighbourhoods form compact inner city areas with a large supply of low quality housing. Today, this housing constitutes a residual private rental sector (residual because it lies at the bottom of the quality range of housing and because one applies for accommodation in this sector when excluded from all other sectors). In the early 1960s, the rapid extension of the middle class and the suburbanization process required the attraction of guestworkers to replace the Belgian population in the lower positions of the urban labour and housing markets. These neighbourhoods are thus characterized by relatively high levels of immigrant concentration. The residual housing sector is partly related to suburbanization, since many abandoned inner city dwellings were converted into rental flats. The selective character of both suburbanization and the housing market processes results in the concentration of the poor population in these inner city neighbourhoods. Deindustrialization and post-Fordist polarization further explain the impoverishment of the population in these areas. In Brussels, this inner city deprived zone is sometimes called the 'poor crescent'. It encompasses nearly one-fifth of the population and since the end of the 1970s it is a clear-cut concentration zone of poverty and immigration (Kesteloot *et al.*, 2002).

In Belgium, most social housing estates are unproblematic. Belgium has never had a postwar housing crisis and the very much-encouraged promotion of self-construction made large social housing building programmes unnecessary. Interwar estates, frequently garden city-like, provided small, but decent housing and are still much appreciated. The few deprived social

housing estates fall in two categories. Some are part of a postwar slum erad-
ication programme and are built on the land released by the clearances in
the inner city. Most of these are high-rise to buffer the substantial land
prices, which have to be calculated into the rents. In other cases, high-rise
estates are built in the periphery. They reflect a poor interpretation of the
postwar ideas on modern urbanism. In Brussels, social housing represents
7 per cent of the total housing stock, but around 55 per cent of the households are eligible. As long as social housing was attractive because of low
rents and fairly good quality, the housing associations could select the
better applicants and reject the others into the private rental sector.

However, the economic crisis of the 1970s and the processes of polarization of the past 20 years have gradually transformed these neighbourhoods
into new areas of deprivation: the traditional clientele of the social housing
association, the lower middle class and the working class, have a much more
fragile financial situation than before the crisis. A second explanation is a
shift in the allocation priorities: devolution of social housing policy in the
wake of the Belgian federalization process has generated a restrictive application of the allocation rules (away from political clientelism) by the Regions,[2]
which facilitated access to social housing to vulnerable population groups.
Basically, access to social housing is limited by an income maximum that
varies according to household size. Allocation is based on a set of social priorities and the order on the waiting list. In Brussels, these rules give precedence
to single parents, disabled persons, households in substandard housing,
young families with at least two children and to a lesser extent, the elderly.

Finally, high-rise estates rapidly lost their attractiveness. In order to avoid
empty dwellings and income losses, housing associations, who tended to
let to Belgians with a regular income, had to accept less desirable applicants. In many cases, high-rise estates offer large apartments to compensate
for the very limited supply of these in the private rental sector, and they
consequently attract large households from immigrant origin. In their eyes,
access to these high-rise apartments is considered as a significant improvement to their housing situation. To other tenants and to the outside world
it sometimes appears as a ghettoization process and it unleashes debates on
social mix.

The Marolles and Kersenhoek in the Brussels context

The peripheral social-housing estates, although never as large as in other
countries, and the poor crescent of Brussels, reflect the neighbourhood contrast sought after in the URBEX research design. However, the selection of
the neighbourhoods had to take earlier similar research in Brussels into
account (Figure 12.1). In a study on the spatial dimension of poverty,
funded by the Belgian federal government, two much larger inner city areas
had already been studied, namely Kuregem, in the central part of the poor

200 Kesteloot and Mistiaen

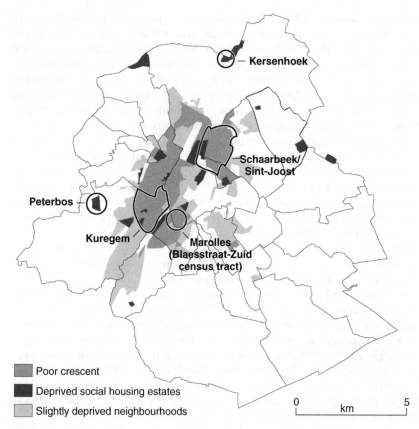

Figure 12.1 Types of deprived areas in Brussels Capital Region and studied areas

crescent, and the northern part of the crescent in the Schaarbeek and Sint-Joost-ten-Node municipalities (Kesteloot *et al.*, 1997). In fact, the URBEX research design largely built on this experience. The same project generated a study comparing both areas with the most emblematic high-rise social housing estate of the city (Peterbos) and a suburban camping site with permanent residents and a poor rural hamlet (Meert, 1998; Meert *et al.*, 1997).

In addition to Schaarbeek/Sint-Joost and Kuregem, the Marolles is also an interesting case of an inner city deprived area. In a study on deprived areas in the 17 Belgian metropolitan regions (for a full account see Kesteloot *et al.*, 2001), it ranked twelfth among 638 poor neighbourhoods on a synthetic deprivation index.[3]

The Marolles is a traditional concentration area of poor people with an important supply of furnished rooms and lots of charities. Because of this tradition, poverty and survival have a much more Belgian flavour than in the other cases. Since the twelfth century, the Marolles has been a repository for the ill and homeless, at that time outside the city walls. The industrial revolution brought the lower working class into the area and a high densification of housing through speculative building. Perceived as a centre of social revolt, the neighbourhood was systematically eroded by large restructuring projects since the end of the nineteenth century, like the building of the Justice Palace in the eastern part of the neighbourhood in 1866. In the south, the Sint-Pieters hospital, originally located on the spot of the early medieval leprosy area of the city, was rebuilt into Brussels' main public hospital. The west was likewise eroded by the construction of the north–south railway connection, started in 1911 and finished after WWII. Within the neighbourhood, similar projects affected the physical and social environment. In the middle of the nineteenth century, unacceptable housing conditions and overcrowding justified the construction of the Blaesstraat, in a pure Haussmann style.

Symbolically, the neighbourhood has known the greatest concentration of urban pilot projects since the early 1970s. When an extension project for the Justice Palace threatened the northeast part of the neighbourhood in 1969, the reactions were channelled by the 'Comité Général d'Action des Marolles' an urban social organization that still exists. The Comité anticipated the speculative processes by formulating a renewal proposal, with four main lines: conservation of the building lines and volumes; respect of the existing population; preserving small local shops and industry; and prevention of a too long displacement of the inhabitants out of their neighbourhood. This project was eventually financed by the Government as one of the first pilot projects in urban renewal in 1973. Although the project has been globally successful – there was a perceptible increase of living satisfaction among the inhabitants – , a lower middle class population partially replaced a majority of deprived people. In 1975, the whole Marolles area was chosen by the European Community as a pilot operation area for the 'Struggle Against Poverty'. Today most of it is integrated in the EU Urban Programme and the Brussels Capital Region has chosen the western part of the area for a neighbourhood contract, the main instrument of urban redevelopment devised by the region, involving the production of social and middle class housing, the restructuring of public space and the strengthening of local social cohesion (De Corte, 1996).

The Marolles is widely known for its Flea Market and antiques and attracts well-off people enjoying a kind of social exoticism in shopping, drinking and dining in the area. Since the 1980s this attractivity has given rise to modest signs of residential gentrification, which are not yet altering the social character of the place. However, it seriously altered the retail sector in the area. In the long run, all these operations resulted in a steady population decline. The area counted more than 15,500 inhabitants in 1970, today only 11,500.

Besides Peterbos, the high-rise social housing estate with the most dramatic increase of foreign tenants during the early 1980s and income decrease is Kersenhoek (ranked 104th on the synthetic deprivation index). Developed in the 1970s and 1980s on the plateau north of the city, it offered apartments with multiple rooms, but was gradually disregarded by Belgian tenants after the oil crisis, because the thermal insulation was very bad and the heating costs could be very high. In reaction, the concerned housing association started to allocate apartments to large immigrant households.

The social housing project was initially part of a larger development plan. As part of the Fordist restructuring of the city, an urban motorway was planned to cross the city from north to south (and incidentally it would also cross the Marolles, doubling the erosion effect of the north–south railway connection). A large housing estate, including private and social housing would be developed on both sides of the motorway. The plan was designed according to the functionalist ideas of the time, with high-rise buildings and a lot of green space between them for leisure and travel. However, the project had to be modified several times. The idea of the motorway was abandoned in 1975 under pressure of the Brussels urban social movements. The inhabitants of the neighbouring private flats worried about the arrival of poor people. Their opposition led to the cancellation of three blocks and to the displacement of two social housing blocks further away from their apartments.

Today, the social housing estate counts 800 dwellings divided into 25 blocks. The total population is about 2,000 people. Most of the apartments have one to three bedrooms and a few of them are duplex with four bedrooms.

Significantly, as a consequence of the worsening financial situation of the housing association in the 1980s, an originally planned social centre has been cancelled. This centre was supposed to be a meeting place for the inhabitants, with a bar, social services and several activities for young and old people. This cancellation reinforces the monofunctional character of the estate, in strong contrast with the Marolles. Evidently, two other contrasting features are the absence of any social tradition rooted in the area and the absence of visitors attracted by the amenities of the area. It was conceived as an urban dormitory and both the employment crisis and the changes in the social housing clientele have transformed it into an even more isolated area of the city.

Poor households in the Marolles and Kersenhoek

Without surprise, the three target groups are relatively well represented in both neighbourhoods and even tend to increase over the past decades (Table 12.1). Both neighbourhoods have a high share of foreigners in which the Moroccans dominate. The 1991 census showed that 33 per cent of the

Table 12.1 Some characteristics of deprived neighbourhoods, the Marolles and Kersenhoek in Brussels 1991–8

	Year	Poor crescent	Among which: Marolles	Deprived social housing estates	Among which: Kersenhoek	Other deprived areas	Brussels average
Dwellings built before WWII (% dwellings)	1991	70	59	12	1	69	42
Tenants (% households)	1991	71	89	88	99	73	61
Annual income per capita in €	1995	3740	3200	4860	3420	5850	8000
Single persons (% households)	1998	47	57	49	44	58	50
Single mothers (% households)	1998		9		20		10
Total foreigners (% population)	1981		47		52		24
	1998		48		31		29
Moroccans (% population)	1981		25		18		6
	1998		29		17		7
Job seekers (% population 15–64)	1981		16		23		10
	1991		30		29		15
Unemployment (% active population)	1998	36	43	32	38	25	14
Population	1999	176618	3859	29726	1827	115970	954000

Brussels Moroccan active population is seeking a job, against 18 per cent for all foreigners and 8 per cent for Belgians. The over-representation of single mothers in the social housing estate results from the regional access rules to this housing type. The free housing market regulation in the Marolles yields a share of single mothers much on a par with the regional one, despite the presence of some shelter institutions for this category. Both labour market participation and unemployment rates in the selected deprived areas present alarming levels and changes in comparison to the Brussels average, leaving no doubt about the presence of local long-term unemployed males. However, several indicators depict a male over-representation in social exclusion in the Marolles against a female one in Kersenhoek.

In selecting the interviewees, we tried to respect the three categories as closely as possible. Nevertheless we retained some interviews of persons not directly corresponding to one of the categories. Thus, in the Marolles we have two single women (a pensioned woman born in Brussels and an ex-bargee from Lille). They were merged into the local unemployed category. The same applies to three Belgian single women in Kersenhoek (one is on pension, the two others on disability benefit). In the immigrants group, respectively one and four women were interviewed instead of men. However, only one was without an immigrated husband (a young Greek women living with her disabled mother).

The local unemployed are dominantly single persons (two couples without children in each neighbourhood). But the immigrants contrast quite sharply: six are single persons in the Marolles against no one in Kersenhoek. Conversely, only two are couples with children, against six in Kersenhoek. The classical labour immigrants of the Fordist era are better represented in Kersenhoek, and the recent political and economic refugees in the Marolles.

The single mothers group reflects quite well the diversity of this household category among the poor. We have in both neighbourhoods Belgian, labour migration, and refugee related single mothers, but again with a better representation of the latter in the Marolles.

In order to explore the interview results in a systematic way, we created a datasheet with a set of categorical variables based on common interview questions. Cross tabulations can be visually explored with principal correspondence analysis. We explore the frequencies of interviewee characteristics and behaviour over the two neighbourhoods and the three categories of interviewees (yielding six categories). Correspondence analysis visualizes interdependencies between rows and columns in a scatter plot. It represents rows and columns profiles as points on a common plane. In this case, we explore over- and under-representation of key characteristics and behaviour over the six categories. The centre of these planes represents the average situation. In other words, if a characteristic of the interviewees is evenly distributed among the six interview categories, it will be in the centre of the plane. Similarly, if a category displays the average characteristics of all the interviewees, it will be projected in the centre of the plane. The more a characteristic or a category diverges from this situation of equipartition, the further it will be placed from the plane centre. Categories with similar characteristics will be placed close together in the plane. Finally, characteristics and categories situated in the same direction from the centre are linked by a common over- or under-representation. In order to avoid any misinterpretation, one has to verify if the concerned profiles are well represented on the plane. If the table has more than three rows or columns it is impossible to represent all the row and column deviations in one single bidimensional plane. The successive dimensions embody the largest possible share of the total deviations (called inertia), but when only two of them are selected to span a plane on which rows and columns are projected, some of them can be poorly represented. In that case their position on that plane can be irrelevant (Greenacre and Blasius, 1994).[4]

Causes of exclusion

On the basis of the trajectories of each interviewee, we assessed the causes of exclusion in terms of the spheres of integration. A person can be socially excluded as a result of several processes and thus the causes can be located simultaneously in more than one sphere.

Since the frequency table contains only three columns (exclusion in each sphere), all the deviations can be captured in one single plane.[5] Both spheres of exclusion and categories of interviewees are perfectly represented on the plane. The first dimension represents 82 per cent of the total inertia (Figure 12.2), the second 18 per cent (Chi-square prob: 0.0837).[6]

The first dimension contrasts exclusion from redistribution with the two other spheres. The second differentiates market exclusion from reciprocity exclusion. The categories are differentiated along this first dimension in the Marolles, and more along the second in Kersenhoek.

As a result of the selection criteria (unemployment) all interviewees have experienced exclusion from the market sphere (except a 65 year old Belgian lady in the Marolles living on a small pension). On the graph, this results in the market sphere having a central position respective to all categories. The only people not well covered by welfare are the refugees. As a result, the immigrants and to a lesser extent the single mothers in the Marolles tend to be excluded in the redistribution sphere (position in the right half of the graph).

Both migrant categories are less prone to reciprocity exclusion because of family migration and stronger kin solidarity among immigrants. The single mothers and the local unemployed appear in the opposite situation (but single women incorporated in the latter category partly explain this exclusion from reciprocity).

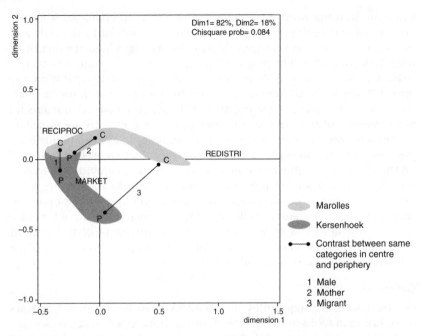

Figure 12.2 Correspondence analysis on causes of exclusion: plot on the first two dimensions

Exclusion from the market sphere alone is most prominent for the Kersenhoek immigrants. The other categories have more complex trajectories, especially in the Marolles (the categories are more scattered in the upper half of the graph).

Within each couple of categories the overall differences between the neighbourhoods is reflected: market exclusion is more important in Kersenhoek and redistribution in the Marolles. In both neighbourhoods, local males are never excluded from redistribution. And in line with the general differences between the neighbourhoods, Kersenhoek locals are more often only victims of market exclusion and Marolles locals from a combination with reciprocity.

To a certain extent, the sources of household income mirror these findings: income from state redistribution (unemployment and work incapacity benefits, pension and minimum income or equivalent social aid) is the most widespread, with only a few exceptions in the Marolles, where some immigrants live from the informal economy. Official labour income is insufficient to cover the needs and usually comes from other household members. Income from informal activities is easier to earn in the Marolles than in Kersenhoek (12 cases against 2).

In summary, exclusion from the market and its compensation by redistribution are general. The notable exceptions are among Marolles immigrants who have access to informal economic activities to compensate for a lack of access to redistribution.

Neighbourhood resources in the sphere of market exchange

Market resources were measured through a set of questions about accessibility from the place of residence. They concern the fact of having worked in the neighbourhood, having an informal job found inside or outside the neighbourhood (in Figure 12.3 referred to as: INFORIN ... INFOROUT) and accessibility of potential workplaces (GOODWACC ... UNKNWACC) on the production side, accessibility of shops for daily goods and for durable goods (GOODDURA ... BADDURA) on the consumption side.

The results show a rather clear correlation between all these elements along the horizontal axis (64 per cent of the total inertia), with good access to market resources on the left and bad access to the right. In general, the Marolles interviewees have a better access to both consumer and producer market exchange, and this appears to be the best for the immigrants of this area. Conversely the effects of the peripheral situation of Kersenhoek and

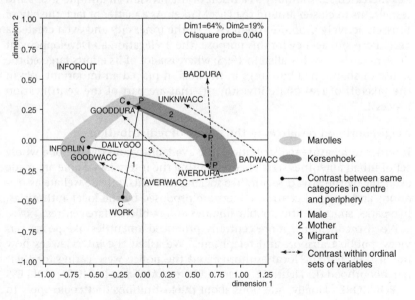

Figure 12.3 Correspondence analysis on resources in the sphere of market exchange: plot on the first two dimensions

its purely residential character affect more the single mothers and the immigrants than the local households. The former have larger households and their larger and more diversified demand is better served for in a super-market than the corner shop. These supermarkets are at least at 20 minutes walking distance from the estate.

The second axis opposes work experience in the neighbourhood and informal labour, especially outside the neighbourhood. This opposition mainly concerns the three target groups in the Marolles. Local males, usually with a long residence in the neighbourhood, have had some work experience there. Informal work is also related to those who live in the Marolles, notwithstanding the fact that such activities are often carried out in other places in the city, because they concern construction activities, farming and domestic help. However, the networks in the neighbourhood sometimes supplied information to find the work. Moreover, the rummage sale provides informal work opportunities (even a Kersenhoek long-term unemployed used to work in the Flea Market).

Even in the centre, single mothers have clearly less market accessibility. On the one hand, the burden of the children makes it more difficult to work, but single mothers in the Marolles also complain about the absence of cheap priced daily goods and of a supermarket in the area. Many shop-keepers took advantage of gentrification and the passage of many city users in the area to raise their prices. Quite probably, the rent for their premises has increased substantially as a result of the pressure of antique shops and restaurants to cluster around the Flea Market. As a matter of fact, the city of Brussels actively promotes the revival of the inner city and even created a very successful agency for this purpose (the 'Délégation au Développement du Pentagone' was installed in 1995; whereas a lot of its efforts targeted the re-use of abandoned buildings in the area, it played an important role in the take-off of real estate investments that are part of the gentrification process).

Neighbourhood resources in the sphere of redistribution

In order to measure redistribution, the availability and the use of a whole set of urban amenities were checked during the interviews. Some are made available by the private sector, like social restaurants, private welfare associ-ations and medical centres. Others are proposed by the local authorities, like parks, sport facilities, public libraries and public welfare centres.

We also considered more centrally produced amenities like postal ser-vices, public transport and telephone.[7] We asked the interviewees how much they felt the local authority and the police were caring for their neighbourhood (In Figure 12.4 referred to as: LALESS ... LAMORE; POLLESS ... POLMORE). Finally, questions about the institutions they could apply to for financial help were included in the analysis (help from private or public welfare institutions).

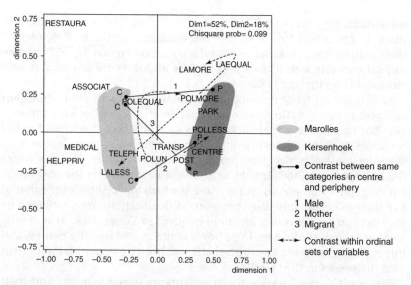

Figure12.4 Correspondence analysis on resources in the sphere of redistribution: plot on the first two dimensions

The separate analysis of the availability of amenities and their actual use did not display any significant differences. In both cases, they show a very clear separation between both neighbourhoods. We consider the use of amenities available in the neighbourhood. The first dimension separates private and public redistribution together with respectively the Marolles and Kersenhoek. The Kersenhoek inhabitants also feel the municipality of Brussels is caring more for their neighbourhood than the Marolles ones. A city alderman is living in the Kersenhoek blocks and takes care of the interests of the inhabitants. Moreover the spatial and social homogeneity of the estate and the action of the housing association helps to see it as a unity and to associate any public care to the benefit of the whole neighbourhood. The social housing association is responsible for the maintenance of the apartments and all collective space inside or outside the blocks. The quality of the maintenance and regular upgrading of the premises encourages its respect. The association has also moved its offices into one of the blocks. It plans to transform the garage of a future building into a hall for youngsters and tries to involve local unemployed in the maintenance works. Finally, it subsidizes a private initiative for children's activities.

In contrast, the long urban struggle tradition in the Marolles involves an antagonistic view of the municipality. The fact that gentrification of the Pentagon is promoted by the city doesn't help to see it as caring for the inhabitants we interviewed. Strangely, the feelings about police interventions do not reflect this view. But the discourses of the interviewees on these matters reveal that opinion on the police very much depends on contingent contacts with it. As a result, these responses are not all very well represented on the first plane.

Among the centrally produced redistribution products, public transport and post offices are also more mentioned by the Kersenhoek inhabitants. One has to remember that these results do not reflect the actual level of resources available in each neighbourhood, but the perception of it by the interviewees. Hence, transport appears somewhat more important to the isolated Kersenhoek inhabitants. The same applies for the post office, although poor households typically use the banking facilities of the post to pay their bills. But very often pensions and allocations are distributed by the post and such incomes are more frequent in Kersenhoek. Also immigrants use the post office for their home contacts and sending money, and this is clearly more the case with the Kersenhoek immigrant families than with the singles in the Marolles.

The availability of several social restaurants in the Marolles and their complete absence in Kersenhoek creates the largest divergence. As a matter of fact, no one in Kersenhoek joins the inner city for cheap restaurant meals (however some respondents enjoy 'meals on wheels' provided by the public welfare centre).

The vertical axis is relevant for the differences between the categories within the neighbourhoods. In the Marolles, single males and to a lesser extent, immigrants are more usually visitors of social restaurants and other private welfare associations, while single mothers rely relatively more on medical centres (higher medical consumption of children) and they also count on private associations for help. The interview recruitment process of single mothers plays a role here, since nine out of twelve were contacted through such associations.

In Kersenhoek, there is at least one doctor in the neighbourhood, but most people have to leave the neighbourhood for appropriate medical services. The differences between the groups concern a more frequent mentioning of the centrally provided services by immigrants and single mothers and a more positive assessment of the efforts of the local authorities by the locals. Foreigners are less sensitive to this aspect since they don't enjoy voting rights (many foreign single mothers and immigrants cannot answer the question).

Finally, it is worthwhile mentioning that the propensity to demand help from the public welfare centre is not well represented on this plane. Immigrants in both neighbourhoods do not consider this option, again because of their weak political status. Single mothers in the Marolles and to a lesser extent locals in Kersenhoek are more inclined to do so.

Neighbourhood resources in the sphere of reciprocity

Reciprocity was analysed with questions regarding the presence of family and friends in the neighbourhood and the quality of relations with the neighbours (EXCHANGE ... NORELATI), places which have the potential to function as nodes in time–space and to open possibilities to build a local social network (public meeting places, primary schools inside or outside the neighbourhood (SCHLIN ... SCHLOUT) and contacts with parents of other pupils). Residential mobility (STABLE ... 2-MOVE) and length of stay in the neighbourhood (SHORTRES ... LONGRES) are measured because they can affect the development of social networks. Finally it was also asked if help from family, neighbours or friends would be received in case of financial problems. Results are shown in Figure 12.5.

The first axis describes the continuum between residential stability and a long period of stay in the neighbourhood versus frequent moves and short stay. The housing conditions, relatively low rents and the tenants' rights in the social housing sector yield a higher stability than in the Marolles, where the transit function for poor and newcomers in the city is reflected for the three categories. However, immigrants are not stable in Kersenhoek. As expected, this stability is important for the availability of friends and good relations in the neighbourhood. The absence of these factors in the Marolles is compensated for by the public meeting places and more short-term helpful relations.

The second dimension relates to the presence of children (attending primary school) and thus immigrants and single mothers are contrasted with the local males. The children generate contacts with other parents in the school, especially when the school is outside the neighbourhood, again necessarily the case in Kersenhoek. Help from family is more frequent when children are at stake. Conversely, the presence of friends, the use of public meeting places and the help from friends are facilitated by the absence of children.

The third dimension still represents 18 per cent of the inertia and relates to two sets of relations (not visible in Figure 12.5): one between immigrants and polite relations with the neighbours (saying hello) and one between single mothers in the Marolles who combine short stay and high residential mobility with a high rate of exchange between neighbours and help from friends. This refers to the peculiar social environment of this category in the Marolles (the semi-collective housing arrangements provided by shelter associations).

In the Marolles, public meeting places are instrumental for the locals (some were recruited in pubs, but this was even more the case for the immigrants). In Kersenhoek, where such meeting places are virtually lacking, the locals and single mothers develop reciprocal attitudes on a micro-local base. Good supportive relations with the neighbours are helpful for

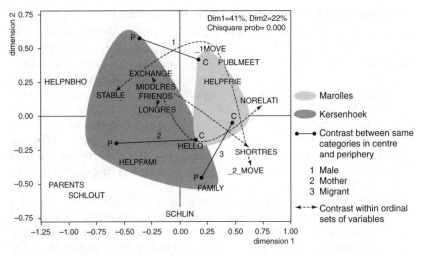

Figure 12.5 Correspondence analysis on resources in the sphere of reciprocity: plot on the first two dimensions

some of them. Kersenhoek immigrants often have family in the area, but familial help is not more developed than for the single mothers. They have less help from friends and neighbours. As a matter of fact, their choice for a social house, which is often regarded as the end stage in their housing career, entails a sharp cut off from the ethnic infrastructure and networks in the inner city concentration areas. There are no ethnic shops, mosques or facilities for the children in the neighbourhood.

Access to means of existence and space

In order to analyse the strategies for access to means of existence in a comparative way, interviewees were questioned for a fixed number of items. For each of them, the sphere of integration in which the access was achieved (including prosumption – which is autoproduction – and under-consumption) and the place where the item was accessed were recorded. The items included bread, table and chairs, the fridge, the car, clothes, clothes washing, haircut, wallpapering, and children care. The last two items appeared to be too case-dependent for comparison. The seven other ones present a bunch of goods and services with which neighbourhoods and categories can be compared in terms of the relative use of each integration sphere and the geography of access to the means of existence. Of course each item is dominantly related to one of the spheres and has a specific distance range, but precisely the small variations are relevant to understand the behaviour of each group in the two neighbourhoods (see Figure 12.6).

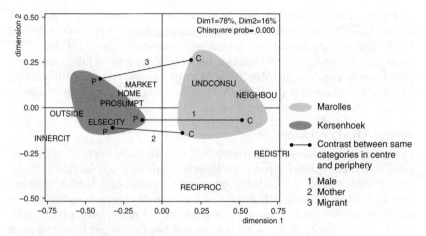

Figure 12.6 Correspondence analysis on access to means of existence and their location on the first two dimensions

The first dimension reveals a consistent difference between both neighbourhoods, with a slight over-representation of the market sphere and prosumption in Kersenhoek and underconsumption, redistribution and reciprocity in the Marolles. Market exchange and prosumption are logically related, since prosumption supposes in most cases the acquisition of the means of (domestic) production on the market. Underconsumption is necessarily aspatial and prosumption is usually home-related. But besides these structural relations, there is a strong over-representation of access to resources in the neighbourhood in the Marolles and elsewhere (inner city, elsewhere in the city and outside the city) in Kersenhoek. However, from the viewpoint of the Kersenhoek inhabitants, the Marolles is part of the inner city. People in both neighbourhoods use partly the same areas to find their means of existence. This is especially the case for the single mothers and the immigrants, the latter taking advantage of the ethnic supplies in the inner city, to which they turned before arriving in Kersenhoek. They visit the same cheap markets in the inner city and some common ethnic shopping areas offering cheap durable goods. As a matter of fact, the spatial range of market exchange is much larger than for the other spheres and the Kersenhoek inhabitants take advantage of the cheap and concentrated offer in the city. This fact also points to the relatively small scale of the city, the well developed public transport system, and the concentration of such resources in the poor crescent (Meert found the same in the case of Peterbos (1998); he could also show that suburban poor turned to the same cheap supply in the Brussels inner city).

The second dimension expresses the use of reciprocity among single mothers (and more slightly Marolles locals) versus market for immigrants and underconsumption specifically for the Marolles immigrants. The most relevant item for underconsumption is the car (absent in 48 cases) followed by the fridge (7 cases). Although there are complaints about the decline of access to daily goods in the Marolles, living without a car is much more feasible than in Kersenhoek. Also in the Marolles, single persons daily visiting a social restaurant and single mothers in a shelter institution with collective appliances don't even need a fridge.

Perception of exclusion

The researchers assessed the perception and attitude towards exclusion, with four behavioural types very loosely inspired from Merton's strain theory: resignation, dependency on welfare institutions, initiative to get out, and other attitudes.[8] The three main attitudes towards exclusion are fairly well differentiated among the categories of interviewees (see Figure 12.7). The 'other' type being exceptional, it has the largest deviation, but this is not very relevant in this matter.

Dependency is typical for the Kersenhoek immigrants, resignation for the Marolles locals, and initiative for the single mothers and even more the Marolles immigrants. The former are evidently pushed by the future of their children to take initiatives, while the latter are very often at the starting point of their immigration project, some of them still in an irregular situation. Overall, dependency is more common among the Kersenhoek

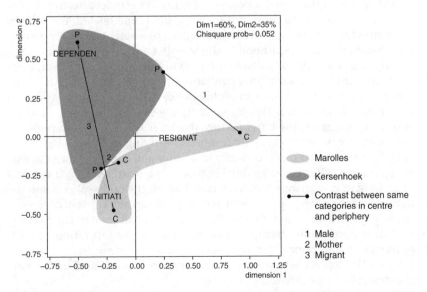

Figure 12.7   Correspondence analysis on attitudes towards exclusion: plot on the first two dimensions

people, initiative and resignation among the Marolles categories. These differences also apply when couples of categories are compared, except for the single mothers. Dependency on institutions in Kersenhoek is of course explained by the reliance on state redistribution in the neighbourhood. This dependency on the welfare state, the exclusion from work-related social networks and the peripheral location of the social housing, undermine the collective dimension of their claims (the inhabitants don't want to be involved in the participatory structures of the social housing association; the association officers gave many examples of tenants asking help for little things they normally should resolve themselves). The culture of rights becomes dominant over the culture of duties. People put themselves in a relation of assistance and their mobilization capacities are weak. Only the single mothers are relatively more inclined to take initiatives than those in the Marolles.

Comparing the poor and their neighbourhoods

When comparing both neighbourhoods in their potentials and constraints towards social integration of their inhabitants, it is worthwhile recalling the conclusions of the former research in Brussels, briefly presented in the first part of the chapter (Kesteloot *et al.*, 1997; Meert *et al.*, 1997; Mistiaen *et al.*, 1995). Neighbourhoods differ by their position in the urban socio-spatial structure. As far as the city centre is not abandoned as a result of the growth of satellite centres or edge cities, inhabitants of centrally located areas enjoy the advantages of concentration and accessibility, which are important both for access to markets, including the labour market, and to collective consumption. The heterogeneity of space, more precisely the diversity of housing and the presence of other land uses like jobs and services, should also function as an asset. Finally, what could be termed the historical thickness of space offers similar morphological and functional heterogeneities, but also memories that can be retrieved when they fuel present issues and struggles. In other words, space is carrying a history, which potentially reinforces certain mechanisms of integration, be it a long tradition of hospitality and mutual help, a workers' history that participated in the struggle for a stronger welfare state or strong traditions of trade and innovation. A complex set of elements and conditions determine if this memory of space can actually play a role in the struggle of the socially excluded. The Turkish neighbourhood in Schaarbeek/Sint-Joost was found to offer a much richer context for all sorts of survival strategies than Kuregem along these lines. Dependency from the welfare state was higher in Kuregem, while in Schaarbeek/Sint-Joost, reciprocity was not so much developed for direct access to means of existence, but as a basis for achieving the conditions to obtain these means in the market and redistribution spheres.

A similar, but stronger contrast between the Marolles and Kersenhoek was expected. The Marolles would present deficiencies in all spheres, but less in reciprocity. But actually, reciprocal exchange is hampered by high residential mobility, access to market resources is easy (yielding also a strong involvement in informal activities), and the availability of private redistribution resources is exceptionally high (probably the best in town).[9] Inhabitants in Kersenhoek would be especially vulnerable in the sphere of market exchange and better off in the redistribution sphere. Both points are verified, but the latter results to a large extent from the electoral sensitivity of the area, with a city alderman living on the estate.[10] Moreover, the market sphere remains essential when actual access to means of existence is at stake. It involves the selective use of resources outside the neighbourhood, including markets and ethnic shopping concentrations in the poor crescent of Brussels.[11]

Nevertheless, the nature of deprivation remains quite unlike in each neighbourhood. The differences are clear-cut on two aspects: private versus public redistribution resources, and local complex versus city market-oriented access to means of existence. In all other cases, the situation is more complex. That could be the result of overarching characteristics and behaviour of the three categories, but the same categories in the two neighbourhoods have similar profiles only in two circumstances: local unemployed tend to experience a similar mix of exclusion processes from reciprocity and the market whatever their neighbourhood, and single mothers in each neighbourhood are taking initiatives to get out of their situation because of their children. In two other cases, different categories have similar positions: single mothers in Kersenhoek and local unemployed in the Marolles have closely resembling exclusion profiles; the Marolles single mothers and the Kersenhoek unemployed have both comparable access to market resources, albeit that this means a better access than the other categories in Kersenhoek and the reverse in the Marolles.

Neither social categories, nor neighbourhoods turn out to be strong independent elements explaining the nature of social exclusion and the consequent behaviour of the interviewees. The common use of a set of market resources supplied in the poor crescent of Brussels, which results from the concentration of poverty in this area, its ethnic character, and relatively good access by public transport, surely plays a role in this finding.

Conclusion

What emerges is a complex dialectical relation between socially excluded groups and relatively well-adapted residential environments to their survival requirements. This dialectic between groups and places is best exposed by the fact that interviewees appearing in the same category, but in other neighbourhoods, are in fact profoundly different. This is not a failure of the research design. Precisely the fact of following as tightly as possible the selection criteria for three social groups, enables us to discover the diversities between the neighbourhoods. Both the selection mechanisms on the housing market and the residential strategies of the poor households concur to create these differences. They relate to different dominant causes of social exclusion and to different attitudes towards this situation.

In order to clarify this, one should know that the Belgian welfare state has been perfected in the mid-1970s, at least in the field of incomes. It covers nearly all imaginable cases of economic poverty. The 1974 law on minimum income secures subsistence to every Belgian adult. This law was seen as the final step in the national social security system. Since this secured income was subjected to a series of conditions (Belgian nationality, the willingness to work and the exhaustion of other social security rights), the law was complemented in 1976 with a new law on social aid, proclaiming in its first article that every person has rights on social aid in order to reach the conditions of living in human dignity. This opens the right to a minimal income to all regular residents in the country. Only homeless people without an official address, illegal residents, and to a lesser extent, not yet recognized political refugees are not covered by the system.

These differences in welfare coverage also appear in housing. Evidently, homeless people fail for one or another reason to access social housing, but also the two last categories have no access to social housing, simply because they don't have the required documents. Thus, a relatively sharp mechanism on the housing market, explains why irregular persons don't live in Kersenhoek. They are precisely over-represented in the Marolles because of its tradition of shelter for poor and isolated people.[12] This shelter function is underpinned by the presence of institutions for homeless people and for abandoned or single mothers, by the Sint-Pieters hospital where the doors are always open for the have-nots and by a substantial offer of cheap furnished rooms on the private rental market. Thus, the Marolles functions as a (hopefully) transit zone for the illegal immigrants, the political refugees and for single mothers, while it is more of an end station for retired and isolated Belgian poor.

In contrast, the social housing regulations tend to concentrate disabled people and lone mothers. People tend to apply to several social housing associations and apply more for a certain housing type than for a precise neighbourhood. Nevertheless, the peculiar characteristics of Kersenhoek and its peripheral location in a green and quiet environment are closest to the best possible housing aspirations of our interviewees.

To a certain extent, these selective processes also shape the neighbourhoods and their social fabric. The networks based on occasional friends and pubs and access to informal activities in the Marolles on the one hand, the networks and solidarity based on vicinity and the pressures on the social housing association to adjust the estate to the individual needs of the inhabitants in Kersenhoek on the other hand, are products of social relations the poor engage in within their residential space.

Notes

1. This chapter is based on the Brussels URBEX report (Guldentops F. *et al.*, 2001) and the interviews, which were conducted by Fred Guldentops and Pascale Mistiaen. Heidi Vandenbroecke and Truus Roesems participated in the collection of other relevant material.
2. The municipalities set up most social housing associations and they appoint their Board Members. However, the Regions decide the legal framework in which they have to operate.
3. The Marolles cover several census tracts. The most representative census tract, called Blaes-Zuid, has been selected for statistical comparison with Kersenhoek and the average figures of the Brussels Capital Region.
4. When that is the case (less than 40% of the row or column inertia), the point is not represented in the graphs that follow, except if it is part of an ordinal sequence of characteristics.
5. To emphasize the intra-neighbourhood differences on the graph, the three Marolles categories are labelled C and encircled by light shading and the three Kersenhoek categories are labelled P and encircled by dark shading. To visualize the contrast between centre and periphery within categories, their corresponding positions in each neighbourhood are connected with a numbered line, where the number refers to the category.
6. For each analysis we give the percentage of the total inertia represented by each axis and the chi-square probability of independence between the six categories and the characteristics under analysis. The latter can only be seen as a comparative measure of interrelation between the successive analyses, not as a statistical test of significance, since the categories can hardly be seen as a representative sample of the population.
7. Privatized, but the offer of public telephones is still strongly related to the public service logic of the former state company.
8. The latter category represents choice to live outside the labour market in two cases, and satisfaction in a third one.
9. This is not to forget that such a concentration of private redistribution is always a sign of weakness of state redistribution. Nevertheless, it is also a sign that the traditional function of the neighbourhood in the city as an area of protection for excluded people is still surviving.
10. By the way, this is exemplifying the gains that inhabitants of deprived areas could obtain from a better political representation.
11. This refutation is partly explained by different research designs. In the first research, information about as many survival strategies as possible were collected and subsequentially a distinction was made between the integrative or exclusive character of the strategies, which revealed the superiority of Schaarbeek/Sint-Joost and the Turkish population in terms of resistance to exclusion. In order to enhance European comparability and to avoid the problem of exhaustivity (one is never sure that indeed all the strategies were mentioned during the interviews), this research considered a fixed number of means of existence and didn't consider the difference between integrative and exclusive strategies.
12. There has been an amnesty for illegal foreigners in 2001 in Belgium and the geography of regularization demands could have corroborated this phenomenon in the Brussels case. However, we couldn't obtain the data for Brussels. They were released and mapped for the Antwerp case and they show unsurprisingly a strong correlation between the deprived areas and the concentration of illegal immigrants (De Decker and Kesteloot 2003). Foreign literature describes the strong dependence of illegal immigrants on places of potential informal jobs and housing and on inbeddedness in conational networks (Engbersen, 1999).

13
European Cities: Neighbourhood Matters

Christian Kesteloot, Alan Murie and Sako Musterd

Neighbourhood within the social exclusion debate

Social exclusion is an encompassing normative concept to address a lack of participation in (urban) societies; it is mainly regarded as something that should be reduced and, although it is not an issue that is reserved to the urban arena, there is a common concern about social exclusion in cities and urban regions, the concentration of deprivation in particular parts of cities and neighbourhood targeting of public policies designed to address social exclusion. The challenge of reducing social exclusion requires a clear view of the meaning of the concept, of the dimensions that are relevant to the understanding of it, and of the potential instruments to reduce the level of social exclusion. In this book we have discussed these dimensions with a particular focus on the significance of neighbourhood.

We recall that social exclusion represents a different tradition in debates about poverty and a change of focus from distributional issues to relational issues (Van Kempen, 2002). It reflects different perspectives on urban inequalities and policies in Europe and in North America. The focus on social exclusion goes beyond low income and refers to participation, redistribution and rights. Having said this, the term is contested and is often a source of confusion. It is frequently used to refer to dualities or divisions (those who are included and those who are excluded), about marginalization (the excluded marginalized versus the included non-marginalized), about polarization (those who are part of the supposedly excluded lower pole versus the included rest), about fragmentation (with some fragments that have and others that have not lost attachment to the remaining fragments), about segregation (those who are spatially separated from the rest) and about the unemployed (versus the employed). Generally, it is about (expected) non-participation versus participation. Few of these concepts attract attention because of their clarity. But all of them refer to questions about processes that affect individual opportunities to be, or to become, a full citizen in terms of participation in society. That 'in' or 'out' of society can be related to all spheres of social life, whether we refer to participation in education, labour or politics or to the use of private services or public facilities and safety nets, or to the size and strength of social ties with friends and relatives.

The definition emerging from the debate on social exclusion is one that embraces more than traditional household and individual measures of poverty and has a spatial dimension. Some authors have particularly emphasized spatial dimensions. This started with the first essays to develop a mere descriptive geography of poverty in the 1970s (Morrill and Wohlenberg 1971), developed later in an effort to understand the nature of spaces of exclusion (Anderson, 2003; Forrest and Kearns, 1999; Sibley, 1995) and today frequently addresses the problem of neighbourhood effect as a spatial dimension of poverty (Atkinson and Kintrea, 2001; Buck, 2001; Friedrichs, 1998; Friedrichs *et al.*, 2003). However, social exclusion has increasingly come to be used to refer to a dynamic process that shuts people off from the benefits enjoyed by full citizens (Walker, 1997: 8). The reference to spatial concentrations of disadvantaged households thus became part of the defining aspects of social exclusion, related to questions about the role of place or neighbourhood in social exclusion. This book has focused on this issue and on the differentiation between neighbourhoods with high concentrations of disadvantaged households. Some of these neighbourhoods are inner city, older neighbourhoods and some are more modern peripheral estates. Some are highly mixed in terms of housing tenure or ethnicity and others are homogeneous.

Not all of the literature assumes that concentrations of disadvantaged households are wholly damaging. For example Wacquant and Wilson (1993: 32) referred to the organized or institutional ghetto of mid-twentieth century American cities where 'activities are ... structured around an internal and relatively autonomous social space that duplicates the institutional structure of the larger society and provides basic minimal resources for social mobility.' This perspective raises the possibility that concentrations of poverty may be functional for the group or groups involved and enables family and other networks to be maintained (see also Bolt *et al.*, 1998 for an overview of positive and negative effects of spatial segregation).

Cities and exclusion

In the introductory chapter of this book we referred to the existing literature on urban changes and the increasingly divided cities and indicated that this literature only partly connects with the importance of neighbourhoods. Over the past decade there have been a number of important accounts of urban change and division but these have tended to emphasize changing economic structures (e.g., Hamnett, 1994; Sassen, 1991; Wilson, 1987). Because housing and labour markets are not well articulated and do not have a simple or predictable interaction it is not clear where the neighbourhood consequences of economic restructuring will occur – and where the concentrations of deprivation arising indirectly as a result of economic restructuring will occur. Thus while we have accounts of polarization and professionalization of cities they do not provide us with accounts of the changing economic structure within the city that link with neighbourhood level concerns about concentrations of deprivation. The contributions focused on economic structure emphasize jobs and employment whereas neighbourhood distributions relate to residence – and changing patterns of residence cannot be read directly off from economic structure. This becomes obvious if one considers that residential changes can also occur independently from economic change. Other contributions have shifted the emphasis and referred to historical (Scott, 1988), ethnic-cultural (Waldinger, 1996), residential and welfare state (Murie, 1997, 1998; Musterd and Ostendorf, 1998) determinants of change in cities but none of these provide a strong neighbourhood dimension. Where neighbourhoods are the focus, they tend to refer to one neighbourhood (e.g., White, 1980) and if more than one neighbourhood is considered, they are within one city or one welfare regime type (e.g., Atkinson and Kintrea, 2001; Forrest and Kearns, 1999; Herlyn *et al.*, 1991; Kesteloot *et al.*, 1997; Morlicchio *et al.*, 1991). While this enables detailed accounts of the neighbourhoods concerned it limits the scope for some types of comparison and assessment – for example of how different welfare regimes impact on neighbourhood differences and dynamics.

It is against this background – a recognition of the importance of neighbourhood within social exclusion and the absence of robust neighbourhood accounts allowing for some international comparison – that this book has been developed. It has directly addressed questions about the different opportunity structures provided by different neighbourhoods. Is there a better opportunity structure for integration in more diverse inner city neighbourhoods than in peripheral and homogeneous neighbourhoods? Do centrally located and mixed tenure neighbourhoods offer better opportunities in terms of access to jobs, and offer a wider variety of all kinds of facilities and better opportunities for mutual exchange of various goods and services? Alternatively is the role of neighbourhood less related to location and housing tenure and more to welfare state regime or to the distinctive history and the political economy of the neighbourhood within the context of the wider city?

Researching the neighbourhood dimension of social exclusion: The problem of comparison

Comparative studies of social exclusion are extremely difficult to carry out. Existing comparative accounts of the processes associated with social exclusion tend to operate in an easier territory. It is easier to compare a selected set of social policies operating at a national level or a series of indicators of the attractiveness and sustainability of cities. The national literatures that seek to explore social exclusion are much more likely to refer to a wide range of contingent factors that affect the experience of social exclusion and are likely to refer to changes over time and place. Many of the most effective accounts of social exclusion are neighbourhood studies or studies of particular communities. It is at this level that researchers and politicians are best able to capture the complex interaction factors, which lead to social exclusion. But it is not easy to capture this complexity and this holistic view of exclusion in international comparative research. Hence there is a tendency for there to be a gap between grounded accounts of neighbourhoods and communities experiencing exclusion in particular countries and cities and normative accounts based on comparisons of urban and other indicators. The research reported in this book seeks to bridge this gap.

Having set out to look at the significance of neighbourhoods in social exclusion at a comparative level, there is a problem in trying to reduce the potential sources of variation, which come into the comparative accounts. If the accounts of social exclusion in different cities involve totally different sections of the community living in totally different neighbourhoods within the structure of the city, the different experiences that emerge from the results of the survey are going to be regarded as wholly unsurprising. At the same time, no generalizations can be made from the lessons of comparison. There is no perfect solution to this problem. By definition differences between cities and cultural and historical differences mean that we cannot develop an experimental design that identifies directly comparable groups or locations in cities that have different histories and cultures. Nevertheless, this research has attempted to limit the sources of variation.

An important way in doing so is the adoption of a common framework to inform data collection and analysis. As briefly presented in the introductory chapter, the theoretical underpinnings of this research and the operationalization of the ideas about social exclusion referred to above derive from Polanyi's work on the modes of economic integration (1944), and later applied in, among other fields, urban studies (Kesteloot, 1998; Kesteloot *et al.*, 1997; Meert *et al.*, 1997). Polanyi argued that the resources, which are necessary for full participation in society, are produced and distributed through three mechanisms: market exchange, redistribution and reciprocity. It is the position in relation to these modes and the way they interact that determines the extent to which households can or cannot be integrated in society.

The spatial dimension, however, should not be regarded as a separated sphere in which additional mechanisms of exclusion develop – as suggested by the literature on neighbourhood effects. In fact, the spatial dimension of social integration and social exclusion is directly linked to the concept of modes of economic integration, assuming that each mode of economic integration requires a different set of socio-spatial conditions. Three main

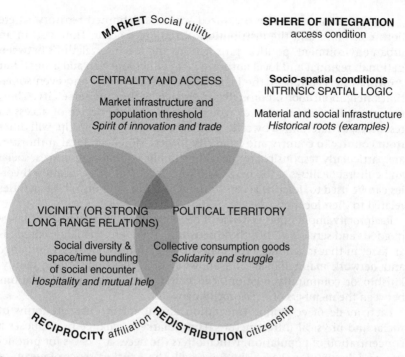

Source: ISEG Ku-Leuven; adapted from Kesteloot (1998)

Figure 13.1   The spatial dimension of the spheres of economic integration

dimensions of this geography of economic integration can be distinguished (Figure 13.1).

The first concerns the intrinsic spatial logic of each mode of integration, the second the presence or absence of the material and social infrastructure that supports the integration activities and the third relates to the historical layers of the socio-spatial structure of the city in which symbols, habits and relations from the past are embedded and possibly reactivated (Meert and Kesteloot, 2000).

In general, one can say that the spatial dimension of market relations is determined by the range of the goods and services offered over space. This can be seen in terms of both production and consumption. Access to employment of each neighbourhood, be it in the neighbourhood itself or in other areas (i.e., selling one's labour or gaining access to sufficient customers in the case of self-employment) are crucial for production. The availability of all necessary goods and services sold on the market is crucial in the case of consumption. This geography of economic integration through the market is well documented in the classic location theories where centrality and access (distance and transportation costs) are the key-factors.

Redistribution is usually organized within a delimited territory where both collection and the distribution of resources occur. However, in an urban environment, political jurisdictions and the interrelations between national, regional and local authorities (to which one can add a small but growing intervention by the EU) will differentiate cities and even sometimes neighbourhoods, boroughs or districts within the same city. Thus, the strength of the system of redistribution and the degree of access to resources, as determined by civil, political and social citizenship, will differ from country to country and from city to city. Moreover, local authorities are particularly responsible for providing public collective resources, social and cultural facilities at the neighbourhood level. The same location theories can be used to describe access to these resources and unveil inequalities related to their location.

Reciprocity implies the existence of networks as well as material exchange of goods and services within these networks. Therefore, spatial proximity is an asset in that it facilitates the dialectical relationship between exchange and network maintenance, and allows trust to develop. Strong family, kinship or community relations can compensate loose spatial relations between the members of a reciprocity network.

Each mode of economic integration also involves different forms of social and physical infrastructure. Thus, market exchange presupposes a concentration of population, which offers the necessary bases for production and distribution. Redistribution entails the actual presence of means of collective consumption and agents for redistribution while reciprocity requires an appropriate arrangement of public and private space, that is, offering places that foster social networks by bundling social relations in space and time. Reciprocal exchange will moreover gain efficiency if the resources held by the members of the network are sufficiently differentiated. Thus, as far as this aspect is concerned, reciprocity has more potential in a socially heterogeneous area than in an area where everyone has similar demands and resources. On the other hand, social relations tend to develop more easily where differences between people are small.

Finally, localities carry with them a history that potentially reinforces certain mechanisms of economic integration, such as a long tradition of hospitality and mutual help in transition zones or immigrant neighbourhoods, a labour movement that fought for a stronger welfare state in nineteenth-century working class areas or strong traditions of trade and innovation in zones where small scale industries and residences are mixed. A complex set of elements and conditions determine if this memory of space is actually playing a role in the economic integration processes. Of course, other historical elements can play a negative role as is clear in the role of reputation and discourses on deprived areas.

Within this analytical framework, it is easy to hypothesize that centrally located areas in the city offer more potential for integration than peripheral ones. Indeed, centrality is crucial for the market and the redistribution spheres when considering their intrinsic spatial logic. Heterogeneity (in terms of functions, social groups employment, services, for example) defines the locally available material and social infrastructure and is usually more important in the older central areas than in the younger peripheral ones. Finally what could be termed the historical thickness of space, offers similar morphological and functional heterogeneities, but also memories that can be retrieved when they fuel present issues and struggles for integration.

We derive a way to enhance comparability from this spatial dimension of integration and exclusion: we have sought, generally, to refer to two contrasting kinds of neighbourhood in this respect, namely older, inner city neighbourhoods where the private sector is the dominant provider of housing and the strongest force in the organization and management of the local economy on the one hand, and more modern housing estates often located towards the periphery of cities and monofunctional in nature on the other hand. These latter neighbourhoods are ones where the state through different housing organizations and through the provision of other services has been particularly influential in shaping the neighbourhood, the services within it and the life chances of the population.

Within these two kinds of neighbourhoods we have also looked at three similar population groups with significant differences in terms of social and spatial opportunities and constraints of integration: long-term unemployed persons, lone parent families, and ethnic minority households. In these respects, in the way that the research was carried out, the contextualization of neighbourhoods and the collection and analysis of data we have sought to enhance the comparability of the cross-national studies and to limit the extent to which differences in the accounts that emerge are explained by differences in the way that the studies have been carried out.

Having said this it is evident that we have not eliminated these differences. Some of the interesting findings of the research are the extent to which it is possible or not possible to identify the three groups in each of the 22 neighbourhoods included in the book. In some estates minority ethnic groups are in a fairly small minority. In other cases the numbers of lone parents in a particular neighbourhood are small. In these cases it is more appropriate to admit that the association between our target groups and our target neighbourhoods differs between the cities rather than insist upon an artificial comparison of groups which are not important in particular neighbourhoods. It is more important to observe the extent to which the interaction between neighbourhood and other factors itself shapes the populations that exist.

However, our theoretical framework captures another dimension of the comparison. The modes of integration are attached to various spatial scales. The city and urban region are the most relevant spatial scales for the functioning of labour markets and thus for *labour market participation* opportun-

226   *Kesteloot, Murie and Musterd*

ities. Of course, superimposed global economic restructuring processes are of major importance too. However, their effects will vary between different regions, dependent on the historically grown economic and social structures in these regions and their ability to get new links to the renewed global economy. Cities and regions with a deeply rooted manufacturing heritage will normally have more problems to realize a transformation to the knowledge and cultural industries and associated business and consumer services industries than cities that already had an economic structure characterized by culture, knowledge (universities), finance, insurance companies and other business and consumer services.

Redistribution is multiple-scaled and, according to the states and the cities considered, differences in welfare state arrangement have to be pinpointed at the relevant set of scales. A full comparison would entail considering the politics of scale in each case.

Reciprocity is mainly a local sphere of relations and exchange. However, the search for networks cannot be confined within the neighbourhood. Especially in the case of networks related to international migration and trade, the neighbourhoods should be framed in a global context.

In this book six different welfare states were included, 11 different cities and 22 different neighbourhoods (two in each city). All of the neighbourhoods included in the research were selected because they had high levels of deprivation relative to the city they formed part of.

Social exclusion and opportunity structures in European cities

In the remaining parts of this chapter we draw together the material reported and make comparisons between the neighbourhoods and reflect on the theoretical and policy consequences of our findings.

Table 13.1 provides an indicative summary of the opportunities associated with each of the neighbourhoods. The first column notes the national welfare state regime type and the second an indication of relative unemployment rates as a measure of the buoyancy of the market context in a cross-city comparison. The final three columns refer to the strength of reciprocity as reported through interviews with the target groups based on the interview data in each city as evaluated in each of the chapters in this book.

The picture emerging from Table 13.1 must be treated with caution. These are not precise summaries but reflect continuities and differences that have emerged from the range of data in the research. If we work back from the reciprocity indicators a number of points emerge:

- There is no dominant or majority pattern emerging. The research does not suggest that certain patterns are associated with welfare regime types or economic circumstances.

Table 13.1 A classification of the opportunities in neighbourhoods in each of the eleven URBEX cities (and their metropolitan areas) in six welfare states

City	Neighbourhood	Redistribution (welfare state)[a]	Market exchange (unemployment)[b]	Reciprocity (support networks)		
				im	sm	nm[c]
Amsterdam	Landlust (c)[d]	++	+	−	+	−
	Osdorp (p)	++	+	−	+	−
Rotterdam	Tarwewijk (c)	++	+	+	+	+
	Hoogvliet (p)	++	+	+	+	+
Berlin	Neukölln (c)	+	−	−	+	+
	Marzahn (p)	+	−	++	+	−
Hamburg	St. Pauli (c)	+	−	+	++	++
	Mummelmannsberg (p)	+	−	+	+	+
Brussels	Marolles (c)	+	+	++	−	+
	Kersenhoek (p)	+	+	−	++	+
Antwerp	Dam (c)	+	+	.	+	+
	Silvertop (p)	+	+	+	+	++
Paris	La Courneuve	+	−	−	−	++
	Montreuil	+	−	−	−	++
London	Ethelred Estate (c)	−	++	+	+	−
	Clapham Park (p)	−	++	+	−	+
Birmingham	Sparkbrook (c)	−	+	+	−	+
	Pool Farm (p)	−	+	.	+	+

Table 13.1 A classification of the opportunities in neighbourhoods in each of the eleven URBEX cities (and their metropolitan areas) in six welfare states *continued*

		Redistribution (welfare state)[a]	Market exchange (unemployment)[b]	Reciprocity (support networks)		
				im	sm	nm[c]
Milan	Baggio (p)	--	++	+	++	+
	Ponte Lambro (p)	--	++	+	++	+
Naples	Mercato Pendino (c)	--	-	+	++	++
	Scampia (p)	--	-	.	-	-

Notes:

[a] redistribution at state level
[b] unemployment (1990s) at city level (based on country reports URBEX programme)
[c] local support networks for immigrants (im), single mothers (sm) and native male (nm)
[d] c: central p: peripheral

Redistribution: ++ soc. democratic, high levels of redistribution
    +   corporatist
    -   liberal
    -- family type, low levels

Market exchange: ++ low unemployment, tight markets
    +   moderate unemployment
    -   relatively high unemployment

Reciprocity: ++ strong support networks
    +   moderately developed support networks (or for selected groups)
    -   weak support networks
    .   not available/not relevant

- Reciprocity strength cannot be read off from either national welfare state regime or market buoyancy.
- Inner-city neighbourhoods appear to be associated with stronger reciprocity in Hamburg and Naples but outer-city neighbourhoods are stronger in Rotterdam and Birmingham. In Berlin, Brussels and London there is no univocal relation between neighbourhood type and reciprocity. The relative strengths of inner- and outer-city neighbourhoods reflect different factors and the potentially weaker access of outer-city neighbourhoods to economic and other opportunities associated with the inner-city are not manifest. The quality of transport links vary between cities as do the community characteristics associated with different places.
- In Amsterdam, Antwerp, Paris and Milan there is the same strength of networks in each of the two neighbourhoods. With the exception of Antwerp, this could partly be explained by the fact that the two neighbourhoods are not as contrasting as assumed in the research design, simply because inner city, private rental poor neighbourhoods do not exist (this is not to say that there are no pockets of poverty in the inner city, but the cities are broadly characterized by a rich inner city and a poor periphery).

There are four common patterns of reciprocity:

1. Central Rotterdam and Central London (moderately developed support networks except for young male unemployed);
2. Peripheral Rotterdam, Hamburg and Antwerp (moderately developed support networks for all three groups);
3. Central Hamburg and Naples (moderately developed support networks for immigrants and strong support networks for others); and
4. Central Antwerp and peripheral Birmingham (moderately developed support networks for the same two groups and the absence of the third).

Although comparison could be further developed in a number of ways (e.g., access to market exchange and resources from distribution, including private welfare and charities, at the neighbourhood level), these results do not support the hypothesis of a crucial opportunities differential between central and peripheral neighbourhoods. This is not to say that the patterns do not hold up the idea that the function and dynamics of neighbourhoods regarding social exclusion relates to history and the political economy of the neighbourhood. But similarities in what is offered by neighbourhoods built in the same era and broad location relative to the city centre and with common elements in terms of design, ownership and other factors, are generally outweighed by sources of difference. In few cases are the continuities strong enough to overcome differences in the economies of cities and in welfare state systems. Both the differences and the similarities suggest that the inner–outer city continuities are weak and represent a contingent possibility rather than an established pattern. The neighbourhoods are unique with distinctive built forms and histories and this distinctiveness emerges in the views of residents and evidence about support networks. The distinctive resources associated with different neighbourhoods and affecting the experience of social exclusion for similar households in different cities are not related to location or welfare regime or economic buoyancy and consequently are not likely to correlate strongly with the kinds of variables included in the larger quantitative analyses of neighbourhood effects.

There are important policy conclusions that can be drawn from these findings. Rather than assume that inner-city areas or peripheral estates have severe problems or problems of a particular type it is important to build up a picture of resources and opportunities from evidence related to particular neighbourhoods and their function within the city.

Discussion

Three themes emerge strongly from the research reported in this book and they are crucial to transcend the apparent contradiction of hypothesis and results.

Levels of explanation

The results of this research can be identified at a number of different levels. First, we are talking about different kinds of neighbourhood effects in this research. For example, we could be discussing whether a neighbourhood effect is important in explaining why households and individuals are experiencing social exclusion or not. Is the neighbourhood crucial in explaining who is in poverty or in triggering poverty? In no cases has this been suggested to be the case. Rather, the argument is that the experience of social exclusion starts somewhere else and is triggered by other factors. It may relate to discrimination or to low employability. It may relate to key events in the household, including ill health, relationship breakdown, or death of a household member. Where the neighbourhood becomes important is in providing a place of residence for households at some stage during their household career. Having accepted this, the questions are about whether the neighbourhood affects the subsequent options of households: whether it provides opportunities for social mobility or whether it reduces life chances. Alternatively, the neighbourhood simply affects the options in relation to coping strategies. Finally, the neighbourhood may affect the experience and quality of life of households.

However, our research also revealed some interesting specific findings regarding the neighbourhood impact. One of these is that the social homogeneity of a peripheral neighbourhood may offer an (temporary) asset, instead of a burden. Homogeneity may help to stimulate interaction and mutual support, which is especially important for newly arrived immigrants, who still have to learn their way in the new place of settlement. We also found some evidence that neighbourhood characteristics are more important in cases where groups are more marginal, that is, where labour market opportunities and welfare state arrangements are less well developed.

The countries with the strongest welfare states, or at least with the most generous social security systems, are most likely to be those where neighbourhood effects are seen to be least important. This would support a view that where the welfare estate is more redistributive and more comprehensive, its impact obscures the significance of local differences. In other situations where the welfare state is less generous and comprehensive, the local welfare state and local resources have more scope to influence the life chances of households.

However, the position is not quite as simple as this. There are some important differences between cities within the same welfare states – between Berlin and Hamburg or between Amsterdam and Rotterdam. There are also problems in the assumptions about the redistributive and comprehensive nature of the welfare state system, especially where issues of citizenship and social rights associated with in-migrant groups and non-nationals exist. Perhaps in these welfare states the impact of neighbourhood is least important for groups that are well-embraced within the welfare state, say, lone parent families and the long-term unemployed, but are most important for groups that have the most marginal rights such as minority ethnic groups. In the German or Italian welfare state systems, rights are strongly linked to citizenship status. In some of the less generous social security systems such as that of Britain, citizenship status has not generally affected eligibility for benefits – although it has applied to the recent wave of asylum seekers. In this case then there is not such a difference between the three target groups in their experience of the welfare state or in terms of their use of local neighbourhood resources.

So we have a number of fault lines rather than one. There is a fault line, which relates to the welfare state and the economy at a national level. This does not neatly divide between countries or cities but is likely to divide certain social groups in certain countries and cities. There is a fault line that relates to citizenship status and social rights irrespective of the generosity of these welfare rights. There is also a fault line that relates to the operation of the local welfare state and the extent to which neighbourhoods are strongly affected by the withdrawal of resources and the decline in the quality of local services such as housing, compared with neighbourhoods that were not in the past major recipients of such resources and so have not been so severely affected by their withdrawal, or even neighbourhoods that are targeted by specific urban policies with positive or negative effects on the living conditions of the poor. There are issues about class, which interact with politics and policy, with housing tenure and with race in European cities. Issues of race and gender operate against this background rather than themselves being the basic fault lines between the neighbourhoods studied. Finally, community strength or weakness can play a role, as far as the poor can share a common belonging. This is often the case with immigrant poor, but in a number of cases, the neighbourhood can be a common ground of reference, especially when a positive reputation or deep historical roots are playing their role.

This list of factors reflects the complexity of neighbourhood difference and the resources that are brought to bear on social exclusion. Neighbourhood effects do not differ along some simple dualism: for example, neighbourhoods within strong welfare state systems and neighbourhoods in weak welfare state systems; or neighbourhoods in strong regional economies or weak regional economies. There is a more complex interaction between a variety of factors that determines the nature of the resources brought to bear on social exclusion. The resources produced in different neighbourhoods are different and are more or less satisfactory for different groups. It is also important that some of these differences may make a qualitative difference to peoples' lives. While neighbourhood effects research may show that neighbourhoods do not generate measurable effects on social or economic mobility, the research reported here involves evidence about different coping opportunities and more or less supportive and safe environments that affect the quality of life.

The neighbourhood and integration

A general finding in the preceding chapters is that neighbourhood types are just valued differently. There were no clear signs that one neighbourhood *type* we distinguished would offer better opportunities for integration than another. A very spatial finding is that public transportation matters. If the quality of connections is not high enough, a peripheral location contributes negatively to the opportunities to become integrated in the urban society, as could be shown in Birmingham and Naples. But the case of Milan shows that remoteness of peripheral neighbourhoods can be offset by very good and relatively cheap transport links.

Peripheral neighbourhoods do not always have a thin infrastructure of neighbourhood and community facilities. Often a single social housing association or company owns the estate. As far as it faces its social role, the landowner aims at improving the living conditions of his tenants. In other cases, the institutional single partner is more sensitive to the collective complaints and demands of the tenants than would be the case with multiple ownership. Sometimes, residents also draw a shared identity, cohesion and solidarity from their common relation with their landowner, as was exemplified by the resistance of the Courneuve inhabitants against the destruction plans of their neighbourhood. In other words, location and housing market tenure structure are less likely to be the keys to differences between neighbourhoods than the factors associated with their dynamics.

Neighbourhoods that look very similar at a certain point in time may experience very different dynamics. The peripheral neighbourhoods in Birmingham, Pool Farm, and Berlin, Marzahn, both have their culturally homogeneous population concentrations and both experience poverty. However Pool Farm is widely regarded as unattractive, whereas the majority of the Marzahn inhabitants regard their place as attractive. Although some of this difference in attitudes may be attributable to the properties themselves the research suggests that it is more to do with the nature of the community and its cohesion.

Another striking finding, especially put forward in Hamburg and Brussels, is that the categories of population we defined actually display significant differences in the central and peripheral neighbourhoods. As far as access to the neighbourhoods is controlled through different mechanisms – the private housing market rules in the centre and the social housing rules in the periphery –, a selection of the groups takes place (e.g., illegal immigrants do not have the right to social housing). On the other hand, housing strategies of the groups involved also consider the opportunities available in each type of neighbourhood. Neighbourhoods that 'specialize' in certain population groups that way, will see the services that are provided change in response to the demands of the population and their desire to set up businesses and organize community activities. The resources that the neighbourhood has are partly the product of the characteristics of the population and the characteristics of the population are in turn partly the product of these resources. The people who choose to stay are those who value these resources and the fact that they use them strengthens the sustainability of these activities.

We see, together with the daily mobility made possible by efficient and cheap public transportation, this residential mobility as a main source to explain the absence of significant contrasts in opportunities between central and peripheral neighbourhoods whose characteristics closely follow the research hypothesis. In other words, the poor also participate in the social production of their residential space and in many cases (but not all) this results in very diversified opportunities for diversified groups according to the socio-spatial setting of their living place.

This social production of space mainly affects institutions and social relations, not so much the built environment as such. However, many of the neighbourhoods are changing, and sometimes these changes are substantial, for example because of demolition or gentrification, not necessarily in the neighbourhood under consideration, but also elsewhere. These processes may cause rapid changes in the position and significance of the neighbourhood in the integration process.

The experience of social exclusion

The overall conclusions presented above indicate that the neighbourhood dimension of social exclusion does not emerge strongly in relation to whether neighbourhoods are set in particular economic or welfare state contexts or are in the inner city or outer city.

In seeking to identify what makes the difference between neighbourhoods the research identified differences in the kind of resources that are available in different neighbourhoods. At one level these are self-evident physical resources that are captured in the description of different places. Beneath these visual images are much more complex social and economic organizational features – facilities that are particular to certain community groups: cafes providing a place of meeting and discussion for male immigrants in Brussels; or facilities developed by a former expatriate community relocating in Berlin. As we already mentioned, these different resources are not built into the neighbourhoods but they develop in response to the characteristics of the communities living there.

It is important that we do not present too romantic a view of these processes. While the neighbourhoods that we have researched do develop services that benefit some residents, we should not imply that all residents make use of these services and that some are not alienated and excluded at this level, nor should we neglect the extent to which these neighbourhoods continue to be affected by discrimination, stigmatization and other adverse processes. It is important, however, that we identify neighbourhoods as dynamic places undergoing change. This perspective connects with that of Wacquant and Wilson (1993) referred to earlier in this chapter. They referred to the organized or institutional ghetto of mid-twentieth century American cities where the activities of the institutional structure of the larger society is duplicated in a relatively autonomous social space that provides basic minimal resources for social mobility. In the European neighbourhoods included in this study, we are not talking about levels of segregation comparable with the American institutional ghetto described by Wacquant and Wilson. The emphasis placed in the present research relates to less segregated neighbourhoods but nevertheless areas with a concentration of disadvantaged households. It highlights that facilities that make a difference to the experience of exclusion have developed in response to the resident population and been shaped by that population. The dynamics that affect the ways that neighbourhoods work for their residents relate to the shaping of these neighbourhood facilities.

All of these factors contribute to the argument that neighbourhoods matter. They may contribute to social exclusion by increasing the entrapment of households or reducing their opportunities because local facilities are poorly resourced or they may contribute to mitigating some of the effects of exclusion or providing opportunities for more effective coping strategies or for long-term social mobility. In some cities and for some groups, (less for lone parents more for other groups), the distinctive resources provided by the neighbourhood do make a difference at least to the experience of social exclusion. This is because of differences associated with the local welfare state and the impact of local policy interventions and the importance of the services that are provided locally in terms of shops, doctors, dentists, community activities, or in terms of faith- and kinship-based networks. It may also be because of discrimination in various spheres. Cultural factors are also likely to be important.

The research suggests, however, that in other cities there is a lack of impact of neighbourhood and the key factors affecting the experience of social exclusion relate to the economy (and are determined at a regional or sub-regional level) or to the welfare state (which is determined at a national level). The opportunities and choices available to lone parents or to long-term unemployed households or to ethnic minorities are determined at these national, regional and sub-regional levels and the impact of the neighbourhood is insignificant or superficial.

Conclusions

Some of the key factors affecting the experience of social exclusion are the product of micro and local factors including those generated by the history of residence and residents. Future research may benefit from adopting a layered approach to the examination and explanation of the importance of neighbourhood on social exclusion. This would refer to context, situation and site. In relation to context it would start with a reference to those factors likely to reduce the extent of neighbourhood difference – including the welfare state, inequalities in income and wealth and national and metropolitan influences. In relation to situation it would locate the neighbourhood (or site) within the wider urban context including position within the sub-regional economy and changing opportunities within it and to the extent of differentiation within the urban housing market: within this it would refer to accessibility, infrastructure and advantages and disadvantages compared with other parts of the urban area and take account of the history of neighbourhood development and path-dependent processes of change. Reference to site involves a more inward looking agenda referring to physical resources and the built environment and local facilities and services including those that have emerged in response to the needs of local residents and those created by the residents themselves. The production of neighbourhood difference involves each of these levels of activity and the individual and household experience of exclusion is also affected by all of them.

What emerges from this is a view of the city and neighbourhood in Europe which is significantly different from the American model that dominates much of the literature. As was indicated in the introduction to this book, the American literature has tended to emphasize the importance of the market and race as the organizing determinants of residence in American cities. The account in this book suggests that Europe has a different set of organizing principles. Perhaps they are more complex and reflect the layering of factors over a longer time through different histories and national policies, but they relate consistently to the influence of the welfare state at a national and local level and relate to power and politics. European cities are not all the same – some are closer because of the nature of the welfare state or trajectories of change but none of them fit the American model. Old Europe has cities that date from Roman times to the Industrial Revolution and are formed by the legacies from these periods. They have gone through a series of changes affected by changes in the economy and technology, government and nationhood, policy and ideology, migration and ethnicity and reputation. The neighbourhood effect in European cities is less about a concentration effect although this may exist in some cases. But where concentration does not exist there can still be social isolation. There are neighbourhood effects but not of the type of which Wilson and Jencks discussed. The operation of the welfare state, the legacies of policy and the built environment and the nature of the urban morphology, the educational system and other institutions are all different.

At the same time there are particular tensions affecting neighbourhoods in Europe. We are often no longer talking about pockets of disadvantage but about large swathes of disadvantage becoming much more comparable with American cities and the reduction in welfare state provision has a particular effect. Again, this is a different effect than in America. The process of neighbourhood change is a path-dependent one. Although superficially there may be some convergence with neighbourhoods more dependent on the market and with discrimination and race more prominent, the path-dependent nature of change in European cities means that race and the market will not be the organizing principles or underpin the nature of neighbourhood effects.

However, the nature of neighbourhood effects in Europe is not determined by the welfare state any more than it is by the market or race or by the environment or the built environment or some cultural tradition – rather they reflect the interaction between all of these. The welfare state in different countries itself embodies conflicts between these different elements and the extent to which it creates or reinforces stigmatization or mitigates stigmatization reflects the working through of conflicts in all of these spheres over an extended period of time.

This takes us on the final issue emerging from the discussions of this research, which relates to its implications for our understanding of the nature of neighbourhood differences and the future impact of these. Neighbourhoods in Europe have attributes and resources that have been produced over a long period. They have different resources and they are more or less able to deal with potential changes in the future. Although neighbourhoods may have a particular continuing function within a city (perhaps as an entry point for newcomers to the city) they are still affected by change. Their function could remain constant but the resources that will exist within the neighbourhood will shift and change as the nature of the communities that are using the neighbourhood changes.

Perhaps more fundamentally the resources that neighbourhoods have are likely to come under different kinds of pressure. In some cases this will be associated with economic change, in other cases it may be associated with changes in the welfare state. For example, we can have two scenarios for the future of European cities: one is of a continuing restructuring of the economy and a further move away from manufacturing production towards service sector employment and the knowledge economy and the second is a further move away from generous welfare state provision towards more limited and less redistributive policies reflecting pressures from globalization and ideas of competitiveness. The implication of this research is that different neighbourhoods will enable people to cope with these changes in different ways. The implication is not that all peripheral or all public sector housing neighbourhoods will experience greater social exclusion in the future while all historical inner-city neighbourhoods have a brighter future. The patterns of change will be rather more complex. The importance of these neighbourhoods and their effects in enhancing or mitigating social exclusion in the future depend not only on the resources they have now but on the way that the economy and the welfare state and other factors in the wider environment change and how they adapt and respond to these changes.

Local and national governments are currently paying substantial attention to reintegration efforts related to community building, neighbourhood targeting and schemes for housing and for specific groups. Major efforts are aimed at improving the local social network base and involving residents and communities. There are also major interventions aimed at improving access to the labour market. This book indicates that local social networks play a moderate role in the entire opportunity structure that affects exclusion and integration in urban society. At the same time it is apparent that spatial targeting and area-based approaches do not always address the underlying structural issues. Action at the neighbourhood level, although relevant, is not always the most appropriate level. Action is also needed at a wider level to address underlying causes in a multidimensional, multiscale setting. In Western capitalist societies, access to labour remains of paramount importance.[1] But social exclusion is context sensitive and a focus on one context only may distract the attention from potentially more relevant contexts. The variation between contexts at various levels (neighbourhood, city, state) and between cities and countries produces enormous differentiation. That does not imply that cities, states and neighbourhoods cannot learn from other situations anymore. However, they should be cautious to copy policies and to accept 'best practice' policies. Differentiated and multiscale context-sensitive types of intervention will probably produce better results.

This is also related to the different histories of the neighbourhoods and cities. What may be labelled as a neighbourhood solution in one context may cause neighbourhood problems in another! Equally importantly the opportunity structures to reduce social exclusion are different. Market opportunities, welfare provisions, social networks and neighbourhood contexts offer potential means to reduce social exclusion. They do so in various combinations. Path dependency, the historically grown urban asset base as Robson *et al.* (2000: 9) put it, are of critical importance. Policy makers should be aware of that, since cities and neighbourhoods that have had different paths, require different strategies.

Note

1. Unless, access to means of existence and labour market integration are unlinked, as advocated by the proponents of a universal basic income.

References

Alisch, M. and J.S. Dangschat (1998) *Armut und Soziale Integration, Strategien Sozialer Stadtentwicklung und Lokaler Nachhaltigkeit*. Opladen: Leske and Budrich.

Allum, P. (1975) *Potere e Società a Napoli nel Dopoguerra*. Torino, Einaudi.

Amato, F. (1993) 'La Città del Disagio: Le Periferie Settentrionali di Napoli'. *Spazi Urbani e Quadri Sociali*, 11–12.

Anderson, E. (1999) *Code of the Street: Decency, Violence and the Moral Life of the Inner City*. New York: W.W Norton.

Anderson, H.T. (2001) 'The New Urban Politics of Europe: The Area-based Approach to Regeneration Policy', in Andersen, H.T. and R. van Kempen (eds), *Governing European Cities: Social Fragmentation, Social Exclusion and Urban Governance*. Aldershot: Ashgate, pp. 233–54.

Anderson, H.S (2003) *Urban Sores: On the Interaction between Segregation, Urban Decay and Deprived Neighbourhoods. Urban and Regional Planning and Development*. Aldershot: Ashgate.

Andersson, R. (2001) 'Spaces of Socialization and Social Network Competition: A Study of Neighbourhood Effects in Stockholm, Sweden', in Andersen, H.T. and R. van Kempen (eds), *Governing European Cities: Social Fragmentation and Urban Governance*. Aldershot: Ashgate, pp. 149–88.

Andreotti, A. and Y. Kazepov (eds) (2001) *The Spatial Dimensions of Urban Social Exclusion and Integration: The Case of Milan, Italy*. URBEX series no.11. Amsterdam: Universiteit van Amsterdam, Amsterdam Study Centre for the Metropolitan Environment.

Arbonville, D., Palomares E. and P. Simon (2000) *Comparative Statistical Analysis at National, Metropolitan, Local and Neighbourhood Level, France: Paris*. URBEX series no.3. Amsterdam: Universiteit van Amsterdam, Amsterdam Study Centre for the Metropolitan Environment.

Atkinson, R. and Kintrea, K. (2001) 'Disentangling Area Effects: Evidence From Deprived And Non-Deprived Neighbourhoods', *Urban Studies*, 38: 2277–98.

Augé, M. (1995) *Non-Places: Introduction to an Anthropology of Supermodernity*. London/New York: Verso.

Authier, J.Y. (ed.) (1999) *Rapports Résidentiels et Contextes Urbains*. Rapport pour le Ministère du Logement, Direction de l'Habitat et de la construction, PUCA. Volume I and II.

Bachmann, C. and L. Basier (1989) *Mise Enlimage d'une Banlieue Ordinaire*. Paris: Syros.

Bacqué, M.H. and Y. Sintomer (2001) 'Affiliations et Désaffiliations en Banlieue. Réflexions à partir des Exemples de Saint-Denis et d'Aubervilliers', *Revue Française de Sociologie*, 42(20): 217–49.

BAGS (Behörde für Arbeit, Gesundheit und Soziales) (1993) *Armut in Hamburg*. Hamburg.

Barbagli, M. (1997) 'Family and Kinship in Italy', in: Gullenstad, M. and M. Segalen (eds), *Family and Kinship in Europe*. London: Pinter, pp. 33–49.

Beaumont, J. (2004) 'De-industrialisation', in Kazepov, Y. (ed.), *Visual Paths through Urban Europe*, CD-Rom accompanying the book *Cities of Europe*. Oxford: Blackwell.

Beaumont, J. and C. Hamnett (2001) *Comparison of Social Exclusion and Integration in Two Neighbourhoods, United Kingdom: London.* URBEX series no. 15. Amsterdam: Universiteit van Amsterdam, Amsterdam Study Centre for the Metropolitan Environment.

Beaumont, J., Hamnett, C., Lee, P., Murie, A and R. Oosthuizen (2000) *Comparative Statistical Analysis at National, Metropolitan, Local and Neighbourhood Level, United Kingdom: London and Birmingham.* URBEX series no. 7. Amsterdam: Universiteit van Amsterdam, Amsterdam Study Centre for the Metropolitan Environment.

Beaumont, J., Loopmans, M. and J. Uitermark (2005) 'Politicization of Research and the Relevance of Geography: Some Experiences and Reflections for an Ongoing Debate', in *Area*, 37(2): 118–26.

Becchi, A. (1989) 'Napoli Contro Napoli. Città Come Economia e Città Come Potere'. *Meridiana*, 5: 143–67.

Becchi, A. (2001) 'Napoli Sostenibile? Logiche di Sopravvivenza e Modelli di Sviluppo'. *Meridiana*, 42: 127–52.

Benassi, D. (2002) *Tra Benessere e Povertà*, Milano: Franco Angeli.

Benassi, D. (ed.) (2005) *Povertà come Condizione e come Percezione. Una Survey a Milano*, Milano: Franco Angeli.

Berthelot, J., Jazulot, W., Marillonnet, J., Rey. H., and M. Verone (1998) 'La Cité des 4000 Logements à La Courneuve', in *Au Cœur de la Ville, en Marge de la Société, ces Quartiers dont on Parle.* Paris: Editions de l'Aube.

Blok, H., Botman, S., Kempen, R van., Langemeijer, M., Musterd, S. and W. Ostendorf (2000) *Comparative Statistical Analysis at National, Metropolitan, Local and Neighbourhood Level, The Netherlands: Amsterdam and Rotterdam.* URBEX series no. 6. Amsterdam: Universiteit van Amsterdam, Amsterdam Study Centre for the Metropolitan Environment.

Blok, H., Musterd, S. and W. Ostendorf (2001) *Spatial Dimensions of Urban Social Exclusion and Integration. The Case of Amsterdam, the Netherlands.* URBEX series no. 9. Amsterdam: Universiteit van Amsterdam, Amsterdam Study Centre for the Metropolitan Environment.

Blokland-Potters, T. (1998) *Wat Stadsbewoners Bindt: Sociale Relaties in een Achterstandswijk.* Kampen: Kok Agora.

Boal, F.W. (1976) 'Ethnic Residential Segregation', in Herbert, D.T. and R.J. Johnston (eds), *Social Areas in Cities.* London: John Wiley and Sons, pp. 41–79.

Bolt, G. and R. van Kempen (2000) 'Concentratie en Segregatie in Nederlandse Steden', in: Kempen, R van., Hooimeijer, P., Bolt, G., Burgers, J., Musterd, S., Ostendorf, W. and E. Snel (eds), *Segregatie en Concentratie in Nederlandse Steden: Mogelijke Effecten en Mogelijk Beleid.* Assen: Van Gorcum.

Bolt, G., Burgers, J. and R. van Kempen, (1998) 'On the Social Significance of Spatial Location: Spatial Segregation and Social Inclusion', *Netherlands Journal of Housing and the Built Environment*, (13): 83–95.

Botman, S. and R. van Kempen (2001) *Spatial Dimensions of Urban Social Exclusion and Integration: The Case of Rotterdam, The Netherlands.* URBEX series no. 19. Amsterdam: Universiteit van Amsterdam, Amsterdam Study Centre for the Metropolitan Environment.

Briggs, A (1952) *History of Birmingham* (vol. 2). Oxford: Oxford University Press.

Brooks-Gunn, J., Duncan, P., Klebanov, P.K., and Sealand, N. (1993) 'Do Neighbourhoods Influence Child and Adolescent Development?', *American Journal of Sociology*, 99(2): 353–95.

Buck, N. (1996) 'Social and Economic Change in Contemporary Britain: The Emergence of a New Underclass?', in Mingione, E. (ed.), *Urban Poverty and the Underclass*, Oxford: Blackwell.

Buck N. (2001) 'Identifying Neighbourhood Effects on Social Exclusion', *Urban Studies*, 38(12): 2251–75.

Burgers, J. (1998) 'In the Margin of the Welfare State: Labour Market Position and Housing Conditions of Undocumented Migrants in Rotterdam', *Urban Studies*, 35: 1855–68.

Burgers, J. and R. Kloosterman (1996) 'Dutch Comfort: Post-industrial Transitions and Social Exclusion in Spangen, Rotterdam', *Area*, 28: 433–45.

Burgers, J. and S. Musterd (2002) 'Understanding Urban Inequality. A Model Based on Existing Theories and an Empirical Illustration', *International Journal of Urban and Regional Research*, 26(2): 403–13.

Burgers, J. and J. Vranken (eds) (2003) *How to Make a Successful Urban Development Programme; Experiences from Nine European Countries*. Antwerp: UGIS.

Burns, D., Forrest, R., Flint, J. and Kearns, A. (2001) *Empowering Communities: The Impact of Registered Social Landlords on Social Capital*. Edinburgh: Scottish Homes.

Campbell, B. (1984) *Wigan Pier Revisited. Poverty and Politics in the 80s*. London: Virago Press Ltd.

Cars, G. (2000) *Social Exclusion in European Neighbourhoods – Processes, Experiences and Responses*. Brussels: European Commission.

Case, A.C. and L.F. Katz (1991) 'The Company You Keep: The Effects of Family and Neighbourhood on Disadvantaged Youths'. *NBER Working Paper* no. 3705.

Castel, R. (1995) *Les Métamorphoses de la Question Sociale*. Paris: Ed. Fayard.

CBS (2000) *Enquête Beroepsbevolking 1999*. Voorburg/Heerlen: Centraal Bureau voor de Statistiek.

CBS (2002) *Statistisch Jaarboek 2002*. Voorburg/Heerlen: Centraal Bureau voor de Statistiek.

Centraal Planbureau (1997) *Economische en Ruimtelijke Versterking van Mainport Rotterdam*. Den Haag: Centraal Planbureau.

Champion, M. and M. Marpsat (1996) 'La Diversité des Quartiers Prioritaires, un Défi pour la Politique de la Ville', *Economie et Statistiques*, 294–5. Paris: Insee.

Comune di Napoli (1991) *Relazione Della Commissione Tecnica Sui Lotti L e M del uartiere Scampia a Napoli*, mimeo.

Comune di Napoli (1999) *Variante al Prg di Napoli: Centro Storico, Zona Orientale, Zona Nord-occidentale*. Napoli: Assessorato alla Vivibilità-Servizio Pianificazione Urbanistica

COS (1998) *Buurten in cijfers*. COS, Rotterdam.

Cotugno, P., Pugliese, E. and E. Rebeggiani (1990) 'Mercato del Lavoro e Occupazione nel Secondo Dopoguerra', in Macry, P. and P. Villani (eds), *Le Regioni dall'Unità ad Oggi*. La Campania, Torino, Einaudi.

CPP (2000) *Our Landmark Place: A New Deal for Clapham Park*. Phase 1 proposals for the New Deal for Communities on Clapham Park. London: Clapham Park Project

Dahya, B. (1974) 'The Nature of Pakistani Ethnicity in Industrial Cities in Britain', in Cohen, A. (ed.), *Urban Ethnicity*. London: Tavistock, pp. 77–118.

Darden, J.T. (1995) 'Black Residential Segregation since 1948: Shelly v. Kraemer Decision', *Journal of Black Studies*, 25: 680–91.

De Corte, S (1996) 'Wijkontwikkeling met Wijkcontracten? Stadsvernieuwing in Brussel', in De Decker, P., Hubeau, B. and S. Nieuwinckel (eds), *In de ban van stad en wijk*. EPO, Berchem, pp. 209–17.

De Decker, P. and C. Kesteloot (2003) *Migration, Housing and Homelessness in Belgium*. Brussels: FEANTSA.

De Decker, P., Meert, H. and K. Peleman (2001) *Combatting Urban Poverty. The Power and Specificity of Territorial Policies*. Paper prepared for and presented at the 'Social Inequality, Redistributive Justice and the City' Conference (Session 1: Poverty in Cities and Social Policies), Amsterdam, June 15–17 (org. International Sociological Association, Research Committee on Urban and Regional Development).

242   *References*

De Decker, P., Van Nieuwenhuyze, I. and J. Vranken (2003) 'Enforced by the Electorate: The Rise of an Urban Policy in Flanders', in De Decker, P., Vranken, J., Beaumont, J. and I. Van Nieuwenhuyze (eds), *On the Origins of Urban Development Programmes in Nine European Countries*. Antwerpen/Apeldoorn: Garant, pp. 17–42.

De Lucia, V. (1998) *Napoli, Cronache Urbanistiche 1994–1997*. Milano: Baldini and Castoldi.

Dorsch, P., Häussermann, H., Kapphan, A., Keim, R., Kronauer, M., Schumann, C., Siebert, I. and B. Vogel (2000) *The Spatial Dimensions of Urban Social Exclusion and Integration: A European Comparison. Comparative Statistical Analysis at National, Metropolitan, Local and Neighbourhood Level, Germany: Berlin and Hamburg*. URBEX series no. 4. Amsterdam: Universiteit van Amsterdam, Amsterdam Study Centre for the Metropolitan Environment.

Dubar, C. (1991) *La socialisation, construction des identités et professionnelles*. Paris: Armand Collin.

Dubet, F. and D. Lapeyronnie (1992) *Les quartiers d'exil*. Paris: Edition du Seuil.

Duchesne, S., F. Haegel, F. Platone and H. Rey (1996) *Les Attitudes Politiques dans la "Cite des 4000 Logements" de La Courneuve*. Paris: CEVIPOF.

Duthe G. (1999) *Analyse de la Sociabilité des Habitants du Quartier Des "4000" à La Courneuve*, memoire de Maîtrise. MST ISHA.

EC (1992) *The Community's Battle Against Social Exclusion*. Brussels: Community of the European Commission.

EDA (1998) *Restructuration du Centre Commercial de la Tour à La Courneuve*. Rapport Remis à la Mairie.

Elias, N. and J.L. Scotson (1965) *The Established and the Outsiders*. London: Sage.

Ellen, I.G. and M.A. Turner (1997) 'Does Neighbourhood Matter? Assessing Recent Evidence', *Housing Policy Debate*, 8(4): 833–66.

Enchautegui, M.E. (1997) 'Latino Neighborhoods and Latino Neighborhood Poverty', *Journal of Urban Affairs*, 19(4): 445–67.

Engbersen, G. (1999) *De Ongekende Stad 2, Inbedding en Uitsluiting van Illegale Vreemdelingen*. Amsterdam: Boom.

Esping-Andersen, G. (1990) *The Three Worlds of Welfare Capitalism*. Cambridge: Polity Press.

Esping-Andersen, G. (ed.) (1996) *Welfare State in Transition: National Adaptations in Global Economies*. London: Sage.

Esping-Andersen, G. (1999) *Social Foundations of Postindustrial Economies*. Oxford: Oxford University Press.

Eurostat (2002) *Employment Rate in the EU. Labour Force Survey*, New Release, August 2002, no.101.

Fainstein, S., Gordon, I. and M. Harloe (eds) (1992) *Divided Cities: New York and London in the Contemporary World*. Oxford: Blackwell.

Fargion, V. (1997) *Geografia della Cittadinanza Sociale in Itali: Regioni e Politiche Assistenziali Dagli anni Settanta agli anni Novanta*. Bologna: Il Mulino.

Farwick, A. (2001) *Segregierte Armut in der Stadt*. Opladen: Leske and Budrich.

Fieldhouse E.A. and R.Tye (1996) 'Deprived People or Deprived Places? Exploring the Ecological Fallacy in Studies of Deprivation with Samples of Anonymised Records', *Environment and Planning A*, 28: 237–59.

Fisher, C. (1982) *To Dwell Among Friends*. Chicago: The University of Chicago Press.

Forrest, R. and A. Kearns (1999) *Joined Up Places? Social Cohesion and Neighbourhood Regeneration*. York: Joseph Rowntree Foundation.

Forrest, R. and A. Murie (1988) *Selling the Welfare State: The Privatisation of Public Housing*. London: Routledge (reprinted 1990).

Forrest, R. and A. Murie (1991) 'Housing Markets, Labour Markets and Housing Histories', in Allen, J. and C. Hamnett (eds), *Housing and Labour Markets: Building the Connections*. London: Unwin Hyman, pp. 63–93.

Friedmann, J. and G. Wolff (1982) 'World City Formation: An Agenda for Research and Action', *International Journal of Urban and Regional Research*, 6(3): 309–43.

Friedrichs, J. (1997) 'Context Effects of Poverty Neighbourhoods on Residents', in Vestergaard, H. (ed.), *Housing in Europe*. Horsholm: Danish Building Research Institute, pp. 141–60.

Friedrichs, J. (1998) 'Do Poor Neighbourhoods Make their Residents Poorer? Context Effects of Poverty Neighbourhoods on Residents', in Andress, H.J. (ed.), *Empirical Poverty Research in a Comparative Perspective*. Aldershot: Ashgate, pp. 77–99.

Friedrichs, J. and J. Blasius (2000) *Leben in Benachteiligten Wohngebieten*. Opladen: Leske and Budrich.

Friedrichs, J., Galster, G. and S. Musterd (2003) 'Neighbourhood Effects on Social Opportunities: The European and American Research and Policy Context', *Housing Studies*, 18: 797–806.

Gallie, D. and S. Paugam (eds) (2000) *Welfare Regimes and the Experiences of Unemployment in Europe*. Oxford: Oxford University Press.

Gans, H. (1993) 'From "Underclass" to "Undercaste": Some Observations about the Future of the Postindustrial Economy and its Major Victims', *International Journal of Urban and Regional Research*, 17(3): 327–25 [reprinted in Mingione, E. (ed.) (1996) *Urban Poverty and the Underclass*, Oxford: Blackwell].

Gilberg, R., Hess, D. and H. Schröder (1999) 'Wiedereingliederung von Langzeitarbeitslosen. Chancen und Risiken im Erwerbsverlauf', *Mitteilungen aus der Arbeitsmarkt- und Berufsforschung*, 32(3): 282–99.

Ginsburg, N. (1992) *Divisions of Welfare: A Critical Introduction to Comparative Social Policy*. London: Sage.

Gornig, M., Ring, P. and R. Staeglin (1999) 'Strategische Dienstleistungen in Hamburg: Im Städtevergleich gut positioniert', DIW-Wochenbericht No. 4. Berlin (DIW).

Granovetter, M.S. (1973) 'The Strength of Weak Ties', *American Journal of Sociology*, 78(6): 1360–80.

Greenacre, M. and J. Blasius (eds) (1994) *Correspondence Analysis in the Social Sciences*. New York: Academic Press.

Groves, R. and P. Niner (1998) *A Good Investment?* Bristol: Policy Press.

Guiducci, R. (1993) *Periferie: le Voci dei Cittadini*. Milano: Franco Angeli.

Guldentops, F., Kesteloot, C., and P. Mistiaen (2001) *Spatial Dimensions of Urban Social Exclusion and Integration. The Case of Brussels, Belgium*. URBEX series no.15, Fourth RTD Framework Programme, Targeted Socio-Economic Research. Amsterdam: Universiteit van Amsterdam, Amsterdam Study Centre for the Metropolitan Environment.

Häussermann, H. (2000) 'Die Krise der "sozialen Stadt'. *Aus Politik und Zeitgeschichte*, 10–11: 13–21.

Häussermann, H. and A. Kapphan (2000) *Berlin: Von der Geteilten zur Gespaltenen Stadt? Sozialraeumlicher Wandel seit 1990*. Opladen: Leske and Budrich.

Häussermann, H. and A. Kapphan (2004) 'Berlin: From Divided into Fragmented City', *The Greek Review of Social Research*, A/2004, 113: 25–61

Hamnett, C. (1994) 'Social Polarisation in Global Cities: Theory and Evidence', *Urban Studies*, 31(3): 401–24.

Hamnett, C (2003) *Unequal City: London in the Global Arena*. London: Routledge.

Hamnett, C. and D. Cross (1998) 'Social Polarisation and Inequality in London: The Earnings Evidence, 1979–95', *Environment and Planning C – Government and Policy*, 16(6): 659–80.

Hatzfeld M., Hatzfeld, H. and Rinjart, N. (1997) *Ville et emploi Interstices Urbains et Nouvelles Formes d'emploi*. Juin.

Hannemann, C. (1996) *Die Platte*. Braunschweig: Vieweg.

Harvey, D. (1973) *Social Justice and the City*. Oxford: Basil Blackwell.

Henderson, J. and V. Karn (1987) *Race, Class and State Housing*. Gower: Aldershot.

Henning, C. and M. Lieberg (1996) 'Strong Ties or Weak Ties? Neighbourhood Networks in a New Perspective', *Scandinavian Housing and Planning Research*, 13: 3–26.

Herlyn, U., Lakemann, U. and B. Lettko (1991) *Armut und Milieu*. Basel et al.: Birkhäuser.

IARD (1995) *I Nuovi Poveri in Lombardia. Sistemi di Welfare e Traiettorie di Esclusione Sociale*. Quaderni Regionali di Ricerca, no. 1, Milano: Regione Lombardia.

Jacobs, J. (1961) *The Death and Life of Great American Cities*. New York: Vintage Books.

Jehoel-Gijsbers, M. (2004) *Sociale Uitsluiting in Nederland*. Den Haag: Sociaal en Cultureel Planbureau.

Jenks C. and S. Mayer (1990) 'The Social Consequences of Growing up in a Poor Neighbourhood: A Review', in Lynn, L. and M. Mc Geary (eds), *Concentrated Urban Poverty in America*. Washington DC: National Academy, pp. 111–86.

Jones, C. and A. Murie (1999) *Reviewing the Right to Buy*. Birmingham: University of Birmingham.

Kapphan, A. (2001) 'Migration und Stadtentwicklung. Die Entstehung ethnischer Konzentrationen und ihre Auswirkungen', in Gesemann, F. (ed.), *Migration und Integration in Berlin*. Wissenschaftliche Analysen und politische Perspektiven. Opladen: Leske and Budrich, pp. 89–108.

Kapphan, A. (2002) *Das arme Berlin. Sozialraeumliche Polarisierung, Armutskonzentration und Ausgrenzung in den 1990er Jahren*. Opladen: Leske and Budrich.

Karn, V, Kemeny, J and P. Williams (1985) *Home Ownership in the Inner City: Salvation or Despair?* Aldershot: Gower.

Keim, R. and R. Neef (2000) 'Ausgrenzung und Milieu: Ueber die Lebensbewaeltigung von Bewohnerinnen und Bewohnern staedtischer Problemgebiete', in Harth, A., Scheller, G. and W. Tessin (eds), *Stadt und soziale Ungleichheit*. Opladen: Leske and Budrich, pp. 248–73.

Kempen, R. van (2001) 'Social Exclusion: The Importance of Context', in Andersen, H.T. and R. van Kempen (eds), *Governing European Cities: Social Fragmentation and Urban Governance*. Aldershot: Ashgate.

Kesteloot C. (1998) 'The Geography of Deprivation In Brussels and Local Development Strategies', in Musterd S. and Ostendorf W. (eds), *Urban Segregation and the Welfare State, Inequality and Exclusion In Western Cities*, London: Routledge, pp. 126–47.

Kesteloot, C., Vandenbroecke H., Van der Haegen H., Vanneste D, and E. Van Hecke (1996) *Atlas van achtergestelde buurten in Vlaanderen en Brussel*, Brussels: Ministerie van de Vlaamse Gemeenschap.

Kesteloot, C., Meert, H., Mistiaen, P., Savenberg, S. and H. Van Der Hegen (1997) *De Geografische Dimensie van de Dualisering in de Maatschappij, Overlevingsstrategieën in Twee Brusselse Wijken*. Brussel: Federale Diensten voor Wetenschappelijke, Technische en Culturele Aangelegenheden, Programma Maatschappelijk Onderzoek.

Kesteloot, C., De Turck A.M., Vandermotten, C., Marissal, P. and G. Can Hamme (2001) 'Structures Sociales et Quartiers en Difficulté dans les Régions Urbaines Belges. Sociale Structuren en Buurten in Moeilijkheden in de Belgische Stadsgewesten', *Politique des Grandes Villes/Grootstedenbeleid*. Brussels, p. 108.

Kesteloot, C., Roesems, T and H. Van den Broecke (2002) *Kansarmoede en Achtergestelde Buurten in het Brussels Hoofdstedelijk Gewest*, Dossiers van het Observatorium voor Gezondheid en Welzijn in Brussel-Hoofdstad, Gemeenschappelijke Gemeenschapscommissie, Brussel, p.128 (also in French).

Knijn, T. (2002) 'Bijstandsmoeders; Burgerschap en de Grondslagen voor Onder-steuning', in Hortulanus, R.P. and J.E.M. Machielse (eds), *Modern Burgerschap. Het Sociaal Debat 6*. 's-Gravenhage: Elsevier.

Kodras, J.E. and J.P. Jones III (1991) 'A Contextual Examination of the Feminization of Poverty', *Geoforum*, 22(2): 159–71.

Kreukels, T. and E. Wever (1996) 'Dealing with Competition: The Port of Rotterdam', *Tijdschrift voor Economische en Sociale Geografie*, 87: 293–309.

Kronauer, M. (1997) '"Soziale Ausgrenzung" und "Underclass": Ueber neue Formen der gesellschaftlichen Spaltung', *Leviathan*, 25(1): 28–49.

Kronauer, M. (1998) 'Social Exclusion and Underclass – New Concepts for the Analysis of Poverty', in Andreβ, H.J. *Empirical Poverty Research in a Comparative Perspective*. Brookfield: Ashgate.

Kronauer, M. (2002) *Exklusion. Die Gefährdung des Sozialen im hoch entwickelten Kapitalismus*. Frankfurt am Main, New York: Campus.

Kronauer, M., Berthold V. and F. Gerlach (1993) *Im Schatten der Arbeitsgesellschaft. Arbeitslose und die Dynamik sozialer Ausgrenzung*. Frankfurt am Main, New York: Campus.

Läpple, D (2003) 'Hamburger Arbeitsmarkt im Globalen Kontext', in Hönekopp, E. and R. Jungnickel (eds), *Internationalisierung der Arbeitsmärkte*. Beiträge zur Arbeitsmarkt- und Berufsforschung. Nürnberg: Institut für Arbeitsmarkt- und Berufsforschung.

Lee, P. (2001) *Spatial Variations in Housing and Health Inequalities in the West Midlands*. Birmingham: University of Birmingham.

Lee, P. and Murie, A. (1997) *Poverty, Housing Tenure and Social Exclusion*. Bristol: Policy Press.

Lee, P., Murie, A. and D. Gordon (1995) *Area Measures of Deprivation: A Study of Current Methods and Best Practices in the Identification of Poor Areas in Great Britain*. Birmingham: Centre for Urban and Regional Studies, University of Birmingham.

Lee P., A. Murie and R. Oosthuizen (2001) *Spatial Dimensions of Urban Social Exclusion and Integration: the Case of Birmingham, United Kingdom*. URBEX series no 12. Amsterdam: Universiteit van Amsterdam, Amsterdam Study Centre for the Metropolitan Environment.

Lepoutre D. (1997) *Cœur de Banlieue. Codes, Rites et Langages*, Paris, Editions Odile Jacob.

Leventhal and Brooks-Gunn, (2003) 'The Early Impacts of Moving to Opportunity on Children and Youth in New York City', in Goering, J. and J. Feins (eds), *Choosing a Better Life: Evaluating the Moving to Opportunity Social Experiment*. Washington, DC: The Urban Institute Press.

Levitas, R. (1998) *The Inclusive Society: Social Exclusion and New Labour*. London: Macmillan (now Palgrave Macmillan).

Lewis, O. (1965) 'Further Observation on the Folk–Urban Continuum and Urbanization with Special Reference to Mexico City', in Hauser, P.H. and L. Schnore (eds), *The Study of Urbanization*. New York: Wiley, pp. 491–503.

Lewis, O. (1966) 'The Culture of Poverty', *Scientific American*, 215: 19–24

Madanipour, A., Cars, G. and J. Allen (eds) (1998) *Social Exclusion in European Cities. Processes, Experiences and Responses*. London: Jessica Kingsley.

Marcuse, P. and R. van Kempen (eds) (2000) *Globalizing Cities: A New Spatial Order?* Oxford: Blackwell.

Marshall, T.H. (1963) *Citizenship and Social Class in Sociology at the Crossroads*. London: Heinemann.

Massey, D. and N.A. Denton (1993) *Segregation and the Making of the Underclass*. USA: Harvard University.

Meert, H. (1998) *De Geografie van het Overleven: Bestaansonzekere Huishoudens en hun Strategieën in een Stedelijke en Rurale Context*. Unpublished PhD thesis, Katholieke Universiteit Leuven, Leuven.

Meert, H. (2002) 'Wederzijdse Dienstverlening en Sociale Netwerken', in Musterd, S. and H. Ottens (eds), *Strijd om de Stad; Sociale en Economische Integratie in de Stedelijke Samenleving.* Assen: Van Gorcum, pp. 99–114.

Meert H. and C. Kesteloot (2000) 'Sociaal-Ruimtelijke Kenmerken Van Economische Integratiesferen', *Tijdschrift Van De Belgische Vereniging Voor Aardrijkskundige Studies,* 69(2): 249–81.

Meert H., Mistiaen P. and C. Kesteloot (1997) 'The Geography Of Survival: Household Strategies. In Urban Settings', *Tijdschrift voor Sociale en Economische Geografie,* 88(2): 69-181.

Menard F., Palomares E. and P. Simon (1999) *Les Populations Immigrées et le Logement à Montreuil.* Mission d'étude pour la ville de Montreuil.

Micheli, G.A. (1997) 'Spezzare il Retaggio, Forse Assecondarlo: Intrecci tra Dinamiche di Povertà e Modelli Familiari', *Polis,* XI(2): 277–98.

Mingione, E. (1991) *Fragmented Societies: A Sociology of Work Beyond the Market Paradigm.* Oxford: Basil Blackwell.

Mingione, E. (1996) 'Urban Poverty in the Advanced Industrial World: Concepts, Analysis, and Debates', in Mingione, E. (ed.), *Urban Poverty and the Underclass: A Reader.* Cambridge, MA: Blackwell.

Mingione, E. (2003) 'Social Exclusion and Local Welfare in European Cities'. EUREX lecture 9, 27 March, 2003.

Mingione, E. (2004) 'Embeddedness/Encastrement', in 'La Sociologie Economique Européenne, une Rencontre Franco-Italien', *Sociologia del Lavoro,* supplemento speciale al 93: 26–44.

Ministerie VROM (1988) *Vierde Nota over de Ruimtelijke Ordening, deel a: Beleidsvoornemen.* SDU Uitgeverij, Den Haag.

Mistiaen P., Meert H. and C. Kesteloot (1995) 'Polarisation Socio-Spatiale et Stratégies de Survie dans Deux Quartiers Bruxellois', *Espace-Populations-Sociétés,* 3: 277–90.

Mollenkopf, J. and M. Castells (1991) *Dual City: Restructuring New York.* New York: Russell Sage Foundation.

Morlicchio, E. (ed.) (2001) *The Spatial Dimensions of Urban Social Exclusion and Integration: The Case of Naples, Italy.* URBEX series no. 12. Amsterdam: Universiteit van Amsterdam, Amsterdam Study Centre for the Metropolitan Environment.

Morlicchio E., Cerase F. and A. Spano (1991) *Disoccupati E Disoccupate A Napoli,* Napoli: Cuen.

Morrill, R.L., and E.H. Wohlenberg (1971) *The Geography of Poverty in the United States.* New York: MacGraw-Hill.

Morris, L. (1995) *Social Division, Economic Decline and social Structural Change.* London: UCL Press.

Murie, A. (1975) *The Sale of Council Houses.* Birmingham: University of Birmingham.

Murie A. (1997) 'The Social Rented Sector, Housing and the Welfare State in the UK', *Housing Studies,* 12(4): 437–61

Murie A (1998) 'Segregation, Exclusion and Housing in The Divided City', in S. Musterd and W Ostendorf (eds), *Urban Segregation and the Welfare State: Inequality and Exclusion in Western Cities.* London: Routledge, pp. 110–25.

Murray, C. (1984) *Losing Ground: American Social Policy 1950–1980.* New York: Basic Books.

Musterd, S. and A. Murie (2002) *The Spatial Dimensions of Urban Social Exclusion and Integration*: Final Report. URBEX series no. 22. Amsterdam: Universiteit van Amsterdam, Amsterdam Study Centre for the Metropolitan Environment.

Musterd, S. and W. Ostendorf (eds) (1998) *Urban Segregation and the Welfare State: Inequality and Exclusion in Western Cities.* London: Routledge.

Musterd, S. and W. Ostendorf (1998) 'Concentratie van Kansarmoede', *Tijdschrift voor de Volkshuivesting*, 3: 27–33.

Musterd, S., Deurloo, R. and W. Ostendorf (1999a) 'Het Omgevingseffect, de Problematiek van het Vaststellen van "Getto-Effecten"', in: Musterd, S. and A. Goethals (eds), *De Invloed van de Buurt*. Amsterdam: SISWO, pp. 13–23.

Musterd, S., Kesteloot, C., Murie, A. and W. Ostendorf (1999b) *Urban Social Exclusion and Modes of Integration: Literature Review*. URBEX series no. 1. Amsterdam: Universiteit van Amsterdam, Amsterdam Study Centre for the Metropolitan Environment.

Musterd. S, Ostendorf, W. and M. Breebaart (1998) *Multi-Ethnic Metropolis: Patterns and Policies*. Dordrecht: Kluwer Academic Publishers.

New Deal for Communities (NDC) (2001) *Advanced Delivery Plan: The Three Estates, Kings Norton, Birmingham*, Birmingham: Three Estates (Kings Norton) New Deal for Communities Interim Partnership Group.

Newman, K. (1999) *No Shame in My Game: The Working Poor in the Inner City*. New York: Russell Sage Foundation and Knopf.

Newman, O. (1972) *Defensible Space: Crime Prevention Through Urban Design*. New York.

Niederlaender, L., Gurske, K. and W. Schumann (1986) *Forschungsbericht 'Wohnen 1986 – Marzahn'*. Berlin: Humboldt Universitaet zu Berlin.

O and S, het Amsterdamse Bureau voor Onderzoek en Statistiek (2002) 'Amsterdam in Cijfers: Jaarboek 2002'.

OECD (2001) *Employment Outlook June 2001*. Paris: Organization for Economic Cooperation and Development.

Offe, C. and R.G. Heinze (1986) 'Am Arbeitsmarkt vorbei. Ueberlegungen "haushaltlicher" Wohlfahrtsproduktion in ihrem Verhaeltnis zu Markt und Staat', *Leviathan*, 14(4): 471–95.

Ostendorf, W., Musterd. S and S. De Vos (2001) 'Social Mix and the Neighbourhood Effect. Policy Ambitions and Empirical Evidence', *Housing Studies*, 16(3): 371–80.

Pahl R. (1984) *Divisions of Labour*. Oxford: Blackwell.

Parkinson, M., Bianchini, F., Dawson, J., Evans, R. and A. Harding (1992) *Urbanisation and the Functions of Cities in the European Community*. Liverpool: European Institute of Urban Affairs. Liverpool John Moores University.

Paugam, S. (1991) *La Disqualification Sociale. Essai sur la Nouvelle Pauvreté*. Paris: Presses Universitaires de France.

Paugam, S. (1996) 'La Constitution d'un Paradigme', in Paugam, S. (ed.), *L'exclusion, l'état des savoirs*. Paris: Edition la découverte, pp. 7–19.

Pedersen, L., Weise, H., Jacobs, S. and M. White (2000) 'Lone Mothers' Poverty and Employment', in Gallie, D. and S. Paugam, *op. cit.*, pp. 175–200.

Philo, C. (ed.) (1995) *Off the Map: The Social Geography of Poverty in the UK*. London: Child Poverty Action Group.

Polanyi, K. (1944) *The Great Transformation*. New York: Rinehart.

Portegeijs, W., Boelens, A. and L. Oltshorn (2004) Emancipatiemonitor 2004. Den Haag: Sociaal en Cultureel Planbureau/Centraal Bureau voor de Statistiek.

Portes, A. (1997) 'Social Capital: Origins and Applications', *Annual Review of Sociology*, 24: 1–24.

Preteceille, E. (2000) 'Segregation, Class, and Politics in Large Cities', in: Bagnasco, A. and P. Le Galès (eds), *Cities in Contemporary Europe*. Cambridge: Cambridge University Press, pp. 74–98.

Pugliese, E. (ed.) (1999) *Oltre le Vele. Rapporto su Scampia*. Napoli: Fridericiana Editrice Universitaria.

Putnam, R. (2000) *Bowling Alone. The Collapse and Revival of American Community*. New York: Simon and Schuster.

Ratcliffe, P (1996) *'Race' and Housing in Bradford*. Bradford: Bradford Housing Forum.

Rex, J. (1988) *The Ghetto and the Underclass: Essays on Race and Social Policy*. Avebury: Aldershot.

Rex, J. and R. Moore (1967) *Race Community and Conflict: A Study of Sparkbrook*. London: Oxford University Press.

Robson, B., Parkinson, M., Boddy, M. and D. Maclennan (2000) *'The State Of English Cities'*, London: Department of the Environment, Transport and the Regions.

Rodman, H. (1963) 'The Lower-Class Family. The Lower Class Value Stretch', *Social Forces*, 42(2): 205–15.

Rodwin, L. and H. Sazanami (eds) (1989) *Deindustrialization and Regional Economic Transformation: The Experience of the United States*. Boston: Unwin Hyman.

Room, G. (1995) 'Poverty In Europe: Competing Paradigms of Analysis', *Policy and Politics*, 23(2): 103–13.

Room, G. (1998) 'Armut und soziale Ausgrenzung: Die Neue Europäische Agenda für Politik und Forschung', in Voges, W. and Y. Kazepov (eds), *Armut in Europa*. Wiesbaden: Chmielorz, pp. 46–55.

Rose, D. and C. le Bourdais (1986) 'Changing Conditions of Female Single Parenthood in Montreal's Inner-city and Suburban Neighbourhoods', *Urban Resources*, 3(2): 45–52.

Saraceno, C. (1998) *Mutamenti Della Famiglia e Politiche Sociali in Italia*. Bologna: Il Mulino.

Saraceno, C. (ed.) (2002) *Social Assistance Dynamics in Europe*. Bristol: Policy Press.

Sassen, S. (1991) *The Global City: New York, London and Tokyo*. Princeton, NJ: Princeton University Press.

Sassen, S. (1994) *Cities in a World Economy*, Thousand Oaks: CA: Sage.

Sassen, S. (2000) *Cities in a World Economy*. 2nd edition. London: Pine Forge Press.

Savitch, H. (1988) *Post-Industrial Cities: Politics and Planning in New York, Paris and London*. Princenton, NJ: Princeton University Press.

Scott, A.J. (1988) *Metropolis. From the Division of Labor To Urban Form*. Berkeley: University Of California Press.

SCP (1983) *Sociale Atlas van de Vrouw 1983*. Den Haag: Sociaal en Cultureel Planbureau.

SCP (1997) *Sociale Atlas van de Vrouw; deel 4. Veranderingen in de Primaire Leefsfeer*. Sociaal en Cultureel Planbureau Cahier 141. Den Haag: VUGA.

SCP/CBS (2001) *Armoedemonitor 2001*. Den Haag: Sociaal en Cultureel Planbureau/ Centraal Bureau voor de Statistiek.

Sen, A. (1999) *Commodities and Capabilities*. Oxford: Oxford University Press.

Sibley, D. (1995) *Geographies of Exclusion: Society and Difference in the West*. London: Routledge.

Siebert, H. (1997) 'Labor Market Rigidities: At the Root of Unemployment in Europe', *Journal of Economic Perspectives*, 11(3): 37–54.

Simon, P. (1995) 'La Politique de la Cille Contre la Ségrégation ou l'Idéal d'une Ville sans Division', *Les Annales de la Recherche Urbaine*: 68–9.

Social networks and support systems, International Social Survey Program, www.za.uni-Koeln.de/data/en/issp

Società Studi Centro Storico di Napoli (eds) (1992) *L'artigianato Produttivo nel centro storico di Napoli*. Roma: SIPI.

Spencer, K., Taylor, A., Smith, B., Mawson, J., Flynn, N. and R. Batley (1986) *Crisis in the Industrial Heartland: A Study of the West Midlands*. Oxford: Clarendon Press.

References 249

Sutcliffe, A. and R. Smith (1974) *Birmingham 1939–70*. Oxford: Oxford University Press.

Suttles, G.D. (1974) *The Social Order of the Slum: Ethnicity and Territory in the Inner City*. Chicago: The University of Chicago Press.

Tanter, A. and J.C. Toubon (1999) 'Mixité Sociale et Politique de Peuplement: Genèse de l'Ethnicisation des Opérations de Réhabilitation', *Sociétés Contemporaines*, 33–4: 59–86.

Thys, R., W. de Raedemaecker, and J. Vranken (2004) *Bruggen over woelig water. Is het mogelijk om uit de generatie-armoede te geraken?* Leuven/Voorburg: Acco.

Townsend, P. (1979) *Poverty in the UK*. London: Penguin.

Van Beckhoven, E. and Kempen, R. van (2002) *Het Belang van de Buurt: De Invloed van Herstructurering op Activiteiten van Blijvers en Nieuwkomers in een Amsterdamse en Utrechtse Buurt*. Utrecht: DGVH/NETHUR.

Van Kempen, E. (2002) '"Poverty Pockets" and Social Exclusion: On the Role of Place in Shaping Social Inequality', in P. Marcuse and R. Van Kempen (eds), *Of States and Cities*. Oxford: Oxford University Press. pp. 240–57.

Van Kempen, R. and Priemus, H. (1999) 'Undivided Cities in the Netherlands: Present Situation and Political Rhetoric', *Housing Studies*, 14(5): 641–57.

Veer, J. van der (2004) *Wonen in Amsterdam 2003. Deel 4 Leefbaarheid*. Amsterdam: Amsterdamse Federatie van Woningcorporaties.

Vijgen, J. and R. van Engelsdorp Gastelaars (1992) *Centrum, Stadsrand, Groeikern. Bewonersprofielen en Leefpatronen in drie Woonmilieus Binnen het Gewest Amsterdam*, Amsterdam: Centrum voor Grootstedelijk Onderzoek, Universiteit van Amsterdam (Stedelijke Netwerken Werkstuk 40).

Vranken, J. and K. Steenssens (1996) *Naar het middelpunt der armoede? Een onderzoek naar de structuren van het dagelijks leven van generatie-armen in een urbane omgeving*, Leuven/Amersfoort: Acco.

Vranken, J. and J. van Ouytsel (2000) *Armoede en sociale uitsluiting, Jaarboek 2000*. Leuven/Leusden: Acco.

Vranken, J. De Boyser, K. and D. Dierckx (2004) *Armoede en sociale uitsluiting. Jaarboek 2004*. Leuven/Leusden: Acco.

Wacquant, L.J. (1992) 'Pour en Finir avec le Mythe des 'Cités-Ghettos'. Les Différences entre la France et les Etats-Unis', *Les Annales de la Recherche Urbaine*, 54: 21–9.

Wacquant, L. (1996) 'Red Belt, Black Belt: Racial Division, Class Inequality and the State in the French Urban Periphery and the American Ghetto', in E. Mingione (ed.), *Urban Poverty and the Underclass. A Reader*. Oxford: Blackwell.

Wacquant, L.J (2002) 'Scrutinizing the Street: Poverty, Morality, and the Pitfalls of Urban Ethnography', *American Journal of Sociology*, 107–6: 1468–532.

Wacquant, L. and Wilson, W. (1993) 'The Cost of Racial and Class Exclusion in the Inner City', in W.J. Wilson (ed.), *The Ghetto Underclass: Social Science Perspectives*. London: Sage. pp. 25–42.

Waldinger, R. (1996) *Still The Promised City? African-Americans and New Immigrants in Postindustrial New York*. Cambridge, MA: Harvard University Press.

Walker, A. (1997) *Britain Divided: The Growth Of Social Exclusion in the 1980s and 1990s*. London: Child Poverty Action Group.

Watt, P. (2003) 'Urban Marginality and Labour Market Restructuring: Local Authority Tenants and Employment in an Inner London Borough', *Urban Studies*, 40(9): 1769–89.

Western, J. (1993) 'Ambivalent Attachments to Place in London: Twelve Barbadian Families', *Environment and Planning D: Society and Space*, 11(2): 147–70.

White, J (1980) *Rothschild Building: Life in an East End Tenement Block 1887–1920.* London: Routledge.

Wilson, W.J. (1987) *The Truly Disadvantaged. The Inner City, the Underclass and Public Policy.* The University of Chicago Press, Chicago.

Wilson, W.J. (1991) 'Studying Inner-City Social Dislocations: The Challenge of Public Agenda Research', *American Sociological Review,* 56: 1–14.

Wilson W.J. (1993) *The Ghetto Underclass: Social Science Perspectives,* London: Sage

Wilson, W.J. (1996) *When Work Disappears: The World of the New Urban Poor.* New York: Knopf.

Index